NATIONALISM AND SOCIAL REFORM IN A COLONIAL SITUATION

NATIONALISM AND SOCIAL REFORM IN IN COLONIAL SITUATION

ARAVIND GANACHARI

KALPAZ

Published by

Kalpaz Publications
C-30, Satyawati Nagar,
Delhi – 110052
Ph.: 011-47034999, 9811692060
www.kalpazpublications.com
E-mail: kalpaz@hotmail.com

Distribution Network
gyanbooks.com
India, USA, Canada, UK, Australia, France

ISBN: 978-81-7835-351-7 (HB)

Reprint in India, 2024
First Published, 2005

Printed at: Gyan Press, Delhi.

Nationalism and Social Reform in a Colonial Situation
Author: Aravind Ganachari

To My Parents
Lalita & Late Gururao

Contents

Acknowledgements

The list of those without whose help this book would have been poorer is much longer than I can acknowledge here. However, to record my gratitude to those who have helped me in the writing of this book is a pleasing task. One of my earliest debts is to Professor J.V. Naik, former Head, Department of History, University of Mumbai, who supervised a few of my original research and whose meticulous standards of scholarship have always been an inspiration. My debt to my friends, Dr. Aroon Tikekar, Senior Journalist, historian and former editor of a popular daily, *Loksatta*; Principal K.J. Purohit, famous Marathi short-story writer and former President of the Marathi Sahitya Sammelan; Dr. K. Jagjit Singh, Guru Gobind Professor for Sikh Studies, Professor Mariam Dossal, University of Mumbai; Dr. Raja Dixit, Reader, University of Pune and Principal Krishna Panikkar, is almost equally long-standing.

The assistance of librarians and archivists has been both rewarding and full of friendship. Equally, I am grateful for the kind and caring help given by the staff at the Director General of Police's Office, where I consulted the *Bombay Presidency Police Abstracts of Intelligence*. Ashok Kharade, the Senior Archivist, and Mr. Pawar of the Maharashtra State Archives, Mumbai, went out of the way to be helpful.

My students at Government of Maharashtra's I. Y. College and at the University Department of History, have helped me in ways most do not know. They patiently and critically listened to the ideas that grew in the course of writing these articles which are included in this book. Special thanks for my friend and esteemed former colleague Prof. Mrs. Flory D'Souza, who took every care of the History Department at the I.Y. College. Over the years librarians at the I.Y. College and the Mumbai University libraries have borne with my requests and queries with exemplary patience.

To my colleagues at the Department of History, University of Mumbai, goes a more general acknowledgement. A few of the articles included here were first presented at the Faculty Seminars in the Department and the critical comments made at that time by my colleagues and students helped immensely in revising the text. I also thank, though in anticipation, the authorities of the University of Mumbai, for giving me partial financial assistance to bring out this volume.

I take this opportunity to specially thank my friends who gave me enough moral support when I needed it most. They are – Prof. Sharad Mestry, Prof. Manoj Bhide, Prof. B. D. Shirole, Dr. Kishor Gaikwad, Shri Uday Ajgoankar, Shri Prem Sumaria, Shri Gurvinder Singh Sahani, Dr. Nimish Sampat, Shri Suresh Jaju and Shri Anil Rajwade. The list also includes my most dear brothers and sisters — Ramesh, Satish, Suhas, Sulbha and Sunita.

My greatest debt is acknowledged in the dedication. I would have loved had this book seen the light of the day before the sad demise of my beloved father on 19th June 2004. I fail in summoning appropriate words to express my debt to them. Also, my wife – Hema and son – Aditya, to them belongs the credit of putting themselves with a difficult person that I am. Formal acknowledgements here can be no more than private words addressed to them in public. Also, I sincerely appreciate the unstinting encouragement my father-in law Shri Anant Joshi provided all these years. My thanks also go to Shri Swapnil Bawaskar, who every time attended my computer related complaints with a broad smile.

My sincere thanks are due to Indian History Congress, the Economic and Political Weekly, and the Popular Prakashan, for permitting to reproduce my articles first published by them.

I am grateful for the pleasant cooperation received from the management, in particular Amit Garg and the staff of the Gyan Publishing House, New Delhi.

The responsibility for errors of fact or argument remains mine alone.

September 11, 2004. **Aravind Ganachari**

Introduction

The essays on different facets of the history of India which are incorporated in this volume were contributed to various symposia and journals over the past decade. There was no definite design while writing these articles. But while researching on various themes — though independent of each other — a more distinct picture emerged that illustrated some common trends or patterns running through these articles. While some of the articles reflect the emergence of national consciousness among the Indians, especially among the Maharashtrians, the others are concerned with the reform movement in Western India during the British colonial rule.

The need to define the concepts of nationalism and social reform in a colonial situation thus arises so as to enable oneself to see every country's case in its proper perspective and in its conditional nature. In a broader sense, the growth of nationalism is the process of integration of the masses of the people into a common political platform. Hans Kohn, an acknowledged authority on the subject and one who has deftly analyzed the origin and growth of nationalism in 18th and 19th century Europe, aptly states as to what constitutes nationalism[1] :

> Nationalism is first and foremost a state of mind, an act of consciousness...The collective or group consciousness can center around entirely different groups, of which some have a more permanent character — the family, the class, the clan, the caste, the village, the sect, the religion. Etc...Each group creates its own symbols and social conventions, is dominated by social traditions....Group consciousness is never exclusive. Men find themselves members of different groups at the same time...With in these pluralistic, and sometimes conflicting, kinds of group-consciousness there is generally one which is recognized by man as the supreme and most important, to which he owes supreme loyalties....

Nationalities are product of the living historical forces and therefore always fluctuating, never rigid....Nationalism is a state of mind...Nationalism is an idea, which fills man's brain and heart with new thoughts and new sentiments, and drives him to translate his consciousness into deeds of organized action. Nationality is there not only a group held together and animated by common consciousness; but it is also a group seeking to find its expression in what it regards as the highest form of organized activity, a sovereign state...

Territory, language, common descent and such other factors are the natural elements out of which nationalism is formed. But the existence of these elements alone need not form the constituents of nationalism, and in that sense, nationalism is not an inherent phenomena but a product of the social and intellectual factors at a certain stage of history. In the background of Hans Kohn's brilliant analysis of emergence of nationalism in Europe, when applied to India, raises a few questions : whether the emergence of nationalist tendencies in India under a colonial regime was only a spasmodic and instant reaction to the oppressive policies of the British Indian administration ? Whether the evolution of Indian national consciousness was west specific in terms of thought, content and methods ? Whether the politics of Indian nationalism was chiefly determined by the kind of education the colonial administration provided to the Indians, 'the genesis of which is clearly linked with those Indians who had been schooled by *Western methods* ?[2]

The introduction and growth of Western liberal education in India, brought about a cultural resurgence by 'cultural induction', taken to mean a direct transfer of ideas.[3] The expression "renaissance" being taken to mean a socio-economic reconstruction, depended on the degree and duration of the contact with English education and Western ideas. The English educated Maharashtrian intellectuals in the nineteenth century regarded English language as a vehicle or a window to the secular-scientific world view and made distinction between the ethos of English society, and the ethos of modern science and scientific world view. While they admitted that there was much to learn from the English, rejected the Englishman and his culture. Hence, ambivalence in their attitude, for they had a sneaking admiration for qualities of the Englishmen, still openly despised him for the ruination their policies brought about in India.[4]

How did the early Maharashtrian intellectuals react to the British rule ? If a few of the intellectuals believed in the benign view of British rule — a belief in "divine dispensation or providence"— it envisaged for them the vision of a new life and society, but one that did not expect the British rule to be permanent. Such a view was revolting to the radical intellectuals who were sharp and quick to perceive the central contradiction between colonial rule and the interests of the Indian people. To them, the sedulously propagated idea of "civilizing mission" of Great Britain appeared to be a myth... To such critics; British rule was not a divine dispensation, "but the most bitter curse India has ever been visited with...."[5]

Prominent among the early Maharashtrian critics of British rule were : Bhaskar Pandurang Tarkhadkar (1816-1847) who made a studied but scathing criticism of all aspects of British colonial rule through a series of letters published in *Bombay Gazette*[6] between June and September 1841 ; Govind Vittul Kunte alias Bhau Mahajan(1815-1890), who consistently and methodically exposed the shady side of British colonial rule through the columns of his powerful Marathi newspaper the *Prabhakar* started in October 1841; and Ramkrishna Vishwanath, the unknown author of a remarkable Marathi book written in 1843, entitled *Hindustanâch Prachin va Sâmpratchi Sthiti Âni Pudhen Kâi Tyâchâ Parinâm Honâr Hyâ Vishayee Vichâr* (Thoughts on India's Past and Present Conditions and Their Impact on the Future). These Marathi writers were forerunners of Dadabhai Naoroji's Drain Theory.[7]

This sentiment, in the post-Revolt of 1857 period, continued within the sphere allowed by the colonial State's[8] regulations that sought to increasingly control the progressively more belligerent vernacular press. Such a press reflected the changing mood of the nation from an earlier liberal phase to the one that got crystallized and culminated into the Extremism in political, social and economic thought. The Deccan Agricultural Riots of 1875-76 were not sporadic incidents to be treated as localized events in Bombay Presidency but one as the effect of oppressive land revenue measures introduced by the British colonial State in this part of the Presidency over a long period. The attitude of the colonial State which was mostly indifferent to the demands for humane social legislations by the Indian reformers and their unwillingness to do anything that would jeopardize their economic and political interests, contributed more than one way to the emergence of nationalist feeling.[9] The repressive measures and the financial opulence of the colonial State displayed in organizing the Delhi Darbar in the face of ruinous wars of Lord Lytton and the Deccan Agricultural Riots of 1875-76, and many such contributing factors did result in the crystallizing and growth of nationalist sentiment. The acerbic writings of Vishnushashtri Chiplunkar in *Nibandhmala*, the activities of the Arya Samaj founded in 1875 in Bombay, are an index of that feeling. The destructive and ruinous nature of British imperialism is well reflected in the articles published in *Mahratta* entitled *The Romans And the English : A Parallel*, and *The Romans and The English : An Apprehension and A Suggestion,* in early 1881. It made comparison between the ancient Roman and the modern English conquests, showed similarities in the form of ruin that was resulted, and further observed that all such imperialist activities of both blossomed under the republican political institutions, the English being monarchy only in name. The comparison is so succinctly brought out that it is worth quoting at length :

> So far, then, Romans and English histories are identical : the Romans prospering while republican enthusiasm was alive in them; the English have been thriving because republican ideas have been gaining a deeper and deeper root in their hearts. The Romans extended their dominion over the greater portion of the then-known world; the English, too, have made vast territorial acquisitions — so vast that the Sun never sets upon them.
>
> Let us extend this parallel to the treatment which the Romans accorded to their subject nations, and the treatment which the English have been giving to theirs... 'The Romans having desolated Europe, set themselves to civilize it. The form of Government which they established in the conquered provinces though sever, was regular and preserved public tranquility. As a consolation for the loss of liberty, they communicated their arts, sciences, language and manners to their new subjects. Europe began to breathe, and to recover strength after the calamities which it had undergone; agriculture was encouraged; population increased; the ruined cities were rebuilt; new towns were founded; an appearance of prosperity succeeded, and repaired, in some degree, the havoc of war.
>
> This state, however, was far from being happy or favourable to the improvement of the human mind. The vanquished nations were disarmed by their conquerors, and overawed by soldiers kept in pay to restrain them. They were given up as prey to rapacious governors, who plundered them with impunity, were drained of their wealth by exorbitant taxes, levied with so little attention to the situation of the provinces that the impositions were often increased in proportion to their inability to support them... It is for our readers to judge how far these observations apply to the present condition of India. We believe the parallel we have drawn above will serve to show how the Romans

and English dealt and are dealing with their respective subject nations....

The form of Government which the English have established over us, sits, we frankly say, very heavy upon us....We have been enjoying the blessings of peace under our present rulers. But by such peace as we have been enjoying, "both Courages", as Lord Bacon says, "will effeminate, and Manners Corrupt"; and this just what has happened.

We are groaning under the most crushing taxes, and the infallible references is : "neither will it be, that people overlaid with taxes, should ever become Valiant and Marshal." Yours laws, your blessing of peace, your taxes and what not, all all conspire to produce one grand effect : a complete demartialisation of India. Agriculture has been encouraged...an appearance of prosperity has succeeded the demolition of Native government and Native independence. But who cannot see that this is only an *appearance* of prosperity, not prosperity itself; an illusion, not a reality?[10]

Such was the indictment of the British rule by Indian nationalists. The above quote is more representative of that genre. A galaxy of brilliant exponents in the last decades of nineteenth century such as Dadabhai Naoroji, M. G. Ranade, G. V. Joshi, G.K. Gokhale, G.S. Iyer, R.C. Dutt, to name a few, contributed in moulding the economic thinking at that time, and thereby challenging the myth of 'White Man's Burden' and also of justifying imperial domination so painstakingly constructed by the colonial historians. The epitome of such well-crafted and unremittingly circulated myth was Rudyard Kipling [1862-1936] : "To be ruled by Britain was India's right; to rule India was Britain's duty".[11] By doing this they gave a new and solid plank for the national movement to stand on and helped the growth of extremism which tremendously helped in unifying the idea of Indian nation.[12] The concept of "nationalism", thus evolved slowly but steadily in the second half of the nineteenth century, from provincial issues taken up by interest groups leading to unified movement called Indian National Congress.[13]

It is argued here that the acceptance of Western liberal education and the ideas it brought about in its wake by the Indians is not be held synonymous to acknowledging the acceptance of British imperialism. The impact of Enlightenment ideas on Indian intellectuals can hardly be interpreted as their acceptance of Western culture system. The assumption by the Cambridge School of historians that the Western thought internalized by English educated Indian nationalists, was in a way an admission of colonizer's duty of improvement or of the "civilizing mission" is reflected in the writings of not a few historians :

"The promotion of Western education turned out to have been 'a story of grave miscalculation'; for although 'it was the clear and imperative duty of the British Government to attempt the intellectual emancipation of India,'..." [14]

> "The major problems associated with those 'founding years' were inherent in the nature of the ambivalent historic realities that gave birth to Congress. For instance, the paradox of 'nationalist' demands emerging from the minds of people trained by their imperialist rulers to articulate them in English language and ideals of Westernization proved to be almost insuperable obstacle. Not were early leaders such as W.C. Bonnerji and S. N. Banerjee, M.G. Ranade and G. K. Gokhale, Dadabhai Naoroji and P. Mehta reared in schools of Victorian decorum and learning, but even the more revolutionary cultural nationalists such as B. G. Tilak, B.C. Pal and L.L. Rai also received ample doses of English education and protective patinas of Western modernity. To some extent all of Congress' founding fathers were, indeed, proto-types of Macaulay's early nineteenth century dream, hybrids 'Indian in blood and colour, but English in taste, in opinion...in intellect".[15]

Earlier generations of imperialist historians[16] had sought to make a critical connection between education and politics. They argued that it was largely English-educated Indian middle class, brought to an awareness of the role of institutions organized along rational and scientific lines in restructuring the society, which recognized that all political activity had to be within the framework of 'Rule of Law' — a condition created by despotic though but altruistic British rule. In support of their contention, they marshaled evidence of the bountiful effects of the civilizing mission, showed judiciousness of British policies, and that Indian nationalism was "the gift of a magnanimous people endowed with enlightened traditions".[17] Ever since Anil Seal, in *The Emergence of Indian Nationalism—Competition and Collaboration in the Later Nineteenth Century*,[18] provided an argument that the politics of Indian nationalism is clearly linked with those Indians who had been schooled by Western methods, and later went on to trace 'vertical alliances' of "bigwigs and followers", factions with "patrons and clients", a host of European scholars with varying differences have been obsessed by this kind of analysis.[19] Some argued the ill-effects of the 'imperial duty' : "The British, although they provided themselves with a steady stream of recruits for their administrative and judicial services, had in many ways also *created a Frankenstein's monster*...It created a group interested in obtaining more and increasingly important positions within the administrative structure; it also *infected* it with western ideas of representative and responsible government and later with concepts of nationalism...."[20] [Emphasis is mine]

Such assumptions provide a sanitized and homogenized view of the West — Western thought and the growth of liberalism as identical with English imperial rule. Interestingly, Guido De Reggiero in his work entitled *The History of European Liberalism* provides an excellent analysis of the contours of Western liberalism— showing the distinct features of English, French, German and Italian liberalism as developed in the 17th to 19th century — a work translated into English by none other than R.G. Collingwood.[21]

It is not the purpose of this author to write a detailed analysis of the origin and growth of Indian nationalism. But it is in the context of Indian response, Maharashtra in specific, and the kind of historiography that has emerged over the years — both colonial and post-colonial — that the articles incorporated in this volume are to be contextualized.

Indeed, any attempt to challenge such assumptions is debunked as a subterfuge of the "Revisionist Nationalist historians".[22] Therefore, it needs to be emphasized that almost all the articles included in this volume are based on the official records maintained in the *Maharashtra State Archives* and such other, i.e. *Bombay Presidency Police Abstracts of Intelligence* available in Directorate of Inspector General's Office, Mumbai.

The first six articles are concerned with various aspects of Indian nationalism, while the remaining are on the theme of social reform movement. The first article attempts to show how in the last decades of nineteenth century and the early years of twentieth century, the press became increasingly critical of repressive official policies and that the British Indian government came down heavily against the press by roping in editors and confiscating press machinery by ever-widening legal net. When legitimate means of ventilating grievances were denied, the Extremists, made intelligent use of indigenous method such as Marathi theatrical art — which included the dramatists, the actors, the theatrical troupes, and the audience— for mass mobilization of nationalist ideas among the masses.[23] How the Epics—*Râmâyana* and *Mahâbhârat*, the Maratha and Rajput histories, and *Swadeshi* movement, provided the themes for the nationalist theatre is shown in this article. Besides, even the oppressive colonial policies also provided new themes. The abridged version of this article was first published in the *Proceedings of Indian History Congress.*

In tracing the "Evolution of the Law of 'Sedition' in the Context of the Indian Freedom Struggle : 1837-1922",[24] the purpose was show how the British Indian administration maintained the legal fiction of the "Rule of Law" on the one hand and on the other, sought to make a travesty of justice, judiciary and judicial procedure with a view to bringing more and more Indians within the legal ambit. In order to repress the nationalists, they invented new definitions of 'sedition' – the Section 124-A of Indian Penal Code,[25] a Section which Gandhi called "the prince among the political sections of the India Penal Code designed to suppress the liberty of the citizen". The increasing exercise of this Section by the colonial State and the progressively more aggressive reaction it evoked from the nationalists is an index of the crystallizing concept of Indian nationalism.

The third article which compares the attitude of both B. G. Tilak and M.K. Gandhi towards the British Indian law and argues that Gandhi's *Satyagraha* movement was not in opposition to the methods undertaken by B.G. Tilak but was an advance over him. The British could anticipate Tilak's faith in British jurisprudence and in British sense of fair play, thereby the administration could fix him within the British legal framework. Gandhi, like Tilak, was a student of British law but in deed a fast learner. With his experience in South Africa and during the First World War, did not work within the British framework but set his own agenda and made the British administration work in it. By setting the tone and pace of that 'agenda' he kept the British officials, both at home and here, guessing on his political moves and made them work in it. It is also contended that Gandhi's *Satyagraha* removed the fear of the "terror of law' and thereby knocking off the important pillar of British imperialism.

How *Bhagwat-Gita* was used as an instrument of mass mobilization during the Extremist phase is being traced in the fourth article. Conversely, the British official perception of *Bhagwat-Gita* did undergo a drastic change. While B.G. Tilak and his followers used religious, historical and cultural iconography as a rallying point for Indian nationalism and events like Ganesh and Shivaji Utsav were deftly used for mass mobilization, such an effort has been termed by European historians as "The Political recruitment of God Ganapati"[26] and "a clear example of 'invented tradition".[27]

One wonders, if the emergence of English nationalism, as pointed out by Hans Kohn, was based on Christianity, why Indian nationalist effort to make use of indigenous historical and cultural iconography be termed as "invention of tradition". Hans Kohn wrote :

> The birth of nationalism in Puritan Revolution determined and still determines the character of English nationalism...From its origin English nationalism preserved it peculiar characteristics; it has always been, and still is, closer than any other to the religious matrix from which it rose, and is imbued with the spirit of liberty asserted in a struggle against ecclesiastical and civil authority. It never made the complete integration of the individual into the nation the aim of nationalism; it always put a great emphasis upon the individual and upon the human community beyond all national divisions. The Calvinist awareness of the infinite value of every individual continued to protect English social organization and uniformity in civil as much as in religious matters. Religious life and sentiment in England were withdrawing into the sanctuary of inner life and inner liberty. They were full of social activism, of feeling of responsibility for the betterment of conditions in this world, conscious of the common commonwealth. The religious and liberal character of English nationalism determined also the peculiar development of English socialism in the nineteenth century...."[28]

Kohn has also shown that factors for emergence of nationalism in England, France and Germany were so very different and were rooted in their respective historical tradition.[29] Hence, there was no homogenized and unified development of nationalist sentiment in Europe. The purpose of this illustration is not to indicate, even remotely, any relation between such development in Europe and usage of religious and cultural iconography by nationalists such as Tilak or Gandhi. The point that needs an emphasis is that every country draws inspiration from its cultural, religious or historical tradition in revitalizing its nationalist sentiment.

The idea of "Civilizing Mission" and disciplining the uncivilized mind of the colonized seem to have provided a favourite theme to a host of European historians of the past and present. Historiography of this idea has worked over-time etching out a historic role that Britain as colonizer had to play : "Torchbearers Upon the Path of Progress' : Britain's Ideology of a 'Moral and Material Progress' in India". [30] It reasoned that, "the British felt obliged to justify their rule in a European idiom. The most powerful tool of self-legitimation was the colonizer's claim to improve the country and to bring the fruits of progress and modernity to the subject people...it is inherent in the logic of colonialism that people who are different because they were regarded as inferior had to be made similar and, hence, equal by being civilized. This was the self-inflicted "duty" of the 'white-man' whose 'burden' derived for the permanent atonement for original sin as well as from the sympathetic attitude of the philanthropic Enlightenment…."[31] Also, to attribute the credit of forcing the gates of the "so-called 'Age of Reform" to Charles Grant and James Mill, is to take out Rudyard Kipling from the grave and consecrate.[32]

When, at the beginning of second half of nineteenth century, colonial administrators found a large number of Europeans, whom they addressed by many names : European pauperism, Luciferism, loaferism, and finally, European vagrants, and feared that their "Prestige" as ruling elite was being eroded; what happened to the self-created myth of "White Man's Burden" and how they invented various ways to protect person of their colour, is illustrated in the article - "White-Man's Embarrassment" : The European Vagrancy In The Second Half of the Nineteenth Century Bombay."[33] By defining 'European British subject' as homogenized European converged into one nationality, the colonial administration invented new tradition and undertook all legal remedial measures to keep the vagrant out of Indian's gaze. All this was long before the white community in India raised the question of "racial superiority" much before the Ilbert Bill controversy in 1883.

To project all "Europeans" as imperialists would equally be blasphemous. There were many Europeans and Americans who raised themselves above the shackles of discrimination in the name of race or colour. The articles on Myron Phelps [1856-1916] and Mary Carpenter (1807 - 1877) highlight their contribution to Indian nationalism and social reform respectively.

The remaining four articles of this volume focus on social reform movement in Maharashtra. The article on the Vijia Lakshmi Case [1881][34] focuses on the infanticide committed by a young Hindu Brahmin widow who gave in to biological urge and later to hide her shame committed infanticide of her illegitimate child. In the judgment, the judges raised the point of morality and awarded her death penalty, while the Indian public opinion felt that they paid scant attention to the social realities in which the offence was committed. They felt that the punishment was very harsh and insensitive to the indignity heaped on her by the orthodox Hindu society. It attempts to show how Justice Pinhey who has been lionized by the reformers for giving a landmark judgment in favour of Rukhmabai in 1986, was so inconsiderate to Vijia Lakshmi that when government referred the judgment back for a sympathetic consideration, reiterated the death penalty as a deterrent punishment. Eventually the government overruled his judgment and reduced to sentence to five years.

The article concerning the daring and erudite Pandita Ramabai is illustrative of her conflicts with Hindu as well as Christian orthodoxy, who attempted to encroach upon her freedom. To the Hindu orthodoxy she was a renegade, and the self appointed Christian benefactors treated her in a manner that undermined her self respect. She strove hard to point out to both that her conversion to Christianity did not denationalize her.

How the East India Company's administration introduced a graded system of liberal education that precluded the lower castes but still conceded 'abstract justice' to Erloo bin Narayan, a Mahar by caste. He was disallowed admission into government run school for fear of alienating the upper and wealthier classes. This case shows that ever since the inception, the colonial administration relinquished their obligations towards their less fortunate sections of the society—the untouchables; they chose to sacrifice their responsibility in order to gain financial patronage from the Indian upper and wealthier classes for educational enterprises so that they had not to incur any expenditure on that account. Interestingly, all the administrative layers of colonial administration — both in India and England, deprived Erloo bin Narayan of the benefits of English education which claimed to impart universalism on the basis of humanism.

References

1. Hans Kohn, *The Idea of Nationalism — A Study in Its Origins and Background*, The Macmillan Company, New York, 1946, Third Revised Edition, pp. 10-19.
2. This has been the claim advanced by a school of historians called "Cambridge school" and in particular by Anil Seal, *The Emergence of Indian Nationalism: Competition and Collaboration in the Late Nineteenth Century*, Cambridge., 1968, p.16. The emphasis on "Western methods" is mine.
3. K. Mukharji, "The Renaissance in Bengal and Maharashtrian Thought from 1850 to 1920" , *Arth-Vijnan*, December 1962, pp.331-41. He aptly argues that induction took place as a result of Indians being exposed to 'Enlightenment' literature. He, even remotely does not ascribe the credit to the colonial masters, for the kind of syllabus that was prescribed in the University and in the pre-Revolt period, was most sanitized by the colonial masters—a kind of inculcation among the Indians that would not go against their imperialist interests.

4. *Ibid.* pp.338-39.

5. J.V. Naik. "Perception of British Rule in Maharashtra : A Selective Study" in *Art and Culture : Endeavours in Interpretation*, Ahsan Jan Quisar & Som Prakash Verma (ed), Abhinav Publications, New Delhi, 1996, pp. 107-18.

6. J.V. Naik, "An Early Appraisal of the British Colonial Policy" *Journal of the Bombay University*, Vol. XLV, No. 80-81, 1975-76, pp. 243-270.

7. For details, see J.V. Naik, "Forerunners of Dadabhai Naoroji's Drain Theory", *Economic and Political Weekly*, 24 November 2001, pp. 4428-4432.

8. In the 'Introduction' to *Ranade's Economic Writings*, Bipan Chandra described the character of the British Colonial State : "British colonialism in India was fully structured during the 19th century—Indian economy was integrated with the British and world capitalist economy in a subservient position and India became a classical economy... But the consequence of colonialism were very different. India was gradually underdeveloped and impoverished. Its traditional handicrafts were ruined; modern industrial growth was delayed and stunted; Indian agriculture first stagnated and then entered a prolonged period of decline and ruin; large sectors of Indian economy – foreign trade, banking, plantations, transport, energy, modern industry and mining – came under foreign control..."

9. As an example, the case of "Age of Consent Controversy" could be cited. It began with the publication of "Notes on Infant Marriage and Enforced Widowhood" by Beheramji Merwanji Malabari on 15th August 1884. It took seven years [1891]to have the legislation passed on this issue.

10. "The Romans and the English : A Parallel", *Mahratta*, 23 January 1881 and "The Romans and The English : An Apprehension and A Suggestion", *Mahratta*, 30 January 1881, [Communicated] The external evidence perhaps shows Gopal Ganesh Agarkar's authorship of these articles for following reasons : Agarkar's acquaintance with the history of Rome. 2. A "Communicated" article, hence Tilak's authorship is ruled out. 3. There is hardly any evidence to show that Vishnushashtri Chiplunkar wrote in *Mahratta*. 4. Agarkar's favourite concept - *Jeet - Jete* (Conquerors and Conquered), on which he later gave a lecture at Akola, as mentioned by his former teacher V.M.Mahajani.

11. Ashish Nandi, *The Intimate Enemy —Loss and Recovery of Self under Colonialism*, OUP, 1983, p.64.

12. Bipan Chandra, *The Rise and Growth of Economic Nationalism in India – Economic Policies on National Leadership, 1880-1903*, People's Publishing House, New Delhi, Reprinted in 1977 [First published 1966 pp. 636-735.

13. Historians like Charles Heimsath have argued differently. He thinks it 'hazardous' to assume that Indian nationalism as a logical historical outgrowth of nineteenth century political activity as they represented only interest groups and that India, in fact, experienced many 'nationalisms'. He argued

that 'there was nothing spontaneous about the appearance in India of nationalism in 19th century and that those who spoke about it were 'an eminent company of intellectuals'. But he admits that in the period after 1880's an all-India nationalism was well established . For further reading, *Indian Nationalism and Hindu Social Reform*, Princeton University Press, 1964, pp.131-146.

14. W. H. Morris-Jones, "If it be Real, What Does it Mean': Some British Perceptions of Indian National Congress" in Richard Sisson and Stanley Wolpert [ed], *Congress and Indian Nationalism – The Pre-Independence Phase*, OUP, Delhi, 1988, p.96.

15. Stanley Wolpert, "Indian National Congress in Nationalist Perspective" in Richard Sisson and Stanley Wolpert [ed], *Congress and Indian Nationalism – The Pre-Independence Phase*, OUP, Delhi, 1988, p.23.

16. The list of this group is very big. Some of the prominent historians, with varying shades, may be mentioned here : James Mill, Sir William Jones, Cunningham, Mountstuart Elphinstone, Thomas Munro, John Malcolm; evangelicals like Shore and Grant; administrator scholars such as Alfred Lyall, Henry Sumner Maine, Leslie Stephen, W.W. Hunter; and modern scholars such as P. E. Roberts, T.G.P. Spear, Professor C.H. Phillips and Professor Holden Furber. Also read, Pramod K. Nayar, "The Sublime Raj — English Writings and India, 1750-1820" in *Economic and Political Weekly*, Vol. XXXIX, No. 34, August 21-27, 2004, pp.3811-17.

17. Vinay Lal, "Walking with the Subalterns, Riding with the Academy : The Curious Ascendancy of Indian History", *Studies in History*, Vol. XVII, No.1, Jan-June 2001, pp.108-13. He makes a penetrative and balanced study of the "Cambridge School" and also the Subaltern studies.

18. Anil Seal, *The Emergence of Indian Nationalism —Competition and Collaboration in the Later Nineteenth Century*, S. Chand & Company Ltd., New Delhi, paperback edition 1971.

19. *Ibid.*

20. Jim Masselos, *Indian Nationalism : An History*, Sterling Publishers Private Ltd., New Delhi, Reprint 1998, p. 50, Revised and Enlarged edition of *Nationalism on the Indian Subcontinent : An Introductory History*,

21. Guido De Reggiero, *The History of European Liberalism*, trans. by R.G. Collingwood, OUP, London, 1927.

22. Richard Sisson, "Congress and Indian Nationalism : Political Ambiguity and the Problems of Social Conflict and Party Control", in Richard Sisson and Stanley Wolpert [ed], *Congress and Indian Nationalism – The Pre-Independence Phase*, OUP, Delhi, 1988, p.5.

23. This was indeed an indigenous method used and does not seem to be remotely influenced by the political drama in England. Hence, until 1876 when Dramatic

Performances Act was enacted, no need was felt to deal with seditious drama. Also, the mental list of prohibited areas of discussion in plays of the licensing authorities in England were the Irish problem, the Reform Bill, Chartism, and the Royal family. For details, John Russell Stephens, *The Censorship of English Drama 1824-1901*, Cambridge University Press, 1980.

24. The article is published in Mariam Dossal and Ruby Malony (ed.), State Intervention and Popular Response - Western India in the Nineteenth Century, Popular Prakashan, Mumbai, 1998.

25. Example could be given of the Tilak Cases of 1897 and 1908. In the first case, the entire jury was composed of Europeans not knowing Marathi; promoted and transferred John Strachey as the judge of Bombay High Court even when there were senior Judges; Justice Strachey invented new definition of Section 124-A of Indian Penal Code, stated what the meaning ought to be and gave judgment accordingly and finally recommended that the concerned law be amended to that effect. The entire Indian press called this as "Strachey Law". In the next case, they brought an obliging Indian Judge to arbitrate over the case, had European jury, two cases were filed in Bombay instead of Poona against two articles that had appeared in *Kesari*, the two cases were simultaneously conducted and judgments were separately given and term of imprisonment not to be undergone concurrently but subsequently.

26. Richard I. Cashman has written a chapter by this title, in his book *The Myth of the Lokmanya*, University of California Press, 1975, pp.75-97. Cashman calls the Lokmanya as a myth, a legendary and fictitious tale. Such a denigrating expression among the Cambridge School historians is common. Stanley Wolpert, in the same line, wrote a book entitled *The Myth of Mahatma*, that is the way he chose to interpret him.

27. C. A. Bayly, *Origins of Nationality in South Asia – Patriotism and Ethical Government in the Making of Modern India*, OUP, Delhi, 1998, pp.108-9. Regarding B. G. Tilak's starting of *Shivaji Utsav*, Bayly commented : "The iconography of Shivaji, had displayed little direct continuity with the political discourse of the *Ajnapatra* ...The themes of self-strengthening and righteous violence in the national cause propagated by *Swadeshi* newspapers were top-dressed with traditional ideas of power [*shakti*], but derived more obviously from current notions of eugenics and race theory coming from Western European sources." Such attributing to the 'western European sources' is, indeed, an "invention of tradition".

28. Hans Kohn, *op. cit.* 178-79. He points out that the Norman Conquest created in England, in spite of its insular situation, certain difficulties in the formation of a continuous national consciousness. The assimilation of the three main racial strains – the Celts, the Saxons and the Normans — proceeded very slowly. It was only in the fourteenth century did the English language gradually replaced French in English law courts and in official life, and also the legal

documents. Not until 1362, the English Parliament did not hold its sessions in English language. pp. 155-56.

29. *Ibid.* pp. 129-83.

30. The colonial and post-colonial historiography including the Cambridge School is very large to write here about. But the latest work engaged in this denigrating "mission" is Harald Fischer-Tine and Michael Mann [ed], *Colonialism As Civilizing Mission – Cultural Ideology in British India*, Anthem Press, London, 2004.

31. *Ibid.* p.5.

32. *Ibid.* pp.12-13.

33. This paper in full is published in *Economic and Political Weekly*, 22-29 July 2002, Vol.XXXVII, No25.

34. This article was published in *Economic and Political Weekly* under the title : "Infanticide in Colonial Western India : The Vijia Lakshmi Case – 1881", March 1-7, 2003, Vol. XXXVIII, No. 9, pp.902-906.

1

"Maharashtra's Response to Colonial State: The Role of the Proscribed Marathi Theatre : 1872-1916"

Of the various devices employed by the nationalists for mass mobilisation, theatre has been both an important and popular one, especially in Maharashtra. The tremendous influence which the Marathi theatre exercised in exciting nationalist sentiment among the masses is aptly summarised in a confidential report in respect of two plays -*Swadeshi Natak* and *Sangit Rashtrodhar Natak*, submitted by A.C. Logan, Commissioner, Central Division, to the Bombay Government in 1907. He wrote: "the performances of such plays is calculated to excite the lowest classes, who would not be reached by newspapers or meetings...."[1] This effective instrument of mass mobilisation for which ample archival material is available, has not received adequate attention of the historians of the Indian national movement. This article seeks to examine the plays written and enacted, which were officially prohibited and proscribed, during the heyday of militant nationalism 1896-1916. An attempt is also made to trace the origin of the enactment of Dramatic Performances Act -1876, to bring out the shift in official attitude in the course of Indian national movement and show how the Marathi theatre and British Government acted and reacted on each other. The more repressive the Government became, the more themes it provided to the nationalist playwrights. As more and more dramas came to be prohibited from performance on slightest allusion to sedition, they created greater interest among the masses, thus promoting the cause of India's struggle for, freedom. Marathi theatre -the playwrights, actors, theatrical troupes, and the audience - devised novel ways of using every aspect of theatrical art for mass mobilisation. Significantly, almost all the dramatists of this period were Tilakaites belonging to the Extremist Camp.

The two plays which prompted the promulgation of ordinance by the Viceroy and later the passage of the Dramatic Performances Act - No. XIX of 1876 (hereinafter DPA) were ***Chaka Darpan*** or the "Mirror of tea Planting" of Girish Chandra Ghosh in Bengali and ***Malharaoche Natak*** of Narayen Bapuji Kanitkar in Marathi.[2] The theme of the first was to exhibit the tea planters and those who were engaged in promoting emigration to the tea districts as "monsters of inequity"[3] and that of the second concerned with the trial of Malharrao, ex- ruler of Baroda and his dethronement. While the opposition to such a legislation came by way of memorial to the Government from the inhabitants of Calcutta, Lucknow and also British Indian Association, which felt that. such a measure was not only "stifling to the rising national literature" but "was not necessary because the existing law was quite sufficient".Since this argument was not wrong, what then prompted the need for a legislation on this issue, is revealed in the proceedings of the Viceroy's Executive Council. When the Bill was introduced by Sir Arther Hobhouse, the Lieutenant Governor of Bengal who was a member of this Council expressed :

> this measure was absolutely necessary; that if it was not passed, mischief would arise of a moral as well as of asocial character - mischief which would be detrimental to the prestige and character of British rule in the metropolis of India...[4]

Although the law was sufficient for protection, he observed, but the offenders "soon took legal advise, and passively defied the authorities" as there was no authority to prevent them. "They obtain a sort of spurious notoriety accrued to them, and this would have encouraged others; and just as fire went on feeding itself; just as snow ball gathered force as it rolled down precipice – *vires acquirit eundo* – so this evil would have gone on increasing until really at last serious mischief would have been done". He also referred to the "public tendency" of such dramatic performances :

> the manner in which all the most revered institutions under which we lived had been brought into contempt by public exhibitions, might not amount to treason, and not even to sedition, yet

nevertheless, everything which politically ought to be treated as sacred in the eyes, not only of Europeans, but more especially of Natives, might be brought day after day, month after month, into greater and greater contempt. And though political danger was not to be feared—indeed, ideas of danger should not lightly be evoked - yet it was undesirable that this sort of thing ought. to be permitted,... Nevertheless, it was possible that, if these objectionable performances were to be repeated for any lengthened period of time, gradually the youth of the country, the educated, quick-witted and aspiring young men of the rising generation, would become - he would not say corrupted or disaffected, but -not so well-affected as we might desire them to be the means of saving them from themselves - from those evil influences to which they might otherwise be subjected...[5]

All the other members of the Executive Council, including the Indian additional member Raja Narendra Krishna Bahadur, concurred with these observations. It was thus an attempt to "discipline" the Indian educated mind and to "punish" the offenders.

The first play against which official action was initiated in the Bombay Presidency was ***Malharaoche Natak*** which was performed in Bombay in 1876.[6] The Correspondence between the Secretary, Judicial Department, his subordinates and the Commissioner of Police of Bombay, Sir Henry Souer, show how some English officials took a liberal view towards dramatic performances which were critical of government action. As Sir Henry Souter thought that the play was calculated to excite the feelings of dissatisfaction against the government, urged the Secretary, Judicial Department (JD), BG, to prohibit the performance and to apply the Section 10 of the DP Act to Bombay. It was imperative that the Bombay Government had to seek prior permission of the Imperial Government to enforce the Act. But when the Secretary, JD, BG, asked Sir Henry to submit a complete report, he could not show anything conclusively to indicate the seditious or immoral part of the play. He admitted that the play was only a verbatim reproduction of the trial itself. Even the Under-Secretary voiced similar apprehension: "the tone of some of the Hindu comedies and farces is not always strictly correct." The Secretary thereupon argued, "the same charges might however be brought with reference to not few of the plays performed, for instance in London, notably at the Criterion and St. James theatres and allowed by the

Lord Chamberlain". Hence, the Secretary refused to comply with Sir Henry's request. When urged reconsideration, he retorted :

> "before prohibiting the performance of this dramatic representation it would be necessary to have fuller information as to the exact nature and the plot, and whether by its incidents or dialogue it is 'likely to excite feeling of dissatisfaction to the British Government'. Unless actually seditious, the Under-Secretary can see little more objection to the representation of this play in Bombay than there is to the representation in Ireland of such dramas... founded on the disturbances in and since 1798. It hardly appears politic to prohibit the performance of dramatised representation of the trial of the ex-Gaekwar unless the play contains absolutely seditious sentiments. To do so would be to seem as if government were afraid to any allusion to the trial."

This note by the Secretary became instructive to government's future policy towards theatrical performances. Hence, the administration refused to take any hard-line attitude in this regard. The only play which came close to government scrutiny in 1889 was Narayen Bapuji Kanitkar's ***Nyaya Vijay,*** a commentary on the British judiciary in the Arther Crawford Case. It must be noted that current political issues did form the subject matter of many a play. They were either supportive of or opposed to certain British policies or criticised European public opinion. The reason why these plays were spared from official repression, perhaps could be that they certainly did not hold the British rule in any sort of contempt.[7] Same was true of those plays which either supported or opposed the official line on matters social.[8] The government tolerated moderated criticism of her liberal policies and nothing seditious was noticed in either political or social plays.

But things began to change in the early 1890' s when B. G. Tilak began mobilizing and canalizing all extant forces into one patriotic current. He inaugurated the Sarvajanik Ganesh Festival in 1893, with a view to achieving the moral and political unity of all Hindus. An innovative feature of the Ganapati festival since 1895, was the introduction of ***mela*** movement of singing parties. The ***melas*** produced salutary effect on the large and eager audiences. "During the ten days festival" wrote S. M Edwardes, the then Police Commissioner of Bombay, in his book *The Bombay City Police,* "bands of young Hindus gave theatrical performances and sang religious songs, in which the legends of Hindu mythology were carefully exploited to arouse hatred of the' foreigner', the word *mlenccha* or 'foreigner' being applied equally to Europeans and Muhammadans"[9] It should, however, be noted here that there is nothing on record to show that the Ganapati festival was in any way directed against the Muslims.[10] To this fervour, the annual Shivaji public festival added more zest and vigour. Such yearly events provided further stimulus to the performance of dramas, which aroused nationalist sentiment particularly through historical and Pauranic themes. How these plays fired the zeal of the youth can be gauged from the statement made by Damu Joshi, an ardent Tilakite and an accused in the Kolhapur Bomb Case of 1908 : "During the Ganapati and Shivaji festivals boys uttered speeches which they committed to memory from dramas like ***Rana Bhimdev, Raghobadada,*** and ***Gunotkarsha....***"[11] The British administration saw sinister design in these developments and started licensing of the *melas* and censoring the songs in 1896.

The widespread famine of 1896, the outbreak of plague in 1897, inadequate relief measures, the murder of the Plague Commissioner, Mr. Rand and Lt. Ayerst, and the Thana Forest Riots, all added to the discontent of the masses. They became utterly dissatisfied with the Moderates' policy of "political mendicancy". Criticism of official policies became increasingly sharp in the native press. The Government, which had earlier attempted to control the nationalist *melas,* now appeared to be even more anxious to strike the press, strike quickly and also hard. Tilak's prosecution as an editor of *Kesari* came at this time.[12] When the Government tried to scuttle the press, the Marathi playwrights made an intelligent use of dramatic art through sarcasm and allegories, to create an anti-colonial feeling and to promote nationalism.

Thus, in the 1890s, assertive nationalism found expression in historical dramas. The Maratha and Rajput histories provided suitable themes for plays such as ***Shiva Chatrapati Vijay*** and ***Maharana Pratapsingh.***[13] Not until 1897, the Government found anything objectionable in such dramas. But in the altered situation, particularly due to Tilak's arrest, they came to convey different meaning to the Government and more so to the public.

The first play after 1897, which came to be banned, was ***Shiva Chatrapati Vijay***, written by Anna Martand Joshi, a clerk in the

Government Central Press, Bombay. This seven act play, written in 1893, was based on the historical events that took place between the invasion of Shaishte Khan (1659) and Shivaji's Coronation (1674). It was scheduled for performance at Alfred Theatre in Bombay, in May 1898. The author himself was to personate Shivaji in it. The Commissioner of Police, Mr. R.H. Vincent urged for its withdrawal on the pretext that it would "infuriate low class Muslims during the Mohurrum period".[14] The author complied with Vincent's request by handing over 320 copies of the play. Despite author's cooperation, official proceedings began. The Oriental Translator (OT), however opined that the intention of the playwright "is to give vent to misfeelings in vehement language regarding the subjection of Hindus to foreign rule, their inherent right to be paramount in their own fatherland, the lack of patriotic ardour among the martial races of India for shaking the yokes of foreign oppressors, and the desirability of union among the Hindus for the achievement of their political independence".[15]

There was now a perceptible change in the earlier relatively liberal British attitude towards the works of art. For example, in 1891, the Government had refused to ban the Urdu play ***Haroon Rashid***, despite a petition from the Muslims that the play had hurt their religious sentiments. The Government stand was that such a prohibition would set a bad precedent and that the original Persian text on which the play was based, had not hurt the sentiments of the people of Persia.[16] But in 1898, the bureaucracy termed Shivaji's soliloquy addressed to Aurangzeb in ***Shiva Chatrapati Vijay*** as likely to incite religious animosity. Since the play could not be covered by DP Act XIX of 1876,[17] the Government considered the prospect of using Indian Penal Code and Criminal Procedure Code, and eventually sought to effect the Bombay City Police Bill of 1898, to cover such cases. The play was not prohibited officially but suppressed at the police level. A departmental investigation was initiated against the author of the play, A.M. Joshi, and his antecedents traced. Joshi was found, "amenable to pressure". Though spared from further disciplinary action, he was black-listed and his name appeared regularly in the Police Abstracts thereafter.

Tilak's arrest and trial in 1898, created tremendous public commotion. It was reflected in the play ***Lokmat Vijay*** written by Anant Waman Barve of Nasik. This play was staged at Mahad on 11

December 1898, by the Manikprabhu Prasadik Mandali. The subject of the play was the diamond jubilee of the Queen Victoria's reign. The objectives of the play were obvious and unmistakable. The character *Ekatantra* (Absolute authority) clearly represented the government, while *Vicharswatantrya* and *Deshabhimani* represented Tilak and Daji Abaji Khare respectively. In *Unmad* (Arrogance), no one could miss in the allusion to Late Mr. Rand and *Ektantra* was none else than the Secretary of State. *Raktapat* was Damodar Hari Chapekar. *Swet-puri* and *Arya-mandal* were England and India respectively. *Unmad* was eventually murdered. The play subscribed to the doctrine that sovereign power *(Rajsatta)* should be controlled by the people *(Lokmat).*[18] While glorifying Tilak as an embodiment of liberty, Barve covertly castigated the Secretary of State, for trying to suppress public opinion as represented by Lokmanya Tilak. This play was staged several times in Pune, until the District Magistrate(DM), Kolaba, S.R. Arther wrote, "the object and intention (of the play) are to represent the government and its officers in an odious light and thereby to bring the government into contempt."[19] It was then that the Government took serious note of this play and was banned under the District Police Act of 1890. Inquiries were made whether the play was staged in other places as well.[20] The proceedings show how the administration was confused over the application of appropriate law in order to give constitutional validity to all its arbitrary actions. It is interesting to note that the British bureaucracy was extremely careful to cover all its repressive measures under the semblance of law. Barve was black-listed and his movements were minutely tracked by the Intelligence Department.

Immediately after Tilak's release in 1898, came another play entitled ***Bandhavimochan*** (Liberation from the Foreign Yoke) by Gopal Govind Soman. The author in his introduction to the play quoted Charles Bradlaugh : "We claim the right to reason, the right to argue, the right to answer, the goal door is no syllogism, the goaler's key is no argument". This was translated into Marathi verse and sung as '***nandi***' at the start of the performance.[21] The play deprecated people's attitude of finding solace in servitude and urged them to inculcate virtues of patriotism, dedication, selflessness, humility and courage. The character *Satyavrat,* representing Tilak was portrayed to possess these virtues. *Anutkarsha,* representing Gokhale, was shown to fight against *Satyavrat.* The characters *Dunnati, Durvilas* represented English officers. The author showed that political rights could be acquired and national welfare achieved if only more persons emulated *Satyavrat*. It was thinly veiled historical account of Tilak's trial, conviction and subsequent release.

The play was advertised through the handbills which carried Tilak's photograph and the names of several prominent persons who urged the people to see its performance. On top of the handbill was printed "God Save the Queen".[22] The handbills provided the necessary proof to the Government to initiate action against the play. The manager of the Arya Subhodh Natak Mandali, Dadabhai Narayan Dhume handed over the copy of the play on demand to the police. The Commissioner of Police, Mr. R.H. Vincent, reported to the government that the play "will have the effect of glorifying Tilak at the expense of the government". He feared that the "enthusiasm evoked by it would become more and more accentuated". The play ***Bandhvimochan*** was performed at Ripon Theatre in Bombay, on December 17, 1898, before a packed audience. It created commotion, especially with regard to unjust treatment meted out to Tilak and whenever his innocence was portrayed. After much bureaucratic battle of wits over the applicability of suitable law, the government arrived at a decision that, "We cannot prohibit a performance on the ground that it is a caricature on the travesty of a judicial trial unless it is a scandalous, defamatory, seditious and immoral", and it could at best attract contempt of the High Court.[23] Nevertheless, the Secretary to the Government suggested in the margin, *"by the unofficial pressure of Commissioner of Police"*. The suggestion was implemented.

The author of the play, Gopal Ganesh Soman, a clerk in the Executive Engineer's office at Thana was charged for transgressing official code of conduct, and of "divergence from the path of rectitude." He was admonished, warned of instant dismissal, and transferred to Ahmedabad. Instead of accepting humiliation, he chose to resign.

II

The ***Swadeshi*** movement and Partition of Bengal gave a big momentum to the nationalist Marathi theatre. The nationalist programme of *Swadeshi*, Boycott and National Education was diligently propagated under a number of dramas written during this period.

The play ***Swadeshi Natak*** (1906) written by Ganesh Ballal Phansalkar, a lawyer from Satara, and a former student of Tilak's Law Classes and a staunch Tilakite, presented British traders as "the most despicable and heartless scoundrels, eating into the marrow of India." The purpose of their trading was described as to "take away all their (Indian's) wealth and to give them in exchange the shell of a coconut". On the first page of the play, God's name was invoked in order to rescue such oppressed Hindus from the clutches of their oppressors. The Englishmen were represented to say, "We will be Satan's auxiliaries, we will foment quarrels among the people... If anyone tries to raise his head above others, we will put out his eyes with the edge of keen and piercing steel". When asked by S.R. Arther, the DM of Satara about the allusions, Phansalkar denied that it was against the Government, called it an "idle remark" and pointed out to him that it was "against the British traders and not the Government".[24] This play was staged in different parts of Maharashtra, also Marathi speaking parts such as Indore, Baroda and Gwalior and at Dharwar, Hubli, Belgaum and Ranibennur in Karnataka. It was staged with two other plays, which Phansalkar jointly wrote with 'Prabhakar', ***Sangit Rashtrodhar Natak*** and ***Bhatji Bovachi Sankrant,*** which too carried the same import. ***Shri Shivaji*** or the ***Sangit Rashtrodhar Natak*** was based on the life of Shivaji and it portrayed the British in the same light as in ***Swadeshi Natak.*** Instead of traditional invocation to Ganapati, the opening verses of this play were addressed to *"freedom" (Swatantryadevata).* These plays were staged by *Swajan Hiteshi Sangit Dramatic Company,* a theatrical troupe founded by the Phansalkar himself. In the course of performance, the audience were asked to further the interest of *Swadeshism.* The principal message was, "fight and obtain independence". Both these plays were banned.[25] Printed copies of these dramas were secretly sold at a nominal price. ***Bhatji Bovachi Sankrant*** (1907) was yet another play written by Phansalkar. Its plot was as follows: Bhatji Bova, the hero, had two wives. By playing one against another, he thought he would have a happy time with both. But contrary to his belief, it only resulted in jealousy and squabbles in the family. The wives ultimately realised that their husband was a cheat, and he became a victim of their wrath. The drama deftly depicted the "divide and rule", especially with reference to the partition of Bengal. Invariably, the members of the troupe burnt foreign manufactured goods in a fire lighted on the stage.[26] Images representing "jealousy" and "self-interest" were thrown into fire lit on the stage, which produced wholesome effect on the audience.[27] The play was finally banned.

The following three plays written by Ganesh Dhonddev Kane were also officially banned. 1] ***Bhu Durg Durg*** [1907] This play dramatised an episode in Shivaji's early career, viz. the storming of the land fortress of Belwadi which was in the possession of the Sultan of Golkonda, and the valiant role played by Yesaji and his wife, in capturing the fort. The virtues of *Swarajya* and the horrors of alien rule were vividly brought out.[28] 2] ***Prithwiraj- Sanyogita*** (1909) This historical drama made references to *Swadeshi* movement. The hero, Prithwiraj, represented Tilak and the Extremist party, and Jaichand, the villain, represented the Moderates. The fictitious character of Kesar Singh was introduced to depict the newspaper, Kesari.[29] 3]***Drauni Mani Haran*** (1910) The play was intended to provide ideological justification to the use of force to put down the evil, which in the present case was the British colonial rule.[30] Even his ***Sangit Lanka Vidwans Natak*** came under official scrutiny. Ganesh Dhonddev Kane was a clerk in the political department of the Secretariat. Since he refused to bind himself by written agreement not to indulge in such adventures, he preferred resigning the job than being dismissed. And although he was obliged to do so, ever since his movements were tracked by the Criminal Intelligence Department.

A number of other Marathi dramas - ***Vanga Vadh*** and ***Barisalchi Dhamdhum*** by Vasudev Purushottam Sathe, ***Maharana Pratapsingh*** and ***Swadeshi Chalwal*** by Anant Waman Barve, ***Samarth Ramdas*** and ***Bhimrao*** by Laxman Narayañ Joshi, ***Swadeshi Chalawal*** by Ismail Yusuf alias Babaji Bhaldar of Kolhapur,[31] which propagated the *swadeshi* programme met with similar fate. Even a children's play - *Sangit Bhatuklicha Khel* by Dhondo Ramchandra Karmarkar, which contained two songs advocating *swadeshi,* was not spared.

The government repressive measures against *Swadeshi* movement provoked strong public reaction. The Surat Split in 1907, was commonly perceived in Maharashtra as the triumph of Extremism. The unearthing of secret revolutionary groups - the Shivaji Club, the Belapur Swami Club, the Peshwe Club and the Khed Club in March-April1909, made the government suspicious of all dramas. ***Kichak Vadh, Vijay Torana*** and ***Rana Bhimdev,*** to cite a few as examples, which were earlier considered to be a-political and as merely entertainments, were now brought under minute scrutiny and came in for action.

Krishnaji Prabhakar Khadilkar, sub-editor of had written in 1894 ***Sawai Madhavraocha Mruttu*** and ***Kanchangadchi Mohana*** in 1896. But now in the altered situation the government held both these plays in suspicion, due to Khadilkar's closeness to Tilak.[32] But the play which hit the eye of the government was his ***Kichak Vadh***, written in 1907 and staged by Maharashtra Natak Mandali. It was a pauranic drama dealing with the state of Pandwas in their exile, when they were serving incognito at the court of Virat as lowly servants. The play compared their condition with that of Indians serving as slaves under the British. Kichak symbolised Lord Curzon, and Draupadi, partition of Bengal. Draupadi's utterances conveyed the oppression to which the country was subjected. Her appeal to Dharma [Yudhisthir] and Bhim to take up arms for her safety and crush enemy, alluded to Gokhale and Tilak and their respective parties. The play also depicted the miserable condition of the Pandits, well versed in the Shashtras, and the exploits of the Extremists were extolled.[33]

Although the seditious tone of the play was reported to the government in 1907, it did not think it to be so, and no action was taken up to November 1909. The reason could perhaps be that the play was seen more as a wrangle between the Extremists and Moderates, and even Viceroy Lord Curzon to whom it alluded to had left India. Besides, the Bombay Government was lulled into a false sense of security after the Surat Split and deportation of Tilak to Mandaley.

During 1907-1909, ***Kichak Vadh*** was a run-away success. It was staged at many places during the Ganesh festival, and was most popular among the amateur dramatic companies. It was specially staged for Tilak, Aurobindo Ghosh and Lala Lajpat Rai, after their return from Surat session of the Congress.[34] Its success alarmed the Government. As there were conflicting opinions among the officials regarding political allusions in the play, the Government asked F.A.M. H. Vincent, the Deputy Commissioner of Police, Bombay, to see the performance in person and report. Vincent did not find anything objectionable in the play. The Secretary of the Judicial Department, thereafter issued instructions to the local officers through the *Police Abstracts of Intelligence* : "The play ***Kichak Vadh*** does not call for police prosecution and further reports about it may be discontinued..."[35] This decision was soon reversed as the Government discovered from disclosures made by Damu Joshi, the accused in the Kolhapur Bomb Case, about Khadilkar's long stay from 1901 to 1905 in Nepal with a view to manufacturing arms.[36] The disclosure of many revolutionary activities, the attack on Viceroy Lord Minto at Ahmedabad and the murder of A.T.M. Jackson, made the panic stricken government urge for a stringent and repressive law to contain such activities and thereby ward off danger to the British government in India. But the Secretary of State, John Morley would not accede to the demand of the Government of India because of his liberal views. The GOI sought the services of Charles Kincaid, a Secretary of the BG and historian of Maratha period, who was at London on furlough. Through the instrumentality of Valentine Chirol of the *Times* of London, Kincaid wrote four articles in the *Times* [18th January 1910] were arranged to create a favourable opinion among the members of the Parliament and to impress the Home Government about the urgency of enacting a stringent law. They were: 1] 'The Chitpavans of Chiplun', 2] 'The Seditious Deccan Press', 3] the ***Kichak Vadh***, and 4] Political Theories of Ancient India. These articles not only hastened the passage of the Indian Press Act of 1910, but immediately called for the attention of the Government toward the banning of *Kichak Vadh.* These articles were reproduced in *The Times of India* and *Bombay Gazette* on 5th and 7th February 1910 respectively. Proceedings for ban were reprocessed on 14th January 1910 and on January 27th, officially the play ***Kichak Vadh*** was finally banned. Khadilkar's two other popular plays also came under official notice, namely ***Bhaubandki*** and ***Manapaman***, but however were spared. ***Bhaubandki***, a historical play concerned about the internecine quarrels among Raghobadada and Peshwa Narayanrao. It was banned in Poona because of an article in *Dnyan Prakash*. But when the editor, Natesh Appaji Dravid, wrote that it was not against the government, it was spared. When Khadilkar was asked by Veer Vamanrao Joshi as to 'why ***Kichak Vadh*** was banned and ***Bhaubandki*** was spared ?', he replied that "the play ***Kichak Vadh*** was viewed by the government as one that encouraged "assassination of high officials, whereas, in ***Bhaubandaki*** regicide had been condemned and therefore, the play promoted loyalty to the state.[37] The play ***Manapaman*** was spared when the Government discovered that the popularity it attained was not due to its seditious allusions but because of the acting of "Bal Gandharva".

The actors had their own share of miseries due to government repression. The best example of this can be had from the proceedings against the play ***Vijaya Torana***, a historical drama. It was written by Ramchandra Mahadev Mahiskar[38] of Sholapur and was performed at Kolaba. This play was based on the story of an episode of conquest of Torna fort by Shivaji, which was written and serialised as ***Kal Kadambari*** in *Karmanuk* magazine by the famous novelist Hari Narayan Apte. Foreigners were referred in the play as *"Parki"* and *"Mlench"*. Patriotic words and ideas such as *Swarajya, Deshbhakta, Deshdroha, Aryamata* and *Dadapshahi* were put in the mouth of the performers. Samarth Ramdas' teachings were highlighted.[39]

J.N. Kabraji, the DM of Kolaba felt that the play ***Vijay Torna*** incited the youth to form secret societies and preached sedition. He thought that the play would breed hatred in the minds of Hindu audience and thus endanger peace. The staging of the play was promptly banned and proceedings were instituted against Laxman Vithal Oak and fourteen other actors of the Mahad Manoranjak Natak Mandali under Indian Penal Code. The actors had to give a bond of Rs. 200 each, with a surety of Rs. 200 each, for one year, to the effect that they would never again act in the play.[40] The two actors, Keshav Shridhar Chaude and Kashinath Narayan Hardikar, who could not furnish the bond and surety, were sentenced to one year's rigorous imprisonment.[41] This is perhaps, the first instance in the history of Modern Maharashtra, nay India, that actors were prosecuted and sent to jail for sedition.

Rana Bhimdev was jointly written by Vasudev Rangnath Shirwalkar and Vinayak Trimbak Modak in 1892. The play was historical, relating to a fight between the Mohammedans and Rajputs, in which the former captured a Rajput prince and his daughter. But Bhimdev, a Rajput nobleman soliloquizes with great feelings on the past greatness of his race and country, deplored its present fallen condition and exhorts his countrymen to develop the qualities of bravery, chivalry, patriotism and valour, for recovering their lost freedom.[42] How popular this play was can be gauged from the fact that it brought into vogue new phrases such as '*Bhimdevi Thaat*' and '*Bhimdevi Garjana*'. V.R. Shirwalkar, who resided in Bhor State, was warned through the Pant-Pratinidhi. V.T. Modak, the joint author, and Yadneshwar Gopal Dixit, the publisher of the play, were warned by the DM of Poona.[43]

The play ***Rana Bhimdev*** was based on the political philosophy of Tilak, was first staged in 1892 and became an instant success. The histrionic talents displayed by the famous actor Ganapatrao Joshi, who played the role of Rana Bhimdev contributed to the popularity of the play, which was finally banned in 1910.

III

Following the disclosure of many revolutionary activities in Bombay Presidency in January 1910, the near panicky administration urged the GOI to legislate stringent laws "on the subject of control of press and dissemination of sedition by means of dramatic performances." A suggestion was also made to make an insertion in the DP Act by way of amendment,[44] which would cover the licensing of theatres. The GOI's detailed reply which was drafted by Sir Harold Stuart, the Secretary to Home Department, outlined the nature and extent of the spirit of dissatisfaction prevalent and suggested certain remedies to fight sedition. The policy GOI advised :

> Remonstrances may often be a better remedy than persecution and it should always be borne in mind that the Government desire to prevent than to punish.... It should be remembered that persuasion will frequently succeed where threats may fail, and that in some cases a private reproof will be most effective, while in others an open discussion will be the best way of gaining the desired end. The most suitable means, in short, will vary with the circumstances and the treatment to be applied in case it demands very careful consideration...If the remonstrances with the managers fail, any tendency towards sedition must be exposed and suppressed. Any attempt to raise money for political purpose by levying a fee on managers of dramatic companies and circuses should be treated with disfavour.[45]

However, the Bombay Government felt that the GOI was unwilling to treat their demand and thereby refusing to grasp the gravity of the situation, created by the Marathi theatre. Instead, it chose to impress GOI again with the necessity of enacting stringent laws. It thought that by way of compromise the GOI might concede the extension of Section 10 to Marathi speaking areas of Bombay Presidency. Frustrated by the indifference of GOI, the Bombay officials - J.B.

DuBoulay, W.T. Morrison, J.E.B. Hotson, J.W.P. Muir Mackenzie, and M.G. Chaubal sought opinion of the Remembrancer of Legal Affairs [RLA], Mr. L. Crump, whether any amendment to DPA or the District Police Act, or the Bombay Police Act could be possible with a view to strengthening the repressive arm of the Government. They also queried if that could be done under the pretext of "safety of the public". While explaining the scope of Section 10 of the DPA, the RLA pointed out that any amendment to the DPA would not only be "inartistic" but also "wholly unacceptable to the GOI". He opined that an amendment to Police Acts could be possible but that would amount to an "innovation of procedure".[46] Realizing the procedural delay that would be involved in having an amendment, the Bombay Government now reverted back to Sir Harold Stuart's letter, which was sent to all the district officials for their comments.

Almost all the Bombay officials reacted in unison to Sir Harold Stuart's letter. They all vehemently opposed the conciliatory approach suggested by him and supported the policy of stern repression. J.B. DuBoulay, the Secretary, J.D., commented :

> "So long as the policy of the Government remains firm, and district officers understand and follow it, as they are now doing, there is no danger of any misunderstanding. I do not believe that any number of letters of this description will do the smallest good: on the contrary I think there is danger of making the government look ridiculous".[47]

W.T.Morrison concurred with DuBoulay. He wrote :

> "I do not agree with the line of action suggested here is suited to present condition in this presidency. We are past the stage where persuasion, 'private reproof' or warnings can stem seditious movements; and the only safe policy at least for some time to come is stern repression of the very sign of sedition".[48]

Morrison thought that it was not only useless but ridiculous to expect local officials to use their influence for the purpose of inducing people to come forward with evidence of sedition, and that the importance of "treating Indians with courtesy and consideration can never be too frequently or too strongly impressed on our officers". The opinions of other European officers were no different. However, M.B. Chaubal, the Indian member of the Governor's Executive Council differed and angrily noted, "It was a mistake to suppose that instances of discourtesy are confined to the half-fledged military officers alone", and urged, "Englishmen, generally are required to be better known to the people in order that they should be able to appreciate them".[49] Thus, the officials were determined to possess far greater powers than they had and therefore, struggled hard to seek constitutional validity to their repressive measures. The more repressive they became, the greater was Indian reaction.

When asked to give their opinion on Sir Henry's letter, the district officials were candid in placing their practical difficulties, their apprehensions, and the procedural innovation they individually made. Their confidential notings in respect of dramatic performances are a proof of the important role that the Marathi theatre played in promoting nationalism and also reflect the helplessness of the existing laws to contain it. The DM of Poona, L.C. Swift did not see any express need for extension of Section 10 of the DPA. While assuring that there exists a system of unofficial licensing of plays, he feared that a formal licensing authority would require an adequate and trustworthy censorial staff. But he detailed inadequacies in the existing law :

> "The mere fact of a certain drama having been licensed could not always be taken as an indication of its harmless representation in practice...Poona politicians are adept at satisfying the letter of the law while infringing its spirit...Seditious words are interpolated by the actors in a play most carefully scrutinised by the local officers. Any law could scrutinize play but the 'Mela' songs, 'most scurrilous and seditious' are not submitted to censorship... Precautionary licensing in this case has hitherto been a signal failure and has perhaps served merely to lull the authorities concerned into a false sense of security : Again actors by their gestures, mannerisms, costume, etc. can and do imitate popular heroes and give voice to sentiments in themselves objectionable, which in peculiar circumstances and coming from the mouth of an actor imitating a popular idol who has been convicted of sedition, do not fail to hit the mark and bring down the house with some obvious political allusion."[50]

For all these reasons Swift thought that the plays have to be watched by persons well-understanding all topical allusions. J.N.K. Kabraji, the District Magistrate of Kolaba, did not think the evil was so great that necessitated extension of Section 10 of DPA. His instruction to the police was to keep watch on plays with quasi-historical and Pauranic themes. Besides he felt the Sections 108 and

144 were sufficient to take drastic action. But Swift's observations were fully endorsed by Mr. Hayter, the Supdt. of Police, Kolaba :

> "A favourite kind of speech (seditious) in these dramas denounce all those who give any information against their countrymen to foreign rulers. The meaning of these references is obvious and they are always greeted with round of applause...Such publicly applauded remarks means another blow, however slight, to the prestige of government among the people. Such plays are chiefly patronised by the castes which principally foster sedition, and the chief merit of any play, in their eyes, lies in the political innuendoes directed against the government..., these dramas definitely constitute one of the agencies used to injure the prestige of the government and demonstrate its insignificance".[51]

B.A. Brendon, the Collector and DM of Belgaum, forwarded a tabulated statement showing the names of the plays and the theatrical troupes performing, its contents and seditious character of those plays, performed in all talukas of Belgaum district.[52] Most of the government officials were convinced that the ban on theatrical performances would not itself put an end to sedition; it would spread, as J. Ghoshal, the Collector of Ratnagiri, pointed out, it would spread in the form of 'Kathas' and 'puranas' at Jatras.[53]

Based on these responses, the GOI conceded the demand of the Bombay Government for an extension of Section 10 of the DPA to the Marathi speaking areas of the Presidency, in September 1910. Having realised the intensity of the danger, the GOI, with the concurrence of the Secretary of State and the British Parliament, came out with the Indian Press Act in 1910. Armed with additional powers, the Bombay Government became most repressive as never before.

IV

A number of nationalist theatrical troupes came into being during the period under review. The names of some were suggestive of the purpose for which they were founded. Their names were: the *Maharashtra Hittechchu Sangit Mandali, the Swajan Hitachintak Dramatic Company, the Swajan Hiteishi Natak Mandali, Maharashtra Dramatic Company, the Young National Dramatic Company, The Rashtroddhar Natak Mandali, the Aryotkarsha*

Mandali. Most of the managers and proprietors were Tilakites.[54] Since all these were touring troupes, their camps were not infrequently places of refuse for many political activists such as Prof. V.G. Vijapurkar, V.N. Joshirao, Veer Vamanrao Joshi, Krishnaji Hari Dixit and many others.[55] Some of these troupes contributed their mite in a very different way. *Shri Manik Prabhu Prasadik Natak Mandali,* which performed A.W. Barve's *Lokmat Vijay* in 1897, contributed to Tilak Defence Fund. This was followed by *Maharashtra Hitechhu Sangit Natak Mandali, Maharashtra Dramatic Company, Belgaumkar Theatrical Company, Swajan Hitechchu Dramatic Company* contributed to the Tilak Paisa Fund.[56] The *Swadeshi Hitchintak Dramatic Company* gave performance of an unobjectionable play - Govind Ballal Deval's *Sangit Sharada,* but the proceeds were handed over for the benefit of "Shivaji Club" of Kolhapur, a revolutionary outfit. These are not solitary instances but the Intelligence records give many such examples and the exact amount they remitted. These being touring companies, they made collections at different places. Many times a subscription list was passed around in the theatre when a non-political play was performed.

Often the time between the two acts of a play was used to address the audience on the gospel of nationalism. At times, some one from the audience spontaneously spoke on some theme of national interest. For example, during the performance of ***Kanchangadchi Mohana*** at Thane, Dhonddev Kashinath Phadke, Narayan Atre and Diler Khan, a guard from the G.I.P. railways, made a speech on the desirability of unity between Hindus and Muslims.[57] Many times, during the intervals, *Swadeshi* items, books and leaflets preaching nationalism and photographs of Lala Lajpat Rai, Bal Gangadhar Tilak and Bipin Chandra Pal were sold.

In 1907, the *Swajan Hiteishi Natak Mandali* founded by the irrepressible G.B. Phansalkar, invented a novel method of using "drop scenes" curtains for spreading anti-British feeling. The CID report mentions that following words were printed on the background curtain, "Have patriotism for your country, Don't take articles from foreign countries, and Don't drink".[58] These words were interposed with three pictures. The first picture depicted a European to a Marwari trader. It was meant to show the time when Europeans first came to India and obtained information on trade and commerce. The second picture showed the Peshwa sitting on the throne with half-drawn sword, flanked by his Sardars, and a European kneeling before them with his cap off. It showed how "humble and crouching" they were initially before the Indian rulers. The third, portrayed a European sitting in a carriage which is pulled by a Brahmin. It was meant to convey the present state in which children of the soil were treated as beasts by their foreign masters.[59] These curtains were in use for a long time and the *Swajan Hiteishi Sangit Natak Mandali* which used them, travelled from Ranibennur and Dharwar in the South, and Indore and Gwalior in the north. Its photocopies were sold in the market. The DM of Satara, S.R.Arther brought this to the notice of the government and -confiscated the curtains under Section 42 of the District Police Act. The Commissioner of Central Division, A.C. Logan, endorsed Arther's view and informed the government that "the prefatory verses... told every spectator what he was to understand by the allusion of the curtain...." When called upon to explain, Phansalkar, the owner of the troupe, pointed out that the pictures in question had been copied from Douglas' book on Western India. The reply nonplussed the DM. It was only later found out that Phansalkar had effected significant changes in the original pictures so as to convey the veiled meaning. Phansalkar, who outwitted the administration was reprimanded and the painter residing at Poona was not only warned but had to give a surety and a bond for good conduct.

V

Indubitably, the period under review constitutes a glorious phase for nationalist Marathi theatre. Undoubtedly, Tilak was the moving spirit behind the assertive nationalism. The dramatists, actors, proprietors and managers of the theatrical troupes, all put their heart, mind and money in spreading his message. In doing so, they withstood the rigorous challenges of British repression. In all, thirty-nine dramas were prosecuted during this period, thirty-one of which were eventually banned under one or the other provision of law, and sixteen of them were proscribed.

With the introduction of *Satyagraha* movement by Gandhi and participation of the masses in the national movement, the fear of the terror of legal oppression was lost. The necessity of using covert method such as the theatrical movement for mass mobilisation gradually faded and it gave way to direct participation under the Gandhian Satyagraha agitation.

Nevertheless, the work of the Marathi theatrical movement in spreading nationalist sentiment among the masses can be neatly summed up in the words of Nilkanth Pandurang Patankar, who spoke on the occasion of an exhibition of theatrical kit organised at Nasik in 1907. He said :

> "the plot in all dramas should be so construed as to impress on the mind of the spectators that they are witnessing the desires and intentions of the nation. The audience should imagine that the actors on the stage actually represent warriors of the present day."[60]

References

1. *Maharashtra State Archives (MSA), Judicial Department (JD),* Year - 1910, Volume 192, Compilation 922, No. P-995, dated August 17, 1907.

2. *MSA/JD/*1876/ Vol. No. 24/ 398. ***Chaka Darpan*** is confused by many scholars with ***Neel Darpan*** *of Girish Chandra Ghosh.* Even the play ***Neel Darpan*** was also written by him.

3. *Abstract of the Proceedings of the Council of the Governor General of India, assembled for the purpose of making Laws and Regulations under the Provisions of the Act of Parliament 24 & 25 Vic.cap. 67.* (hereinafter *APCGGI)* 1876. Vol. XV, p.74. Except these proceedings, no other source mentions the promulgation to the Ordinance by the Viceroy Lord Lytton in this regard.

4. *Ibid.* p.348.

.5 *Ibid.* p. 349. The Council met on 6th December 1876 to enact the Bill. The meeting was presided over by Major-General Sir H. W. Norman, and was attended by : Arther Hobhouse, E.C. Bayley, Sir A. J. Arbuthnot, R. A. Dalyell, T.C. Hope, Raja Narendra Krishna Bahadur, and F.R. Cockrell.

6. *MSA/JD/*1877/ Vol. 58/699.

7. To quote a few plays which were supportive of government policies were: Shankar Moro Ranade's ***Doctor Va Vaidya Prahasan*** (1881) on government order regarding registration of doctors, ***Adhikardanvivechan*** (1882) on Rippon's Local Self Government Bill, ***Gaurnyayamimansa*** (1884) on the hue and cry raised by Europeans regarding the Ilbert Bill, or Balawant Raoji Patil's ***Nyayadan Athawa Chokh Nivada*** (1884) on the same subject. Many of such plays supported liberal attitude of the

Government but criticised the aggressive and racist European public opinion.

8. During the period between 1880 - 1895, a number of plays were written either supportive of or opposing the contemporary social issues such as infant marriages, evil effects of prostitution, widow's plight, or age of consent or female education. A few examples could be given. The play ***Jayapal*** showed the evil effects of an old man marrying a young girl, and also hints at love marriage. Annasaheb Kirloskar's ***Sangit Saubhadra*** too has love-marriage as the central theme and supported marriages by consent. The plays – ***Manorama*** and ***Swairkesha*** painted gaudy picture of social evils concerning women. Eknath Ganesh Bhandare's ***Kamakandala*** (1881), M. V. Kelkar's ***Tara Naikeen*** (1886) and V.N. Dongre's ***Rangi Naikeen***, showed the evil effects of prostitution. Anna Martand Joshi's ***Sangit Savitri*** and ***Sangit Saubhagyarama*** were written in support of female education and widow marriage. Narayen Bapuji Kanitkar's ***Taruni Shikshan Natika*** (1886) & ***Sammativayache Natak*** (1892) presented the other side of social reforms. Only when Narayen Hari Bhagwat crossed legitimate boundaries in criticising social reforms in ***Mor El. El. Bee. Prahasan***, was sued for vulgarity.

9. S.M. Edwardes, *The Bombay City Police – A Historical Sketch* 1672-1916. Oxford University Press, London, 1923, p.105.

10. For details see J. V. Naik, "British View of the Ganapati Festival", in *Sarvaianik Ganeshotsav - Shatakachi Vatchal*, Mauj Printing Bureau, Bombay, 1992, pp. 109-117.

11. *Bombav Presidencv Police Abstracts of Intelligence (BPPAI)*. 1909, Vol. XXII, Para 2276; November 17,1909. Statement of Damu Joshi before Mr. Wallinger, Supdt. of Police on Spl. Duty, Kolhapur; December 11, 1909.

12. For details regarding Tilak Case (1897) and the *Pratod* Case, in which law was used as an instrument of political coercion in the form of "Stratchey Law", see Aravind Ganachari, "Evolution of the Law of 'Sedition' in the Context of The Indian Freedom Struggle: 1837-1922", in *State Intervention and Popular Response : Western India in the Nineteenth Century*, Popular Prakashan, Mumbai, 1998, pp. 147-171.

13. A few examples could be cited : N.B. Kanitkar's ***Shivaji Natak*** (1889), ***Bajirao-Mastani*** (1892), and ***Baji Deshpande****(1893)*; H.P. Wagle's ***Prabhav Darshan Athwa Sangit Shivaji*** (1891); A.M.Pathare's ***Shri Chatrapati Sambhaji Natak*** (1891); V.D. Bhilwadikar's ***Naravir Tanaji Malusare*** (1898). For a detailed study of the historical plays, refer

Bhimrao Kulkarni, *Eitihasik Marathi Natake*, Joshi- Lokhande Prakashan, Poona, 1971, pp. 141-225.

14. *MSA/JD*/1898/Vol.178/1523; Mr. R. H. Vincent to the Government of Bombay, Confdl. No. 4066/C of 1898, June 24, 1898.

15. *Ibid.*, No.1086 of 1898, June 24, 1898.

16. *MSA/JD/* 1898/Vol. 178/1523; *JD/* 1892/ Vol. 6/436, Minute by the Secretary to the Government, Sir Raymond West.

17. To bring a play under the purview of DP Act of 1876, it had to be of "a scandalous or defamatory nature or likely to excite feelings of dissatisfaction to the Government established by law in British India, or likely to deprave or corrupt persons present at such performances". The Act did not cover "inciting religious animosity". Hence, it was covered under the Section 153 of the Criminal Procedure Code.

18. *MSA/JD*/1899 / Vol. 167/580.

19. *Ibid.*, Letter No.4 (Confdl.) December 23, 1898.

20. *Ibid.*, No.6752, September 29, 1899. It was earlier staged at Poona and Nasik. When asked to explain, the DM of Poona shifted the blame on his subordinates, and DM of Nasik blamed the Deputy Collector K.B. Pendse. The Secretary, JD, BG, reprimanded the DM of Nasik : "You will be so good as to point out to K.B. Pendse that however admirable the ostensible moral may be, still that a dramatic performance, in which the Secretary of State is held up, under a thin disguise, to exercation and a person who has been imprisoned for sedition is held up as virtuous model, is not precisely the kind of thing that the DM would have expected a Native Officer of experience and presumably of good judgement, to approve of".

21. Gopal Govind Soman, *Sangit Bandhavimochan Athwa 1897 Salatil Raikopkahar*, Saraswati - Shrungal Press, Mumbai, 1900, Introduction.; It was translated into Marathi verse :

    Kārasthāni Suneetivād Karuni Prashnôttaré Vhāvayā

    Lokāā Dyāchi mubhā Ase Chir mani Thévitaśe To tayā

    Bandivās na alp ji Upajavi Bheeti Kadā Kālihee

    Taisā vāādvivādee bandh na aasā Hôyeel Upoddhātahi

22. *MSA/JD*/1899/ Vol. 167/319. The handbill of the play ***Bandhavimochan*** is in the file. The system of free distribution of handbills in the town was started by Prof. Vasudeorao Kelkar for Shahunagarvasi Natak Mandali. A few such handbills have been given in Laxman Narayan Joshi, *Ganapatrao Joshi Yanche Charitra*. Vangmaya-Vihar-Mandal, Pune, 1923, pp. 132-138.

23. *Ibid.*, No.9366/ C of 1898, December 17, 1898.

24. *MSA/JD/* 1907/ Vol. 192/922, No. 5834 (Confdl.) August 7, 1907.

25. *Ibid.*

26. *BPPAI/*1907/XX/ NO.10 of 1907/ 16th March/ Para 212[c]

27. *BPPAI/*1907/ Vol. XXI, Para 307/ April 20, 1907.

28. *MSA/JD/*1910/Vol. 192/922; Papers are not found in the original compilation. *JD/*1910/ Vol. 169/ 862 [Confidential].

29. *BPPAI/*1909/ Vol. XXII, Para 1516, July 24, 1909.

30. *MSA/JD/* 1910/ Vol. 192/922.

31. *BPPAI/*1911/ Vol. XXIV / Supplement dt. November 4, 1911. *List of Prohibited Publications.*

32. *BPPAI/* 1907/ Vol. XX / Para 229[b], March 16, 1907.

33. *MSA/JD/*1910/ Vol.192/ 922, and *HD/*(Spl) Comp. 265 (Confdl.) 1910.

34. Keshav Trimbak Datey, "*Maharashtra Natak Mandali* : *Ek Drishtikshep* 1907-1929" in *Marathi Rangabhumi : Marathi Natak -Ghatana Ani Parampara* Dr. Amrutrao Narayan Bhalerao Memorial Volume, Mauj, Bombay, 1971, p.75. Keshavrao Datey was himself an actor of renown. He was a contemporary.These are his recollections.

35. *BPPAI/*1909/Vol. XXII, Para 2146[c], November 13, 1909.

36. An excellent account of the Nepal Affair is given by Y. D. Phadke, *Lokmanva Tilak Ani Krantikarak,* Srividya Prakashan, Pune, 1985, pp. 40-61; Also *Khadilkar Smaranika,* Y.K.Khadilkar [ed.], Shri Dattatryaya Printing Press, Bombay, 1949.; Khadilkar had stayed with Damu Joshi, with a view to manufacturing arms. Joshi gave out information under duress caused by third degree torture to Wallinger, regarding their Nepal venture. *BPPAI/*1909/ Vol.XXII, Para 2276, December 11, 1909.

37. Quoted by M.S. Kanade, *Kalache Natak-kar,* Joshi-Lokhande Prakashan, Pune, 1967, p.8. Proceedings of *Bhaubandki* in *MSA/JD/* 1910/ Vol.192/ 1452, are not found.

38. The intelligence records give following information. Ramchandra Mahadev Mahiskar was a native of Haripur in Miraj State. He was 27 years of age in 1910 and has passed vernacular third grade Public Final Exam from Sholapur in 1902. He joined as an untrained teacher on 15 September 1904 in Sholapur Municipality School No.6 on a salary of Rs. 8/-. He did not know English and taught lower classes. He is described

as a man of 'quite disposition and having good character'. The CID were of the opinion that he wrote this play with a view to making profit and did not have sufficient knowledge to form opinions on politics. He was officially given a warning and an undertaking was taken that he would not indulge in such activities again. *BPPAI*/1910/ Vol. XXIII, No.18/ 7th May 1910/ Para 1295[i].

39. *MSA./JD/* 1910 / V0l. 192/ 922. The compilation is not found in the original volume : *JD*/1909/ V0l. 135/2018[Confdl.]

40. *MSA/JD*/1910/ Vol.216/1272; *BPPAI*/ 1909/ Vol. XXII/ Para 2267.

41. *MSA/JD*/ 1911/ No. P-334/43, dated 18.6.1910. This play was actually based on Sheridon's *Pizzaro*.

42. L.N.Joshi, *op.cit.*; Also, Ganesh Govind Bodas, *Mazi Bhumika*. Shri Dnyaneshwar Press, Kolhapur, 1940, pp.52-53.

43. *MSA/JD*/ 1911/ Vol.233/ 2307 [Confdl.] After being warned, Shirwalkar turned to different themes and wrote *Sant Tukaram*, which also became an instant hit.

44. *MSA/JD*/1910/ Vol. 235/1553, Bombay Government's Letter No.332 dated 19 January 1910.

45. *Ibid.*, Sir Harold Stuart, the Secretary to GOI, Home/ Political Department, writing to the GB, No. 345, dated 4.3.1910.

46. *Ibid.*, Circular No. 1800, dated 30 March 1910

47. *Ibid.*

48. *Ibid.*

49. *Ibid.*

50. *MSA/JD*/ 1910/ Vo1.192/922 [Confdl.]; L.C. Swift, the DM of Poona to the Under-Secretary, JD, No. C-23, June 25, 1910.

51. *Ibid.*, No.25, May 13,1910.

52. The list of 85 plays with comments was submitted by Brendon through the Commissioner, Southern Division, No. P.334/43 [Confdl.] dated 18.6. 1910. *MSA/JD*/1910/ Vol. 192.

53. When the DPA was passed in 1876, the mover of the Bill Arther Hobhouse had categorically stated that they did not intend to interfere with religious ceremonies and that "nothing in this Act should apply to any *Jatras* or performances of a like kind at religious festivals." APCGGI. Vol. XVI 1876, p.340.

54. Raoji Gopal Mhaiskar, Manager of Swadesh Hitachintak; G.B.Phansalkar, owner of Swajan Hiteishi, and its manager Krishnaji Abaji Guruji, one who was jailed for writing *Bhavani Talawar* in 1896; Maharashtra Dramatic Company -Manager: Dattopant Deshpande and Trimbak Sitaram Karkhanis; Young National Dramatic Company: founder Sitaram Keshav Damle, younger brother of the famous poet' *Keshavsut* 'and editor of *Rashtramat and Rashtrodava*; Patankar Dramatic Company: Madhav Narayan Patankar; Belgaumkar Theatrical Company: Proprietor D. V. Newalkar.

55. *BPPAI*/1911/ Vol. XXIV / Para 2244, October 21, 1911.

56. *BPPAI*/1908/Vol. XXI/ Para 718; Vol. XXI / Para 769, July 25, 1908; 1908/ Vol. XXI / Para 571, June 27, 1908.

57. *BPPAI*/1908/Vol. XXI/ Para 389/ 14 May 1908

58. *MSA/JD/* 1910 / Vol. 192 /922, No. 955-P [Confdl.] August 17, 1907.

59. *BPPAI*/ 1907/ VOL.XX/ Para 739/ August 3, 1907.

60. *BPPAI* /1908/ Vol. XXI, Para 514, June 3, 1908.

2

Evolution of the Law of 'Sedition' in the Context of The Indian Freedom Struggle: 1837 - 1922

The law of 'Sedition' was an import *from* English law into the Indian Penal Code, in the colonial period. During the freedom struggle, on the one hand the British Indian administration, under changing political exigencies, sought to repress any hostile criticism of its rule by ever widening the legal scope of the term 'sedition', and on the other, the nationalists questioned the very basis of it. Was it sedition of the people against the colonial government *(rājdroha)* or of the Government against the Indian people *(deshdroha)* ?[1]

This article seeks to trace the evolution of the Indo-British law of sedition through the diverse phases of India's freedom struggle, and to point out how the law of sedition and the Indian nationalists acted and reacted on each other. With ever increasing repression, the nationalists found different ways of disseminating ideas of 'freedom' other than the press, through *me a* songs, the theatre, *kirtans, pravachanas* and public lectures. Unable to stem the tide of nationalism, the Government sought to contain 'sedition', firstly, by prosecuting the newspapers and secondly, by amending the Indian Penal Code (IPC) and Criminal Procedure Code (Cr. PC); applying different existing laws and enacting new cognate laws such as the Sea Customs Act (1878). the Seditious Meeting Act (1908), and the Indian Press Act (1910), to name a few. The chain reaction continued until Mahatma Gandhi inaugurated an era of *Satyagraha* when the 'terror of law' was lost.

The article also seeks to argue that the bureaucracy at various levels was at pains to maintain a legal fiction while using every conceivable means to suppress nationalist agitation. The law of sedition as it came to be applied to the Indian situation reflected a tension between the British adherence to democratic ideas in theory and its actual recourse to repression as a means of political survival. Likewise, the article seeks to establish that in this process the Anglo-Indian press generally acted as an agent and the judiciary as the coercive arm of the executive.

The Origin and Enactment of the Law of Sedition - Section 124-A

The clause on 'sedition' stood as Section 113 in Macaulay's draft Indian Penal Code (IPC) of 1837, and was shelved for twenty years until the enactment of IPC in 1860. But when enacted, the said clause was curiously omitted, only to be inserted into the IPC by way of an amendment in 1870. This raises a few pertinent questions, i.e. why was the draft shelved for 20 years? Why was the said clause on sedition omitted in 1860 while enacting the IPC despite the Revolt of 1857? And, what prompted the Government to insert the clause by an amendment in 1870? A few probable reasons could be offered.

Firstly, in Bombay, "Rules, Ordinances and Regulations" for preventing 'the mischief' arising from the printing and publishing of newspapers and periodicals was enacted in March 1825. These regulations continued in force until September 15, 1835, when they were replaced by Act XI of the year. Besides, the press was liberated by Sir Charles Metcalfe in 1835. It remained practically free until the Revolt of 1857, for the restrictions were never put in force and Government had no intention of enforcing them.[2] As a result, fairly sharp criticism of the British rule was not seen as bringing the Government into disrepute or contempt. Examples of such criticism could be cited of Bhaskar Tarkhadkar's letters under the pseudonym of 'A Hindu' in the *Bombay Gazette* of 1841,[3] and Bhau Mahajan's hard hitting editorials in *Prabhakar* on the dethronement of Raja Pratapsingh of Satara.[4] Macaulay's draft survived the ordeal of 20 years of detailed criticism from many quarters. Auckland had referred it to the Sadr and Supreme Court judges of Presidencies. Their comments were compiled by C.H. Cameron in two extensive reports in

1846 and 1847. He recommended the enactment of the IPC but the Government took no action as Lord Dalhousie was busy in the Second Sikh War and his Law Member Drinkwater Bethune was uncompromisingly hostile to the draft IPC. Bethune produced a draft of his own as he was opposed to the Benthamite features. Dalhousie referred the question to London as he felt undecided about such widely differing proposals. Meanwhile, after the Charter Act of 1853, the Second Law Commission was constituted comprising Cameron, Millett and Sir John Romily which decided in favour of Macaulay's Code.[5] It took six years thereafter to enact the Cr. PC (1860) and IPC (1861).

After the Revolt of 1857, the nationalists generally eschewed violence, and took to constitutional form of agitation. Violence was not given up altogether; it went underground only to surface periodically. Lord Canning immediately brought the press under official scrutiny. The earlier Act XI of 1835 was not replaced but supplemented by Act XV of 1857, passed two months after the outbreak of Revolt. It did away with the liberal attitude of the earlier period and gave to the Government a more absolute and summary control over the press than before.[6]

The omission of clause 113 pertaining to sedition from the IPC, when enacted in 1861, however was very surprising. Sir Barnes Peacock who moved the IPC Bill in 1860, when asked by Sir James Stephen in 1870, was quite unable to account for its omission. He recalled, "I have looked into my notes and I think the omission of a section in lieu of section 113 of the original Penal Code must have been through mistake... I feel, however, that it was an oversight on the part of the Committee not to substitute for section 113".[7] This was officially stated by Sir James in 1870. This explanation lacks credibility considering the fact that the IPC was enacted immediately after the Revolt. Perhaps, a few possible reasons for omission could be offered that, 1) the so called seditious tone of the press was already brought under official scrutiny under Act XV of 1857; 2) attempts at rebellion were covered in the IPC under Section 121 and 121-A, i.e. waging war against the Government and abetting to wage a war[8]; 3) under the recommendation of the Peel Commission of 1859, the army was so recognized as to prevent any future rebellion[9]; and 4) the rebellion by the Bengali Muslim Police during the Revolt led to a reduction of the number of Bengali Muslims in force. Instead, there was a large scale recruitment of non-Bengalis—Biharis and Punjabis, into the Bengal Police.[10] Under the circumstances, an inclusion of a clause on sedition could have been thought as disturbing the already hurt Indian psyche, and that the assuaging effect of the promises given in the Queen's Proclamation could have been lost.

What then prompted the insertion of a clause on 'sedition' by an amendment to the IPC? A legislation could only be necessitated either to unify the existing laws or to bring a new one due to political exigencies. As the enactment of the IPC unified the earlier laws, political necessity of a serious nature alone could have prompted the insertion. The fact that Sir James Stephen could not give any conclusive evidence, and that 'disapprobation' of official measures was allowed, rules out the possibility of a seditious vernacular press. Besides, Act XXV of 1876, which necessitated declaration from editors, printers, publishers and owners of printing presses, and made their registration compulsory, was intended to be a deterrent and a preventive measure against cognate seditious offences.

Interestingly, Sir James Stephen's speech while introducing the amendment was an eyewash. His justification was that it brought about uniformity and removed incongruities in the existing law.[11] He pointed out that the new section aimed to punish attempts to excite feelings of 'disaffection' against the Government and made a distinction between 'disaffection' and 'disapprobation'.[12] In fact, the insertion of a section on 'sedition' was prompted by the increasing Wahabi activities between 1863-1870.[13] Despite the Ambala and Patna trials of 1864-65, the Wahabis continued to draw men and money from parts of Bengal and Bihar, and their agents moved freely amongst a large Muslim populace for this purpose. To book these 'agents of sedition', E.C. Bayley, Secretary to Government of India (GOI), Home Department, suggested "the necessity of amending law with the object of enabling the government to deal more satisfactorily with seditious proceedings not amounting to waging, or attempting to or abetting to wage war against the Queen, that it cannot now do under the provisions of the Indian Penal Code."[14] Also, the murders of Viceroy Lord Mayo and Justice Norman of the Calcutta High Court must have precipitated the situation. Accordingly, comments were invited from the Government of Bengal and enquiries were made with the Bombay Government (BG) about connection of the Bombay Wahabis with those of Bengal. All the officials favoured a legislation amending the

IPC, so that the Wahabis could no longer be detained under Regulation III of 1818. The concluding remark of A. Eden, Secretary, Judicial Department (JD), GOI, is indicative of the real motives, "There can be no doubt that where a population is at once ignorant and fanatical, as are the Mohammedans of India, seditious teaching are to be made a substantive offence".[15]

Thus, the Bill containing the law of sedition, i.e. Section 124-A, was passed on November 25, 1870 as Act XXVII, an amendment to the IPC and continued to remain in force unmodified till 18 February, 1898.[16] Accordingly, an act or writing which smacked of 'disapprobation' of certain government measures was allowed but any attempt to spread 'disaffection' was considered sedition. Curiously, no case came up under this clause until 1891.

It is significant to note that the official records classified the case against Vasudev Balwant Phadke as 'decoity'. Phadke was charged under Section 121-A, 122, 395 and 400 of the IPC. The government's effort to bring him under more stern laws than Section 124-A which dealt with sedition, is clear from the comments of Judge W.H. Newnham of the Poona Sessions Court: "His attempt at treason might be negligible. Nevertheless it was an attempt at Sedition and inciting dissatisfaction by spoken words... His attempt to do this had not the slightest possibility of success in it. But you must not forget that a good deal of mischief would have been done and serious consequences would have followed because of it."[17]

While the administration was discreet in not using the law of sedition against criticism of official measures, it dealt severely with any attempt of uprising, however negligible.

Sedition and the Cognate Offence – the Preventive Measures

After 1870, the administration did not amend the law of sedition until 1898 but sought to cover sedition by enacting two cognate laws, i.e. the Dramatic Performances Act XIX of 1876 (DPA) and the Vernacular Press Act (IX) of 1878. If there was criticism, it was against the official measures and did not aim at the Government itself. Hence. these Acts were termed 'preventive measures'.

The passage of the first Act was prompted by two plays - *Cha-Ka Durpan* (The Mirror of Tea Planting) in Bengali and *Malharraoche Natak* by Narayan Bapuji Kanitkar in Marathi.[18] The Government was quick to realize the impact of this medium in spreading sedition. This is evident from the comments of Mr. Hobhouse, who introduced the Bill. He observed, "Now in all times and countries, the drama has been found to be one of the strongest stimulants that can be applied to the passion of men. And in times of excitement no surer mode has been found of directing public feeling against an individual, a class or a Government than to bring them on the stage in an odious light... Prevention was worth all the punishment in the world. That was particularly true in times of excitement and in case where the play was of a seditious character. If the performance took place few times, the mischief was done, and it was poor satisfaction to punish the offenders."[19]

A case was initiated under this law against the play *Malharraoche Natak*, which dealt with the trial of the ex-Maharaja Gaekwar of Baroda that took place in the British court. The prosecution was dropped because it appeared to show that the Government was afraid to allow the play which depicted proceedings of its own court.[20]

The second cognate law -the Vernacular Press Act of 1876 - was brought by Lord Lytton to suppress criticism of British policies in the native press because of the events of 1875-76, namely, the Deccan Agricultural riots. It aimed to control the publishers and printers of periodical magazines in native languages by means of a system of personal security. The only prosecution in Maharashtra for seditious writing under this Act was of *Pune Vaibhav* in 1881, which had commented in the editorial note that, 'the failure of his (Irish leader Parnell's) efforts in Ireland only suggest the futility of such civilized methods. The only remedy for any country to attain independence could perhaps be the use of the barbarous means as those of Cabul".[21] The, Bombay officials favoured prosecution under Section 124-A of IPC and requested the Government of India for permission to implement the Section. It was turned down because the thinly veiled seditious allusions did not carry force. Both the cases show that the conservative Bombay Government was ever ready to use Section 124-A against the slightest hint of criticism.

The *Bangobasi* Case

The first trial on record for sedition was Queen Empress v. Jogendra Chander Bose and Others, more commonly known as the *Bangobasi* case of 1891, which brought up the question of limits of legitimate criticism against the official measures. The *Bangobasi*, a newspaper edited by Jogendra Chandra, while reacting to the passage of the Age of Consent Bill (1891), raised the cry of 'religion in danger', and charged the Government for Europeanising India by brute force, and held it responsible for the economic deprivation of Indians. However, it also stated that Hindus neither believed in rebellion nor were they capable of it.[22]

The question that was discussed in the case was: Did the *Bangobasi* exceed the bounds of legitimate criticism? The prosecution charged that the intention was to bring the people into a frame of mind – 'we would rebel if we could', and that the religious feelings of the people were so excited that public peace was imperiled. The defence argued that there was no reference to 'rebellion', and that it only differentiated between "European and native method of thought". However, the judge 'thought that *Bangobasi* excited the feelings of ill-will against the Government and attempted to hold it up to the hatred and contempt of the people."[23] In the meanwhile, the accused tendered an apology and the proceedings were dropped. In 1891, unlike the earlier period, the official attitude showed that it was increasingly becoming intolerant of the slightest criticism not just of British rule but of minor measures as well. The observation of the judge was noteworthy, for it related to legislation that came after the Tilak case in 1898.

Political Atmosphere and Amendment to Section 124-A

Two cases made a significant contribution to ' the evolution of-the, law of sedition in 1897. The Tilak Case and the *Pratod* Case, the events of 1896-97, the hostile criticism 'of the native press' against the failure of government measures and the growing popularity of B.G. Tilak, alarmed the government. The officials decided him to fix him by any means but within the legal framework. On 12 June 1897, Tilak took the lead in celebrating the Shivaji Coronation ceremony with lectures and patriotic songs. Although the function went off peacefully, the report of this function which appeared in *Kesari*, was followed by the murder of Plague' Commissioner Rand and Lt. Ayerst on June 22. Legal proceedings against Tilak on the charge of sedition were then pressed. This case is important on several counts : first, it was a classic example of how the imperialist Anglo-Indian press goaded government into arresting Tilak on charges of sedition and also prejudiced the judiciary; second it illustrated how the law and the legal system were twisted to suit the official purpose; and lastly, it precipitated the amendment to the existing law of Sedition [Section 124-A of IPC] to make it more comprehensive and draconian.

The alleged seditious report in *Kesari* of 15 June 1897, carried two different series of publications. The first was a metaphorical rhapsody in verse entitled 'Shivaji's utterances'. It was alleged that the verse depicted Shivaji's deliverance of *Swarajya* against foreigners and made allusions to tribulation of the people under British rule and that the sign of the *Bhawani* sword affixed at the end of the verse symbolized taking up arms. The second was a report that contained speeches in which Shivaji was compared with other historical personages such as Caesar, Napoleon and Mazzini. It also included Professor S. G. Jinsiwale's justification of Shivaji's murder of Afzal Khan.

The legal proceedings against Tilak were precipitated by a venomous campaign launched by the *Times of India* and *Bombay Gazette*. Not only the letters of 'Justice' and 'Shackles' but also the editorials of the *Times* charged Tilak's articles in *Kesari* as seditious and faulted the Government for allowing such a man to be on the Governor's Executive Council. On June 28, 'Shackles' connected Tilak to Rand's murder and thereby suggested his complicity in the murder. The *Times* advocated to the Government on July 6, to prosecute Tilak under Section 124-A. The Anglo-Indian press in India and England echoed the charge. This prompted Sir E. Ashmead Barlette to question the Secretary of State for India in the Parliament on June 9. Tilak's retort to the mischievous writings of the *Times* appeared in the *Kesari* of June 30.[24] As expected, Tilak was arrested on charges of sedition on August 27th and the trial began on September 8th, 1897.

Significantly, while applying Section 124-A, Justice James Strachey rejected the defence argument that the articles describing the sufferings of the people were quite consistent with loyalty, the object of the accused was to "create a national sentiment" and that "no suggestion to overthrowing the British Government" was made. Further, he transcended the argument of the prosecution and gave his own interpretation on, the "feelings of disaffection" : it meant "hatred, enmity, dislike, hostility, contempt and every form of ill-will to the Government". He equated disaffection to disloyalty, comprehending every possible form of bad feeling and held that "the amount or the intensity of the disaffection is absolutely immaterial except perhaps in dealing with the question of punishment". On the 'disapprobation' allowed in the explanation to clause 124-A, he remarked, "It does not apply to any writing which consists not merely of comments upon Government measures, but of attacks upon the Government itself, its existence, its essential characteristic, its motives, or its feelings towards the people".[25] In view of the significant interpretation, the obvious necessity of importing plainer language into the law of sedition was at once recognised and legislation speedily followed in 1898. Justice Strachey's remarks were very often cited in subsequent cases and confirmed.

Tilak was aware that the case for prosecution was weak but he feared the bias of a non-Marathi knowing and European dominated jury. He knew that the law was twisted to suit the administration. The native press called it "the Strachey Law".[26] Justice Strachey, who was the junior most on the bench and was known for his bias against the natives, was especially asked to preside over the case. Tilak's conviction was resented by almost the entire vernacular press and it did contribute to mass mobilization.

The *Pratod* case, concerned with a newspaper from Islampur in Satara district that published the article "Preparation for becoming independent" (27 May 1897). The article described Canadian nationalist resistance to colonial exploitation and the manner by which Canadians acquired political democratic rights, and urged the Indians to follow suit. The judge, H.F. Aston sentenced the first accused, R.N. Kashalkar, the publisher, to transportation for life and the other, K. D. Hamalkar, the printer, for seven years imprisonment. His remark explains the bias against Indians, "The sentence should be such as to bring home to the minds of all, the gravity of the offence committed by those who seek to undermine the foundation on which the greatest strength of the Government in India rests".[27]

This case came up on appeal to the High Court, a few months after the Tilak Case, before the full bench consisting of Chief Justice Farran, Justice Parson and Justice M.G. Ranade. All the judges unanimously held that animus was to excite a feeling of aversion and hatred against the Government. They believed that the attack was not against any particular act or measure of Government or its officers, but was an outcome of a vague disaffection against the existing political system. Significantly, the judges made further interpretation of the terms 'disaffection' and 'disapprobation' but within the framework provided by 'the Strachey Law'. Justice Farran felt that the word "disaffection" used in Section 124-A "cannot be construed as meaning an absence of or the contrary of affection of love, that is to say dislike or hatred". It is an attempt "to excite political discontent and alienation from their allegiance". He concluded the enigmatic exposition by saying that "the article as a whole has the object of making its readers impatient of their allegiance to a foreign sovereign and creating in them the desire of casting off their dependence upon England". Justice Parson concurred with Farran. Justice Ranade generally concurred with other judges but made a studied observation: "Disaffection is a positive political distemper, and not a mere absence or negation of love and good-will. It is a positive feeling of aversion which is akin to disloyalty, a defiant insubordination of authority or when it is not defiant, it secretly seeks to alienate people, weaken the bond of allegiance, and prepossess the minds of the people with avowed or secret animosity to Government, a feeling which tends to bring the Government into hatred or contempt by imputing base or corrupt motives to it, makes men indispose to obey or support the laws of realm, and promotes discontent and public disorder".[28]

Ranade's definition of the same term was a model of precision and apt phraseology and did not differ content-wise from his European counterparts. Perhaps, he over-zealously provided new armoury to the biased judges and thereby alienated himself from many nationalists.

The conviction of both the accused were confirmed, but the sentences were found to be out of proportion to the gravity of the offence. It was reduced to one year's and three months simple imprisonment respectively. The reasons given for this reduction were far from convincing, but certainly gives us an idea of the differing perception of Aston and other High Court judges in the altered political conditions, and how the law could be powerfully used for terrorizing the people.

Against this background, the *raison d'etre* of the amendment to the law of sedition — Section 124-A, was provided by Mr. Chalmers, the member in charge of the Bill. He said, "...recent events in India have called prominent attention to the law relating to seditious utterances and writings. We have had anxiously to consider the state of law regarding these matters and to decide whether, and in what respects, it required an amendment... But we are also determined that the law shall not be a dead letter...."

He made references to the defence arguments in the Tilak Case that "resort to actual violence was not advocated", and therefore thought that the law be expressed in clearer and less equivocal terms.[29] In the amended Section 124-A, the words 'hatred and contempt' were inserted along with the term 'disaffection'. 'The expression 'disaffection' was made inclusive of 'disloyalty and all feelings of enmity'. 'Disapprobation' of the measures or any other-action of the Government without creating hatred, contempt or disaffection did not constitute an offence; but was left to the mercy of biased judicial interpretation.

The changed political atmosphere of 1897-98 also brought three amendments to the IPC and the Criminal Procedure Code (Cr. PC), to suppress slightest allusion of sedition. I) In terms of importance, Section 153-A was inserted in the IPC in the chapter relating to offences against public tranquility to cover the offence of stirring up class-hatred. 2) Section 505 of the IPC was found unworkable and, therefore, was repealed and re-enacted. This section made the dissemination of certain false statements and rumours, likely to produce adverse effects on either imperial troops, or the public or might create class-hatred, punishable. 3) The last, Section 108 was included in Cr. C.P. It empowered the Chief Presidency and District Magistrate to bound a person with a bond of good behaviour and sureties for a limited period, who either orally or in writing disseminated or abetted the dissemination of seditious matter under Section 124-A or 153-A, or any matter concerning a judge which amounted to criminal intimidation or deformation under the IPC.

When critically viewed, these amendments in 1898, gave extensive powers to the executive and judiciary. .Importantly, the words 'hatred and contempt' used by Justice Ranade in his exposition, in the *Pratod* Case were inserted to supplement the word 'disaffection' in the main clause of Section 124-A. Although the declared intention of the Government was to use plain and simple language, it left all important words - 'hatred and contempt' undefined. Also, the new explanation made explicit that the term disaffection was synonymous to "disloyalty". Though 'disapprobation' of official measures or acts was legally permissible, the intention of not producing 'hatred and contempt or disaffection' was most difficult to prove for the defence and that too before a biased judiciary. Besides, Section.124-A read along with Section 153-A, left hardly any action of the nationalists uncovered. Under Section 153-A, any adverse comment against the Government could be brought under legal scrutiny for fomenting dissension against the 'whites', or the 'Europeans', or 'the ruling class' or the Christians'.

Against such wide powers, the Government contended that the mandatory prior sanction of the central or the local administration for instituting proceeding under Section 124-A was a safeguard against its possible abuse. But this safeguard was most elusive. In fact, Section 108 of Cr. P.C. gave unlimited powers to the District Magistrates to book persons for sedition of a lesser degree without a legal process. The Government, thus armed with all these amendments, sought to terrorize the nationalists, for which many examples are available. The nationalists were quick to realise the Government's game-plan. In Poona, a public meeting was convened under the auspices of the Deccan Sabha on February 20,1898, to protest against the said changes.[30]

Unmindful of Indian reaction, the Government was very clear in its design. No wonder, Lord Elgin, the Viceroy, said, "All that we, the Government, can say is that we desire the powers necessary to put down sedition. W e ask for nothing more but we can be satisfied with nothing less". [31]

Immediately after the enactment of the amendments, the Bombay Government charged a host of newspapers on grounds of sedition. Proceedings were instituted against the *Sudharak, Muslim Herald, Arunodaya, Kalidas, Indu Prakash* and *Gurakhi,* to name a few. In the case *Indu Prakash,* the Poona district officials started proceedings under Section 153 -A; i.e. class-hatred, for describing Englishmen as "adept in the art of trickery".[32] The Solicitor General felt that such a comment, could incite a hot-headed Englishman to assault the editor *Indu Prakash.* The case against *Gurakhi* also went up to conviction.[33]

In the midst of such repression was the case of Imperatix v. Henry Wilson, which evoked considerable criticism in the vernacular press. Henry, the accused, was a stud-keeper of the Governor of Bombay, who caused the death of one Bapu bin Raoji, a servant of the stud farm, by what way as termed as a "rash and negligent act". Judge H.F. Aston, who had earlier awarded a harsh sentence in the *Pratod* Case, fined Rs. 25/- for fatally attacking Raoji. This was glaring instance of judicial discrimination on the basis of race. Such bias against Indians was held by many European officials of the ilk of Aston.[34]

Different Perception of the Bureaucracy: The Kal Case

A prosecution under Sections 124-A and 153-A required, a prior sanction of the Government of India. This was done more as a safeguard against possible abuse. Most of the cases referred by the Bombay Government were negatived by the Government of India, on the ground that legal opinion 'was not hopeful of a conviction in the court. It felt that the Bombay Government was quite arbitrary in seeking its permission, and therefore it repeatedly advised the Bombay Government to seek legal opinion before hand. The Bombay Government on the other hand, repeatedly said that it had taken legal aid, and increasingly felt that the Government of India was not able to read the gravity of situation in this part of the country.[35] In fact, the Bombay Government was in a panic situation due to the events of 1898- 1900. Unable to apply Section 124-A and 153-A effectively for want of prior sanction, it chose to use Section 108 of Cr. PC and bound many persons through bonds for good behaviour and sureties. The Bombay Government requested to the Government of India to amend Act XXV of 1867 regarding the press. The Viceroy, Lord Sandhurst, informed that the time was not ripe for an amendment and that the Bombay Government could use Section 108 of Cr. C.P., as a preventive measure. The Bombay Government restarted the desirability of an amendment. It argued that initiating legal proceedings under the said section would not be successful unless the commission of an offence punishable under Section 124-A or 153-A could be established, and that the delay in ascertaining the advisability of legal proceedings under Section 124-A was an obstacle under the section. However, after inquiring about a similar need in other provinces, the Government of India refused to amend Act XXV of 1867.[36] The correspondence between the Government of India and Bombay Government shows differing perception of the political situation. Increasingly frustrated the apathy of the Government of India and instead of making fresh proposals, the Bombay Government choose to apply the different local laws such as the District Police Act of 1890, made up the want by inserting relevant clauses in the draft Bombay City Police Bill, which was enacted in 1902; and also used extra-constitutional methods to deal with sedition.

The legal proceedings against *Kal* in 1900 and 1904 provide an insight into the nature of the differing perception of bureaucracy at different levels, even while it unanimously believed in the need to stamp out sedition. In the Tilak Case (1898), the Anglo-Indian press pressurized the Bombay Government, but in the *Kal* Case it acted as an agent of the Bombay Government. When the Bombay Government approached the Government of India for prior sanction to prosecute the *Kal* for the article "An Englishman's experiences in India" (March 9, 1900), the latter believed that it was not sufficiently seditious to justify prosecution under Section 124-A.[37] The Government of India expected a reasonable hope of conviction in the court and criticised the needless delay of the Bombay Government in seeking permission. In fact, the Bombay Government first sought legal opinion, and consequently lost time. However, in 1904, when the *Kal* persistently kept up the same tone in its articles, C. L Hill, Secretary, Judicial Department, Bombay Government sought the help of the *Times of India* to draw Government of India's attention. In a personal letter to the editor, L.G. Fraser, Hill wrote about his difficulties, "You know many objections to taking up prosecutions makes a hero or martyr of the accused and brings him into undesirable prominence. On the other hand, there is a point beyond which it is impossible to allow things to go... *The Times of India* or some prominent English paper might take up and reproduce the articles of their stamp which are published in the *Kal* and comment upon them..."[38]

The Times of India obliged to produce the desired effect. As a result, the Government of India, on their own asked the Bombay Government to make enquiries and seek legal opinion on the articles in which were made comparison between M. de Plehve and Lord Curzon. The Bombay Government quickly replied in favour of prosecution. However, the Government of India deplored that "the case had been rendered, highly inexpedient by the unfortunate circumstances, that the leading articles of *The Times of India*... was based on the translations furnished by the Government of Bombay", and feared that "the Native Press has already drawn the obvious conclusion that the Editor of the *Times of India* was assisted by the Bombay Government... and that there can be little doubt that in the event of a prosecution, the point would be brought out and pressed home, by the defence to the prejudices of the Government case...."[39] The Government of India termed the action of the Bombay Government as "a somewhat unfortunate error of judgment" and reasserted the need to take prior sanction. The effort of the Bombay Government was thus unsuccessful. It was only in 1908, that Professor S.M. Paranjape, editor of the *Kal* could be convicted for seditious writings.

The Nationalist Reaction — The Other Forms of Mass Mobilization

One of the most innovative features of mass mobilization since 1895 was introduction of the *Mela* movement of singing-parties, which produced a salutary effect on large and eager audiences. The British Government saw a sinister design in this development and started licensing *the mela* songs in 1896.[40] The CID report of 1905 on the *mela* songs Of the *Sadvartan Pravartak Mandali* and the *Sanmitra Samaj,* is indicative of the influence it exerted on the masses.

The case - Emperor v. Ganesh Damodar Savarkar in 1909, is a fine example of how the Government used the judiciary to scuttle the *mela* songs within the legal framework. The accused, G.D. Savarkar, had published a book of Marathi poems called *Laghu Abhinav Bharat Mala* in 1908. He was charged under Section 121 and 121-A, i.e. waging war against the State and abetting to wage war, and 124-A of IPC.[41] The defence argued that the poems charged had no reference to the British Government or the present times, that they did not constitute abatement to waging war, and that the "poems are puerile and must not be taken very seriously... at the very worst the poet inculcates revolutionary ideas into minds of readers". Though Justice N.G. Chandavarkar admitted that the poet "has in mind the *Ganapati Melas* of the present times", he charged that "the venom is too transparent to be mistaken for anything else than to call people to wage (and)... preach war against the present Government". He held the invocation to Lord Ganesh, Rama, Krishna and Shivaji to destroy the 'foreign demons' as 'unmistaken innuendoes against the Government'. Justice Heaton went still further in his interpretation. He felt that it was "an instigation of an unknown person", for the author had sold three thousand copies of the book. Both the judges held Savarkar guilty under the sections charged in the plaint and sentenced him to two years of rigorous imprisonment. The charges show the extent to which the Government used law with a view to terrorize. When Indian judges like Justice Chandavarkar gave such an interpretation, they became the target of public ridicule for obsequiously obliging their white masters.

In the late 1890s, when government tried to scuttle the press and *Mela* movements, the Marathi theatre made an intelligent use of dramatic art through sarcasm and allegory, to create anti-colonial feelings and to promote nationalism. The Maratha and Rajput histories, and the epics provided suitable themes. Not until 1897, did the Government find anything objectionable in such dramas. But in the altered situation, particularly due to Tilak's arrest, they came to convey a different meaning to the Government and more so to the public.[42]

During the heyday of militant nationalism (1897-1916) as many as 39 dramas were prosecuted for dissemination of sedition, 32 of which were eventually banned and 16 were proscribed. The Government banned these dramas under one or the other provision of law. Wherever the Dramatic Performances Act (DPA) (1876) could not be used since the enforcement required prior sanction from the GOI, it applied the District Police Act (1890), Bombay City Police Act (1902), the IPC, Cr. C P, and even extra-constitutional methods. Dramatists such as G.D. Kane, K.H. Dixit, K.P. Khadilkar were harassed and black-listed. Actors were sent to jail under the IPC and a few of them Were bound Section 108 of Cr. CP. Descriptive rolls of the members of the theatrical troupes were maintained by the Intelligence Department, as they were suspected to be conduits between the nationalists and the revolutionaries.

Another indigenous method of spreading national sentiment that the nationalists followed and the Government found difficult to curb, was through *Kirtans and puran* reading, The following official note addressed to the district officials and published in the *Bombay Presidency Police Abstracts of Intelligence,* explains Government's concern against the *kirtan buwas* and *puran* readers: "the *Kirtan Buwas* and the *Puran* readers are the most dangerous of the lot. These men are invariably Brahmins and being of the superior intellect, they know how to win the people to their cause by touching their susceptibilities. I am firmly of opinion that these men play more substantial mischief than the more reckless Extremist newspapers. What they generally do is this - they select a passage or verse from some *purans,* more especially from the *Bhagwat Gita* for their theme... (and impress) the advise given by Shri Krishna to Arjun that it is no sin to destroy the enemy that the destruction of the material or physical body is not the destruction of the *Atma* of the person destroyed, as *Alma* is immortal, that destinies of human beings are governed by *karmas* or the actions of his former life... that God alone is the destroyer of the world and everything in it, and the actual perpetrator of the deed is a mere instrument to carry out His Will. Then they carefully twist the subject and apply these principles to the present day politics... and the Europeans are their enemies and that their presence in India is an evil and block to the advancement and attainment of Swarajya. When murders are thus shown to be justified even by the most sacred of the Shastras, it seems to be no wonder that such preaching should turn the heads of irrational youths like the murderers of Sir Curzon Wyllie and Mr. Jackson".[43]

Apart from the *Bhagwat Gita* and the *Purans,* the most common themes of the *kirtans* and *pravachanas* were the life and teachings of Shivaji and Ramdas.

The Government which had kept a close surveillance on the Arya Samajists, maintained descriptive rolls of even *Haridasas,* the *Ramdasi Sadhus.* the swamis of Ramkrishna Math and termed them as "political Sadhus". In 1910, it prosecuted Keshav N. Damle and Shankar S. Dev for authoring and printing respectively, the *Ekaslokigita*[44] under Section 124-A. Later many commentaries on *Bhagwatgita* were brought under official ban and proscribed.

Swadeshi and the Official Repressive Measures

With the background of the Partition of Bengal (1905), the Swadeshi Movement with its programme of *swadeshi,* boycott, national education, and temperance, any criticism in the native press against the official repressive measures caused much consternation to the Government. The said Section 124-A was further reinterpreted in the case against the newspaper *Bhala,* to suit official repression. The article it published – "A Durbar in Hell" (Oct. 11, 1905) - was an allegory applying to no government but giving a description of Hell and its rulers, The defence argued that the accused, L.B. Bhopatkar, the editor, was educated enough to know the limits of disapprobation, and that as a journalist he was entitled to criticise the conduct of Anglo-Indians. But in Justice Blatty's opinion Bhopatkar had made allusions to the forgery committed by Robert Clive, the treatment meted to the Begam of Awadh, the Income Tax, the Salt Tax and the Arms Act, and thereby did attempt to create hatred and disaffection against the Government. He further clarified, "Disaffection is a feeling and not the want of feeling. It is not the absence of affection. It is not indifference but a positive emotion not necessarily prompting to action, but with a tendency to influence conduct just as all our feelings do...[45] Bhopatkar was sentenced to six months imprisonment, and the scope of Section 124-A was further enlarged.

The events of 1905-7 and the triumph of Extremism in Congress led to more severe repressive measures by the Government. The native press became more vocal in its criticism and even admired revolutionaries, though tacitly. The administration came out with two repressive legislations against sedition related offences - the Newspapers (Incitement to offences) Act VII of 1908 and the Seditious Meeting Act of 1908. The first, empowered the District Magistrates to confiscate the printing press used or intended to be used for, publishing seditious matter.[46] The title of the second article makes the intentions of the Government clear. The nationalists quickly understood the intentions and organized protest meeting against the Seditious Meeting Act. Tilak's comments aptly describe the nationalists' perception of the Bill. He pointed out that, "the Government of India is giving itself powers to stop meetings where more than twenty people assemble... It will create tyranny on people... Such things are done in Russia". He doubted the necessity of such an enactment when the administration had Section 124-A at their command and further said, *"they have made up their mind to pass the Bill into law. We only meet and discuss for formality's sake... The police can enter the house where such a meeting is held, arrest its promoters without a warrant. If there are* 18 *persons, the police will supply remaining two to make up the complement. It is not that I am suggesting this idea to the police. It will suggest itself to them..."* Emphasis is mine).[47]

Tilak concluded that such oppressive laws might compel the people to find out ways and means to evade them, and forewarned the administration that too much of repression breads revolution. But the Government was in no mood to listen.

In the wake of this development, the Muzzafarpur bomb incident took place. The *Kesari* wrote strong articles pointing out the evil effects of repression. The Government was waiting for an opportunity to prosecute Tilak. It was aware that K.P. Khadilkar had written the articles but judging from Tilak's conduct in the past they knew that, if prosecuted, he would own responsibility as editor.[48] Proceedings were initiated against Tilak as editor for publishing two articles – "*Deshache Durdaiva*" (The Country's Misfortune, *Kesari*, May 12, 1908) and "*He Upaya Tikau Nahit*" (These Remedies Are Not Lasting, June 9, 1908). Two separate cases were filed for the two articles under Section 124-A and 153 -A. The case was committed to the High Court by Judge Aston Jr. on both charges. It came up before Justice D.D. Davar, who was elevated to the bench just before this case, and who was assisted by a non-Marathi knowing European dominated jury. Tilak defended himself. Branson, who had defended him in the Barve Defamation Case in 1882, appeared for the State. In 1908, Tilak was the only leader of note among the Extremist leaders yet to be sent to jail. Davar accomplished the task assigned. Tilak's arrest on July 24, evoked nation-wide protests.

Justice Davar did not depart from the line suggested by Strachey. Tilak was sentenced to six years rigorous imprisonment with transportation, three years in each case, to be undergone simultaneously. Tilak's reply to the judge is too well-known to be repeated. Justice Davar's harsh remarks speak volumes about predetermined deliberations by the .administration. He said, "it must be a diseased mind, a most perverted mind, that can think that the articles you have written are legitimate articles in political agitation. They are seething with sedition : they preach violence, they speak of murders with approval. I say such journalism is a curse to the country... I have decided to pass a sentence which I consider will be stigmatized as an instance of what is called misplaced leniency..."[49] Tilak's transportation was resented by the people through out the country. In Bombay, it resulted in the mill-hands strike and disturbances.[50]

On the heels of Tilak's conviction, came the conviction of S.M. Paranjape, the editor of *Kal*. The significant feature of this case was that "for the first time in the history of prosecution for sedition in India, *partriotism was recognised in the jury-box to be a ground for palliation of sedition*".[51] (Emphasis is mine)

Tilak and Paranjape's conviction resulted in a spurt of revolutionary activities in Maharashtra, which made the Bombay Government perturbed. The unearthing of secret societies such as the Shivaji Club, Pen Club and Belapur Swami Club; the murder of Jackson, and the attempt on the life of Lord Minto in December 1909 prompted a panic stricken Bombay Government to urge the

Government of India to legislate more stringent laws to control the press and dramatic performances.

Sir Harold Stuart, Secretary, Home Department. GOI, explained the nature and extent of the spirit of dissatisfaction against the British government. He detailed the various groups of agitators and suggested remedies. The policy he proposed: "Remonstrance may often be a better remedy than prosecution and it should always be borne in mind that the Government desires to prevent rather than to punish... Persuasion will frequently succeed where threats may fail and that in some case a private reproof will be most effective, while in others an open discussion will be the best way of gaining the desired end. The most suitable means will vary with the circumstances and the district officer must understand that the treatment to be applied in each case demands very cafeful consideration."[52]

However, frustrated by the meek attitude of Government of India, the Bombay Government evolved different plans. It discussed the idea of amending local laws such as the District Police Act and Bombay City Police Act, but eventually gave up due to legal complexity. The observations of the Bombay Government officials on Sir Harold's letter are illustrative of their stern attitude. Sir James DuBoulay, Secretary, JD, BG, wrote, "So long as the policy of the Government remains firm, and the district officers understand and follow it, as they are now doing, there is no danger of any misunderstanding. I do not believe that any number of letters of this description will do the smallest good : on the contrary I think there is a danger of making the government look ridiculous." While concurring with Du Boulay, J.B. Morrison, Under Secretary, JD, BG, recorded, "I do not agree that the line of action suggested here are suited to present condition in this Presidency. *We are past the stage where persuasion, private reproof or warnings can stem seditious movements; and the only safe policy at least for some time to come is stern repression of the very sign of sedition*".[53] These comments finally impressed the Government of India and accordingly Section 10 of the Dramatic Performances Act was extended to many parts of Maharashtra.

The conflict between the conservative Viceroy Lord Minto and liberal Secretary of State, Lord Morley, which complicated the situation, represents the tension between the British theoretical adherence to democratic ideas and in practice ultimate recourse to repression as a means of political survival.[54] It also reveals differing perceptions on the Indian situation, by the Government of India and Lord Morley, as in the case of the passing of the Indian Press Act of 1910.

With the sudden rise in the revolutionary activities in 1909, the Government of India requested Lord Morley to accord sanction to the Press Act in India. Afraid of a hostile reaction from English public opinion and the "Friends of India" members in the Parliament, Morley refused the permission for the enactment. Sir William Lee-Warner, senior member of the Council of the Secretary of State found Morley difficult to convince and therefore devised a different plan. He asked Charles A. Kincaid, member of the Bombay Governor's Executive Council, who was in London on furlough, to write articles on the seditious climate fostered by the native papers, with a view to strengthen his hands. Kincaid approached Valentine Chirol, the Director of Foreign Intelligence of the *Times* (London), through his friend R.E. Enthoven. Sir Valentine, himself an imperialist, promised to do the needful. Thus Kincaid wrote four articles in the *Times* : 1. "A Seditious Play of the Deccan", critique of the Marathi play *Kichak Vadh* by Krishnaji Prabhakar Khadilkar; 2. "Mr.Tilak and the Seditious Deccan Press", in which Tilak's influence on Indian youths was described; 3. "The Chitpawans of Chiplun", and lastly, 4. "Ancient Indian Theories of Government". These articles were published under the by-line "A Political Correspondence"[55] in January 1910.

Morley conceded the demand of the Government of India and the Indian Press Act was passed on February 9, 1910. The above account shows how the European press and Anglo-Indian fraternity worked as agents of the Government in dealing with the administrative problems.

The Law of Sedition and Post-1910 Period

After 1910, press censorship and proscription of seditious books began. Sanads of 'seditious' pleaders were suspended and even Inams were confiscated. *The Bombay Presidency Police Abstracts of Intelligence* discloses interesting facts about government's efforts to contain sedition. Interception of post under the Sea Customs Act [1878] began to be stringently enforced since 1907. A list of "dangerous characters" and their weekly movements began to tracked down from 1908. After 1911, a list of proscribed literature was regularly appended to the intelligence reports.

In the process, the Government also sought the help of native Princely States to curb sedition. For example, in 1909, the Kolhapur State convicted Professor V.G. Vijapurkar, Tilakite and of the Samarth Vidyalaya fame, Vaman Malhar Joshi, the famous Marathi poet, and V.N. Joshirao, in the *Vishwavrutta* newspaper case under Section 124-A.

In 1916, Tilak was again prosecuted under the charges of sedition, for delivering objectionable speeches. He had stated that the salaries of the British officials were too high, Indians had no effective control over finance, and the present officials being in fact alien by race, did not really understand the needs of the people. This was termed as causing "hatred" against the European bureaucracy, and therefore, seditious against the government. Barrister Mohammed Ali Jinnah ably defended Tilak and secured his acquittal. He argued that criticism of English bureaucracy did not represent 'disaffection' against the Government. Justice Stanley Batchlor and Justice Shah, upheld the defence argument.[56]

With the outbreak of the First World War, the Government came out with more draconian laws to suppress sedition. A Sedition Committee was constituted under S.A.T. Rowlat, which submitted its report in 1918.

The said report contained a comprehensive account of the seditious movements in different parts of the country, particularly revolutionary activities. It listed the difficulties faced by the Government in trying to contain sedition and suggested legislation, both preventive and punitive along with the emergency powers for the executive.[57] It mainly provided justification for official measures against sedition.

CONCLUSION

The chain reaction between the repressive law of sedition and the cognate laws and the Indian nationalists continued until Mahatma Gandhi inaugurated an 'era of *Satyagraha*', when the 'terror of law' was lost. In all his *satyagrahas*, Gandhi pointed out the oppressive nature of British colonial law and openly declared his duty to spread dissatisfaction against the oppressive State.[58]

When Gandhiji was tried for sedition in 1922 for his articles in *Young India,* he said "Section 124-A under which I am happily charged is perhaps the prince among the political sections of the Indian Penal Code designed to suppress the liberty of the citizen... Holding such a belief I consider it to be a sin to have affection for the system." And when the Judge told him that his offence was similar to Tilak's and sentenced him to six years imprisonment, Gandhiji replied, "Since you have done me the honour of recalling the trial of the Late Lokmanya Bal Gangadhar Tilak, I just want to say that I consider it to be the proudest privilege and honour to be associated with his name".[59] The difference between Lokmanya Tilak and Mahatma Gandhi was that while Tilak consistently contended in 1897, 1908 and 1916 against the charge of committing sedition and thereby being 'disloyal' to the State, Gandhiji pleaded guilty. He called the British Indian State evil and removed the spell of fear of the 'terror of law'. This was also the measure of distance which the nationalists had traveled in relation to the "law of sedition".

References

1. *Bombay Presidency Police Abstracts of Intelligence (BPPAI*), 1907, Vol-XXI, No, June 20,1907, Para 537 (c).

2. The measures of 1835 drafted by Macaulay was explained by Metcalfe as an "Act to establish perfect uniformity in the laws... Every person would be at liberty to set up a newspaper without applying for previous permission; but no person would be able to print or publish sedition or calumny without imminent risk of punishment". Quoted by Walter Russell Donogh, *The History and Law of Sedition and Cognate Offences in India,* Thacker Spink and Co., Calcutta. 1914, 2nd ed., p.180. This book is mainly based on Law Reports and presents the British viewpoint.

3. J.V. Naik, "An Early Appraisal of the British Colonial Policy", *Journal of the University of Bombay,* Vol. XLIV and XLV. Nos. 81-82, pp. 241-70.

4. J.V.Naik, "Bhau Mahajan and his *Prabhakar, Dhumketu and Dnyan Darshan", The Indian Historical Review,* July 1896 and Jan. 1897, Vol. XIII, Nos. 1 & 2, pp. 135-152.

5. Erie Stokes, *The English Utilitarians and India,* The Oxford University Press, Bombay, Paperback 1989, pp. 260-262.

6. While introducing the Bill in the Council, Lord Canning said, "I doubt whether it is fully understood or known to what an extent sedition has been poured into the hearts of native population in India..I know no means by which this can be effectively accomplished other than a law which shall give to the Government a more absolute and summary control over the press than it has in its hands...", Donogh, *op.cit.*, p.183.

7. *Ibid.*, p.2.

8. Edmond C. Cox, *Police and Crime in India,* Stanley Paul and Co.,London, n.d., pp. 86-7; Chapters VI & VII of the IPC related to offences against Army, Navy and Public Tranquility.

9. Hira Lal Singh, *Problems and Policies in British India,* Asia Publishing House, Bombay, 1963, pp.137-43.

10. Percival Griffith, *The History of Indian Police,* Allied Publishers Pvt. Ltd., 2nd Imp., 1972, pp. 88-94.

11. The criminal law which prevailed before the passing of the Penal Code was still in force, 'as to make such offences as sedition unpunishable by the Code. In Bombay and Madras seditious libel was only punishable with penalties. In many mofussil areas, Mohammedan Criminal Law prevailed which had nothing on the subject of seditious libel, but had much on the subject of rebellion. The law of sedition was based on the Law of England, which consisted of the Treason-Felony Act, the Common law with regard to seditious libels and the law relating to the seditious words. Donogh, *op.cit.*, p.6.

12. Disapprobation or disapproval of any official measures was allowed so long as it was compatible with a disposition to obedience to Government.

13. For more details see R.C. Majumdar (ed.) *British Paramountcy and Indian Renaissance,* Part I, Bharatiya Vidya Bhavari, Bombay, 1963, pp. 883-901; Also, Narahari Kaviraj, *Wahabi and Farazi Rebels of Bengal,* People's Publishing House, New Delhi, 1982.

14. *Maharashtra State Archives* (*MSA*)/ *Judicial Department* (*JD*),Vol. 14/ 767; No. A52, March 24,1869.

15. *Ibid.*, No.2813, Dated April 22, 1869.

16. Section 124-A read thus: "Whosoever by words, either spoken or intended to be read or by signs or by visible representations or otherwise excite or attempts to excite feelings of disaffection to the Government established by law in British India, shall be punishable with transportation of life...to three years to which fine may be added. Donogh, *op.cit.*, p.9.

17. V.S. Joshi, *Vasudev Balawant Phadke : First Indian Rebel Against British Rule,* India Printing Works, Bombay, 1959. The sections under which Phadke was charged were - 121-A of IPC : "waging war against the British Government. Section 122: "collecting men, arms and ammunition or exciting disaffection against the British Government", Sec. 395 & 400 : committing decoities; For information on Trial of V.B. Phadke, *MSA/JD/*1880/Vol. 58 & 59*;* Donogh does not make a mention of this case regarding sedition.

18. *MSA/JD/*1876/Vol.24/398.

19. Donogh, *op.cit.*, p.187.

20. *MSA/JD/*1877/ Vol. 58/699.

21. *MSA/JD/*1881/Vol. 125/1315.

22. Donogh, *op.cit.*, pp. 38-9.

23. *Ibid.*, p. 40.

24. S. S. Setlur and K.G. Deshpande (ed.), *A Full and Authentic Report of the Tilak Case (1897)...at the Criminal Sessions.* n.d. pp. 90-6. Also, Queen Empress v. B.G. Tilak, *Indian Decisions.* New Series, Vol. XL 1897-98, pp.656-683.

25. Donogh, *op.cit.*, pp.47-50.

26. Setlur and Deshpande, *op.cit.;* Appendix-D, Pp.30-1. Tilak's letter quoted in *The Indian Nation* of Calcutta, Sept. 1897.

27. *MSA/JD/*1897/ Vol. 233/2039.

28. Queen Empress v. Ramchandra Narayan, *Indian Decisions,* New Series, Vol. XI, 1897-98, pp. 683-91.

29. Donogh *op.cit.*, pp. 60-1.

30. *BPPAI/1898/No.7/Feb.22/Para* 226.

31. *Donogh, op.cit.*, p.70.

32. *MSA/JD/*1899/ Vol. 147/619 (Confdl.) pp.889-90.

33. *MSA/JD/1900/* Vol.27 /749; JD/1901/Vol. 193/1599 (Confdl).

34. *MSA/JD/*1899 /Vol.145-A/139-A (Confdl.)

35. *MSA/JD/*1899/Vol.147/618(Confdl.); *JD/*1900/ Vol.155/645, Part I (Confdl.)

36. *MSA/JD/*1900/Vol. 214/ 1759 (Confdl.)

37. *Source Material for A History of the Freedom Movement in India (SMFM)*, M.R. Palande (ed.) Government of Bombay, Bombay, Vol. II, 1958, pp.647-8.

38. *Ibid.*, Hill to Fraser, pp.649-50.

39. *Ibid.*, H.H. Risley, Secretary, HD.GOI to Hill, pp.654-5.

40. Richard L. Cashman. *The* Myth *of Lokmanya,* University of California Press, 1975, pp.81-2.

41. *The Bombay Law Reporter* , Vol. XII, pp. 105-21, The sedition charges were with regard to poems Nos. - 5,7,9,17.

42. Aravind G. Ganachari, "The Contribution of Marathi Theatre to The Growth of Nationalism- 1897-1916", *Proceedings of The Indian History Congress,* 54th Session (1993), Delhi, 1994, pp.582-590.

43. BPPAI/XXII/No.18/May7, 1910/para 1295(ii)

44. Emperor v. S.S. Dev, *The Bombay* Law *Reporter,* Vol. XII. pp.675-88. Keshav N. Damle was the author of the *Ekshlokigita* and was father of the famed Marathi poet *Keshavsut.* S.S. Dev was the publisher.

45. *Ibid.*

46. A case was registered under this Act against D.K. Phadke. He printed the newspaper *Hindu Punch,* which had carried a seditious article. The press was confiscated. *The Bombay Law Reporter,* Vol. XII, pp.120-121.

47. *BPPAI/* 1907/ XX/No.43 /12 Nov. /Para 1113.

48. *BPPAI*/1908/XXI/No.27/July 11/ Para 674.

49. Emperor v. B.G. Tilak, *The Bombay* Law *Reporter,* Vol. X, pp.848-903. The full case was immediately published in Marathi and it became a means of spreading Tilak's message. Sitaram K. Damle, *Tilak Yanchyavaril Rajdrohacha Khatala* (1908), National Publishing, Bombay, 1908, This book was later proscribed. Sitaram K. Damle was poet *Keshavsut*'s younger brother.

50. *MSA/JD/*/1910/Vol. 99/1562.

51. *SMFM, op.cit.*, pp. 647-55.

52. *MSA/JD*/1910/ Vol. 235/1553.

53. *Ibid.*

54. M.N. Das, *India Under Morley and Minto,* George Allen and Unwin Ltd., London, 1964, pp. 46-87.

55. Aroon Tikekar, *The Kincaids,* Promilla & Co. Publishers, New Delhi, 1992, Pp. 20-1.

56. Emperor v. B.G. Tilak, *The Bombay Law Reporter,* Vol. XIX, pp. 111-73.

57. *Sedition Committee Report* - 1918, New Age Publisters Private Limited, New Delhi, New Print 1973.

58. *Navjivan,* July 4, 1920, "Non-cooperation"; He later repeated it in the artice in *Young India,* "Duty of Disloyalty", March 27, 1930.

59. M.K. Gandhi, *The Law and Lawyer,* Navajivan Publishing House, Ahmedabad, Second Reprint, 1962, pp. 113-22.

3

Tilak and Gandhi Towards British Indian Law in their Political Agitation : A Study of Strategies

The article attempts to make a comparative study of the attitude of B.G. Tilak and M.K. Gandhi to the British colonial law, and seeks to show how it reflected in their respective modes of political agitation for the attainment of swarajya.

Lokmanya B.G. Tilak, who adopted a policy of 'responsive co-operation' on the one hand and confrontation on the other in political agitation, worked within the framework of British Indian legal system. He never openly defied the existing laws. He, in fact, had faith in British jurisprudence. In his political career, Tilak had to defend himself in as many as five legal cases brought against him by the Government, four of them on the charge of sedition. He consistently contested the charge of disloyalty against the Government. As the Government used law as the most effective instrument of political repression by prosecuting newspapers, enacting new laws and amending the old ones, and the judiciary generally acting as the coercive arm of the executive, Tilak deftly used these cases to arouse political consciousness of the masses. The fundamental moral question he raised : Was it sedition of the people against the British Indian Government (*Râjdroha*) or of the Government against the Indian People (*Deshdroha*).[1]

With the experience in South Africa as well as from the lessons drawn from the Tilak trials, Mahatma Gandhi adopted totally a different strategy. He, unlike Tilak, did not work within the British framework of law; in fact, he set the agenda which was designed to defy law and the legal system, and even to ridicule it. In this, the British authorities could not anticipate Gandhi. By inaugurating an 'era of Satyagraha' he sought to attack the very basis of British rule - the 'oppressive' law. His individual Satyagrahas, No-tax campaigns, Non-cooperation, Civil Disobedience, culminating into Quit India Movement, were illustrative of the design. With the progressive mobilization of mass participation in the national movement the 'terror of law' so characteristic of the earlier phase was lost. Therein lays the success of Gandhi's political acumen. The article attempts to show how Tilak paved the way for Gandhi's mass mobilization and their seemingly conflicting attitudes to British law were really complementary to each other.

The paper, which is based on archival source material [*Maharashtra State Archives and the Police Records*] and seeks to provide a new dimension to an understanding of the development of the Indian national movement.

In 1882, Tilak and his colleague G.G.Agarkar, who were editors of *Mahratta* and *Kesari* respectively, were taken to the court by Mahadev Wasudev Barve, the State-Karbharee of the Kolhapur State for publishing certain letters supposedly written by Barve, and writing articles indicating Barve's conspiracy along with his European officials to declare the Maharaja Shivaji III as insane and thereby dethrone him. Though the defamation suit was filed by Barve, the fight, in fact, was between the Bombay Government and defendants.[2] Despite their unconditional apology, the editors were sentenced to four months imprisonment. The native press unequivocally condemned the sentence as biased and harsh, as they were not the main accused. Memorials from all over Maharashtra were sent to seek their acquittal, but with no avail.[3] However the case enhanced their reputation as selfless patriots, which is reflected in the manifold increase in the subscription *Kesari*.[4]

By 1893, Tilak had realized that the Moderate leadership of the Congress was against any widespread agitation and that it was scared if the bogey of sedition was raised by the Government. This was clearly demonstrated in the threatened split between the liberals and the Extremists at the time of Hume circular, which described the untold miseries of the Indians.[5] He was also disillusioned by the 'class interest' which it sought to protect[6] by their belief in the "providential" nature of British rule.

Tilak inaugurated the *Sarvajanik Ganesh* Festival (1893) and *Shivaji Birth* Anniversary (1896) with a view to bringing masses into the movement and to achieve the moral and political unity of all classes. The British Government saw sinister design in this and viewed Tilak's activities as seditious.

However, as a member of the Bombay Legislative Council, Tilak's attitude towards the Government was one of "responsible co-operation". When severe famine visited Maharashtra in 1896, Tilak through the columns of *Kesari* tried to educated people on the Famine Code and did his best to dissuade people from rioting and looting. He urged them to make applications to the officials for remission in land revenue, to provide them work and loans. Tilak's faith in the British law and the legal system is clearly reflected in his editorial in *Kesari* of 15 December 1896. He wrote, "This Government is based on law and not aggression. If you have to fight, you must fight legally, and then alone we can get rights".[7] While urging to adopt legal ways for the redressal of their grievances, Tilak asked the farmers to resist any official attempt to collect land revenue during the famine. Even though Tilak was trying to keep the agitation strictly within the purview of law, the tone of his language was such as to make the people bold and defiant. When the Government refused to recognise the Sarvajanik Sabha as a representative body, he wrote, "so long as the Sabha was fighting legally, it was the duty of the Government to answer it legally."[8] When the administration filed suits against his three co-workers, he wrote, "If Prof. Sathe is prosecuted for explaining to the people the meaning of law, there is all the more reason why I should be prosecuted because I do the same thing on much wider scale".[9] The Anglo-Indian press raised the cry of sedition and accused Tilak for attempting to start a no-rent campaign on the model of Irish no-tax campaign.

When, in 1897, bubonic plague struck Pune, Tilak strongly supported the various measures adopted by the Government but advised their being carried out in a humane and conciliatory spirit. He advised the people not to resist the segregation of plague patients and house-searching, and took the Pune 'educated leaders' to task for running away at the time of distress. His service in this respect were acknowledged not only the Government but even by Justice

Strachey, while passing sentencing against him in 1898. The Government was alarmed at Tilak's growing popularity and decided to fix him by hook or crook but within the legal fiction.

Tilak took the lead in celebrating Shivaji's coronation ceremony with lectures and patriotic songs on June 12, 1897. Although the function passed off peacefully, it was on the report of this function, which was followed by the murder of Mr.. Rand, the Plague Commissioner and Lt. Ayerst on June 22 that the legal proceedings against Tilak on the charge of sedition were started.[10] This case is important for several counts: firstly, it was a classic example of how the imperialist Anglo-Indian press goaded the Government into arresting Tilak on the charges of sedition and also prejudiced the judiciary[11]; secondly, it illustrates how the law and legal system was twisted to suit the official purpose; and lastly, it precipitated the amendment to the existing law of sedition (Section 124-A of *IPC*)[12] to make it more comprehensive and draconian.

While applying the Section 124-A of *IPC*, Justice James Strachey twisted and interpreted the Section to suit the official policy which was to put Tilak behind the bars. He said, 'feeling of disaffection' meant "hatred, enmity, dislike, hostility, contempt and every form of ill-will to the Government". He equated 'disaffection' to disloyalty, and opined that the "disapprobation" allowed in the explanation to the clause 124-A does not apply to any writing which consists not merely of comments upon Government measures, but of "attacks upon government itself, its existence, its essential characteristics, its motives, or its feelings towards the people".[13] In view of this comment, the necessity of an amendment to the Section 124-A was immediately recognized, which followed in 1898. Tilak was found guilty by a majority of six to three. Justice Strachey, who was the junior most on the High Court Bench and one who was known for bias against the natives was specially asked to preside over. Curiously, the entire jury was non-Marathi knowing.

Tilak's letter to a Calcutta friend written shortly before the trial is indicative of his attitude to the whole issue of disloyalty. He wrote:

> The other side expects me to what amounts to pleading guilty. I am not prepared to do so. My position amongst the people entirely depends upon my character; and if I am cowed down by the prosecution, in the heart of hearts —I know the case for the prosecution is the weakest that was ever placed before a jury —

> ***I think, living in Maharashtra is as good as living in the Andamans***...I am afraid only of a non-Mahratta- knowing jury, and not of justice. You as well as I know that we are incapable of nourishing any sinister feeling against British rule, and it is thus impossible for any of us to be convicted of such a heinous charge as sedition. Such risks, however, we must take if we dabble in politics. They are the risks of our profession, and I am prepared to face them. If you all advise, I am prepared to go only so far as this : I don't think that the articles are seditious, but the advisers of the government think otherwise. I am sorry for it. But this will not satisfy the Government. Their object is to humiliate the Poona leaders, and I think in me they will not find a Kutcha reed as they did in Professor Gokhale and the editor of *Dnyan Prakash*. Then you must remember beyond a certain stage we are all servants of the people. You will be betraying and disappointing them if you show a lamentable want of courage at a critical time. But above all, as an honest and honourable man, how can I plead guilty to the charge of entertaining sedition when I had none? If I am convicted, the sympathy of my countrymen will support me in my trouble. (Emphasis is mine)[14]

Tilak's conviction was resented by almost the entire native press throughout the length and breadth of India and it did certainly contribute to mass mobilization of nationalist sentiment by his commendable example.

In the late 1890's, when the Government tried to scuttle the press, the nationalists found different ways of disseminating ideas of "freedom", through the *Mela* songs, Marathi theatre[15], *Kirtans* (religious discourse based on *Pauranic* themes, a form commonly used by medieval saints in Maharashtra and which is very popular), *Pravachanas* and public lectures. Between 1901-3, the Government tried to implicate Tilak on criminal charge of perjury in the *Tai Maharaj Case*. After the Partition of Bengal (1905), the Government tried to counter the nationalist upsurge by enacting new cognate laws such as Seditious Meeting Act (1908), Newspapers (Incitement to Offences) Act (1908), the Indian Press Act (1910) to name a few. Tilak commented that such enactments were unnecessary when the administration had Section 124-A at their command, "It will tyrannize people...Such things are done in Russia". He warned that, "people must have opportunities to give vent their grievances. If those opportunities are withdrawn, the result will be far from agreeable". When *Kesari* published articles[16] on the evil effects of official repression, the Government seized the opportunity to prosecute Tilak as editor. The Government knew that K.P. Khadilkar[17] had written those articles, but seemed to be predetermined to deport Tilak. In Justice Aston Jr. in the lower court and Justice J.D. Davar and non-Marathi knowing European majority in jury of High Court, the Government found a perfect alibi to effect the desired end. Tilak was sentenced for six years imprisonment and transportation. Justice Davar's concluding remarks, "I say such journalism is a curse to the country... I have decided to pass a sentence which I consider will be stigmatized as an instance of what is called misplaced leniency...", shows the animus against Tilak. Tilak's reaction to the verdict is well-known.[18] Tilak's transportation created commotion in the country. In Bombay, mill-hand's spontaneously resorted to strike.[19] This case discredited legal system and promoted the nationalist cause which was what precisely Tilak wanted.

After the return from Mandaley in 1914, Tilak was again prosecuted under the charge of sedition in 1916. But this time Jinnah ably defended Tilak and got his acquittal.[20] At the fag end of his political career, Tilak seems to have thought of mobilizing liberal Englishmen in favour of India through Valentine Chirol Libel Case fought in the Privy Council in England.

From 1900 onwards, Tilak followed a two-fold policy for the spread of Extremist thought, namely, attempting mass mobilization for Swaraj through certain new techniques which came to called passive resistance and through the legal cases on the one hand, and a tacit support to the *revolutionary terrorism* on the other.[21] The Government throughout suspected his connections with the revolutionaries but failed to get clear evidence. It is important to note that Tilak consistently contested the charge of disloyalty.

II

The South African experience (1893-1914) of Mahatma Gandhi contributed in a number of ways to the foundation of his ideology and methods to fight every from of injustice and oppression. He faced three trials there in South Africa : in 1907 for violating Transvaal ordinance on compulsory registration and passes for Indians; in 1908 for disobeying the order of the Court to leave the Colony; and in 1913 over immigration restrictions, the de-recognition of non-Christian marriages and the 3 pound tax on ex-indentured labourers. In all these instances, he used his novel weapon of *Satyagraha* to peacefully disobey the oppressive laws; it shows a definite pattern in approach and method. In every case, at the very outset Gandhi pleaded 'guilty' and made a statement, except in the first instance when he was denied the permission. In 1908, he requested that he be awarded the heaviest penalty under the law, at least not less than his co-agitators in Pretoria. In 1913, he stated that he had only done his duty in advising his countrymen, that until the tax was removed, they should leave work and subsist upon rations obtained by charity. This uncommon presentation nonplused the respective judges and the administration.[22] Gandhi had made the point by showing the hollowness of the law and of legal procedure. He wrote in 1908 that the laws of the land are not inviolable and that "The selfsame law is now about to fall apart".[23] He later recalled,

> In opposing the atrocious laws of the Government of South Africa, it was this method that we adopted...no State is possible without two entities, the ruler and the ruled. You are our sovereign, our Government, only so long as we consider ourselves your subjects. When we are not subjects, you are not the sovereign either...If you make laws to keep us suppressed in a wrongful manner and without taking us into confidence, these laws will merely adorn the statute-books. We will never obey them. Send us to prison and we will live there as in a prison...[24]

This became the pattern even in India, but on a large scale.

In Champaran (1917), he decided to disobey the order of the District Magistrate W.B. Heycock to quit Champaran, as 'he was danger to the public peace'. This was an individual satyagraha. The bureaucratic correspondence reveals the un-preparedness of the Government in dealing with Gandhi. In fact, it considered that the externment order was of dubious legality and Heycock was reprimanded for "unjust Magistracy".[25] The nationalist press condemned the order and hailed Gandhi as a hero, which endeared him to the title *Mahâtmâ*. Judith Brown, who attempted to trace origin of his rise to leadership, in her work *Gandhi's Rise to Political Power*, has either overtly or covertly failed to understand the new phenomenon that Gandhi was and has attributed the causes of his success to the "inner power battle" between the Government of India and the Government of Bihar, and to the "middle-tier of Bihari society", the professionals and businessmen.[26]

In Kaira (1917), he made a further advance in introducing Satyagraha, from individual to a group. When the Magistrate served him with an order to quit the district, he disobeyed. He told the Court, "I have ventured to make this statement not in any way in extenuation of the penalty to be awarded against me, but to show that I have disregarded the order served upon me, not for want of respect for lawful authority, but in obedience of the higher law of our being - the voice of conscience".[27] In his statement, Gandhi raised the most fundamental issue : *Is moral law, the law of conscience, higher than the law of the State which is oppressive ?* (Emphasis is mine.) Though, Kaira Satyagraha was small in size and number of people involved, it was this question which touched the heart and mind of Indian masses. Gandhi was not just addressing it to the Government but more to the people. The officials were confounded, one said, "Gandhi is, this time, on a thoroughly bad wicket". Lord Willingdon, the Governor of Bombay, called him "honest, but a Bolshevik and for that reason very dangerous".[28] However, he advised his volunteers, "We are opposing the intoxication of power, that is, the blind application of law, and not authority as such". A similar issue was taken up next in Kheda. He experimented the efficacy of the weapon of Satyagraha against Indian employers in Ahmedabad.

Gandhi was sincere in co-operation in war efforts. But he was soon disillusioned with the introduction of Rowlatt Bills. He quickly learnt the lesson and denounced them as they had disobeyed the fundamental laws of God. He told the Secretary of State, "This retention of Rowlatt legislation in the teeth of universal opposition is an *affront* to the nation. Its repeal is necessary to appease national honour."[29] It provided him a national political issue. Quickly followed the *hartals*, mass courting of arrests and Satyagraha throughout the country. A vow was to be taken to refuse to obey the laws, should they be implemented. Chelmsford's reaction to Gandhi's call was one of a confused person. He told Montagu, "I think he is trying to frighten us and I propose to call it a 'bluff'. In any case no other course is open to us". He finally said, "I am quite happy in defending my present position". Judith Brown, however, thinks that 'Chelmsford judged correctly that Gandhi was not on firm ground'.[30] Even the Home Member, Sir William Vincent wrote to Surendranath Banerjee, "I think you will agree he has crossed the boundary....It is quite impossible to treat with him".[31] Gandhi set for Delhi and Amritsar, the Government confined him to Bombay. The news of his arrest led to far more violent protest in Ahmedabad. On 13 April 1919, took place the tragic event of Jallianwala Bagh.

These events, along with Khilafat Movement and the inadequate Mont-Ford reforms, led him to introduce the Non-Cooperation movement. His article in *Navjivan* on this subject, is very illuminating as to why the lawyers in particular should boycott the courts. He wrote:

> It is my firm belief that every Government masks its brute force and maintains its control over the people through civil and criminal courts, for it is cheaper, simpler and more honourable for a ruler that, instead of his controlling the people through naked force, they themselves, lured into slavery through courts, etc., submit to him of their own accord. If people settle among themselves and the lawyer, unmindful of self-interest, boycott the courts in the interest of the people...every State tries to perpetuate its power through lawyers.[32]

Gandhi's belief in the absolutism of ethical values, that moral norms are absolute and are objective and eternal, and completely removed from the canons of expediency and opportunism, was unquestionable. Hence eternal values such as truth and non-violence were, for him, beyond the relativism of time and space and absolutely binding on all persons.[33] According to Gandhi, the essence of religion was morality. Hence, if he found the Moderate's method unworkable, nevertheless condemned violence in no uncertain terms.

Gandhi was arrested in March 10, 1922, on charges of sedition, for publishing certain articles in *Young India*.[34] His written statement before Judge Kennedy shows clearly how he was led to form the ideas on Satyagraha, and also his attack on the oppressive British colonial law and the legal system. He said:

> I came reluctantly to the conclusion that the British connection had made India more helpless than she ever was before, politically and economically. A disarmed India has no power of resistance against any aggressor if she wanted to engage in an armed conflict with him... Little do I realise that the Government established

> by law in British India is carried on for this exploitation of the masses...The law itself in this country has been used to serve the foreign exploiter. My unbiased examination of the Punjab Martial Law cases has led me to believe that at least ninety-five per cent of convictions were wholly bad. My experience of political cases in India leads me to the conclusion that in nine out of ten the condemned were totally innocent. Their crime consists in the love of their country...the administration of law is thus prostituted consciously for the benefit of the exploiter....Section 124-A under which I am happily charged is perhaps the prince among the political sections of the India Penal Code designed to suppress the liberty of the citizen...Holding such a belief I consider it to be a sin to have affection for the system.... I am endeavoring to show to my countrymen that violent non-cooperation only multiplies evil and that as evil can only be sustained by violence, withdrawal of support of evil requires complete abstention from violence...I submit to what in law is a deliberate crime and what appears to me to be the highest duty of a citizen. (Emphasis is mine)

He then addressed the Judge, "The only course open to you is either to resign your post and thus dissociate yourself from evil, if you feel that the law that you are called upon to administer is an evil...; or to inflict the severest penalty..." Finally, he thanked the Judge for associating his name with the Late Lokmanya Bal Gangadhar Tilak.[35]

Gandhi raised again the same fundamental issue. Unlike Tilak, Gandhi never disclaimed his disloyalty towards the Government and that there was no half-way between active loyalty and active disloyalty. In the editorial- "Duty of disloyalty" (27 March 1930), he wrote, "When you are disloyal you seek not to destroy persons but institutions. The present State is an institution which can never evoke loyalty. It is corrupt...They represent not the interest of the people but those of their foreign masters...Disobedience to the law of an evil State is therefore a duty."[36] Gandhi, thereby, called the British Indian State as an evil and questioned the very basis of its existence. In doing so, he removed the spell of fear of the "terror of law" from the hearts of the people, which became so characteristic of all of his movements, and thus knocked off an important pillar of imperialism. Countless people went fearlessly to prisons, which Gandhi called "His Majesty's Hotels". He struck at the very root of British imperialism in India.

Under the Non-Cooperation, he exhorted the people not to co-operate with the unjust system. The point he made was, one can bring a person to obedience to State law under the impending fear of punishment, but not to the Moral Law, which was superior. To bring the people to conformity with that Moral Law, their sense of morality has to be elevated. And that can take place only through belief in truth (*soul-force*) and non-violence. He further clarified, "Violent disobedience deals with men who can be replaced. It leaves the evil itself untouched and often accentuates it.[37] Gandhi always differentiated between persons and institutions. If the British Empire was ostensibly his enemy, it was as a system of control, he had no particular animosity towards British people.[38]

Gandhi was changing all the time. Once he successfully tested the weapon of Non-Cooperation, he advanced to the next step, the Civil Disobedience. Under this, there has to be not only non-cooperation with the oppressive laws, but one must break the unjust civil laws. This was experimented in Bardoli Satyagraha and also in Dandi March to break the oppressive salt laws.

In 1942, he was not just condemning the evil law or the system that perpetrated it, but felt that the evil British Government ought to go out of India. He, thereby, refused to work his movement within the British framework. From 1917 to 1947, his method of Satyagraha kept the British officials, both in India and England, baffled. In fact, he set the agenda for national movement, and the administration had to work in it.

Gandhi's method created a dilemma for the British. If there had been an upsurge in revolutionary activities, the problem would have been simple. Throughout, he first condemned violence in any form if it had been committed during his agitation and subtly pointed out the role of repression that was responsible for it. Even a faint justification of it would have helped the authorities to deal with him like Tilak. They found that neither indifference nor repression really worked against Gandhi. Furthermore, the bureaucracy at various levels was at pain to maintain legal fiction, while using every conceivable means to suppress nationalist agitation. Equally, he was as bewildering to the Indian political elite of the day as it was to the British authorities.

In the final analysis, though there were many differences between Tilak and Gandhi in their temperament and approach, it is important to note that Tilak prepared the ground for Gandhi to take over the leadership of the national movement. The forward which he wrote to Gandhi's biography written by Avantikabai Gokhale, who was in Champaran with Gandhi, is revealing : "to strive for bettering a system of administration which appears unjust is no sedition, speaking from the point of view of justice. To call it sedition amounts to saying that the rulers do not want their subjects to be inculcated with principles of justice, morality and the ability to fight against injustice and they are not prepared, further, to confer on them the right of equality. We hold that the welfare of the people is the real ideal and strength of the State. Once this is accepted, it follows that wherever we oppose injustice and work for its removal we are strengthening the hands of the State...." While both agreed on the basic belief on the British colonial law, they differed in their means. Tilak finally concluded that "At this time devotees of the nation who wish to bring about a proposed reform by constitutional methods, find their path beset with numerous difficulties...The way found out by Mahatma Gandhi is thus a way out of this difficulty - it is a way of passive resistance, of obstruction, or to put it in his own words, a way of Satyagraha. He has used it and has undergone sufferings for it. It has thus acquired sacerdotal sanctity".[39] No wonder, the staunchest Tilakites, such as Senapati Bapat, Annasaheb Khaparde, K.P.Khadilkar, Vir Vamanrao Joshi, Gangadhar Deshpande, to name a few, realized the revolutionary character of Gandhiji's movement and became his ardent followers.

References

1. This question was openly raised in the paper by one of the loyal supporters of Tilak. *Bombay Presidency Police Abstracts of Intelligence(BPPAI)*, 1907/ Vol.XXI/ No.24/ June 20/ Para 537(c).

2. *Maharashtra State Archives(MSA) Report of the Trial At The Bombay Third Criminal Sessions,1882*. The other co-accused were Sadashiv Pandurang Bhide, Keshav Narayan Bhakhale and Waman Govind Ranade. This report gives the official view of the proceedings. While Mr. Lang, acting Advocate General and Mr. Inverarity appeared for the prosecution, Messers Branson, Pherozshah Mehta, K.T. Telang instructed by Shapurjee and Thakordas appeared for the defense.

3. *MSA/JD* /1882/ Vol.125; Petition for the release of Tilak and Agarkar. The signatures collected from different parts of Maharashtra cover nearly 200 pages.

4. MSA/ *Report on the Native Newspapers(RNN)*, 1882; The subscription shot up from 500 copies at the beginning of the case to 3750 copies at the end of the Case.

5. Hume issued a confidential circular for the Congress members in which he described the miseries of the Indian people and voiced the need to arouse the public opinion in England. The Anglo-Indian press raised a hue and cry over it urged the Government to try him for sedition. For details, *Source Material for A History of the Freedom Movement In India*, M.R. Palande (ed.) Vol. II, Government Central Press, Bombay, 1958, pp.112-128.

6. While seconding a resolution on Land Tenures in Lahore Congress, Tilak remarked ,"We are not seeking to benefit that class (educated) but the poor classes and I shall point out, coming as I do from Bombay, I do not plead for the Zemindars but the ryots of Bombay". G.P. Pradhan and A.K.Bhagwat, *Lokmanya Tilak - A Biography*, Jaico Publishing House, Bombay, 1858, p.83.

7. *Lokmanya Tilakanche Kesaritil Lekh*, Political, Vol.I, Kesari-Maratha Sanstha, Pune, 1922, pp.190-93.

8. *Kesari*, '*Puné Sârvajanik Sabhâ Âni Sarkâr*', March 23, 1896.

9. Pradhan & Bhagwat, *op.cit.*, p.103.

10. The legal proceedings against Tilak were precipitated by a venomous campaign launched by *Times of India*, *Bombay Gazette*. Not only the letters of "*Justice*" and "*Shackles*" but also the editorials of the *Times* charged Tilak's articles in *Kesari* as seditious and faulted the Government for allowing such a man to on the Governor's Executive Council. On June 28, 1897, "*Shackle*" connected Tilak to Rand's murder. The *Times* urged the Government on July 6, to prosecute Tilak under 124-A of the *IPC*. The Anglo-Indian press in India and England echoed the charge. This prompted Sir E.Ashmead Barlette to question the Secretary of State in the parliament on June 9, as to how such a person could continue as Executive Councilor. Tilak replied in *Kesari* on June 30, but the government was hell bent roping him in the legal net. He was arrested on August 27. Setlur S.S. and Deshpande. K.G. (ed), *A Full and Authentic Report of the Tilak Case(1897) at the 4th Criminal Sessions*, n.d.

11. Tilak was accused as the editor of Kesari which carried two different series of publication - 1. a metaphorical rhapsody in verse entitled

"Shivaji's Utterances", and 2. A report of the Shivaji Coronation festival with a summary of the speeches delivered, including his own as the President of the function. The verse depicted Shivaji's deliverance of Swarajya against foreigners and at the bottom of the verse the sign of *Bhavâni* Sword was affixed. The report contained Prof. Jinsiwale's justification of Shivaji's killing of Afzal Khan, the noted noble of the Bijapur Sultan. Although the prosecution admitted nothing disloyal in the celebration of Shivaji, it charged that the language used with reference to the British was intended to excite disaffection and the sign of *Bhavâni* Sword symbolised taking up arms. Whereas the defense argued that the articles describing the miserable conditions of the people were quite consistent with loyalty, and the object of the accused was to create a national sentiment.; The discussion on the Afzal Khan episode began with the reading of a paper on that topic in The Royal Asiatic Society in 1896 by Mr. Karkaria and by Prof. Bhanu in the Deccan College. It was also reported in the *Times of India.* But the prosecution contended that it was an innocent discussion in 1896. Setlur and Deshpande, *op.cit.*, pp.90-6.

12. Section 124-A of the *IPC* under the 1870 amendment read thus: "Whosoever, by words, either spoken or intended to be read or by signs or by visible representations or otherwise excite or attempt to excite feelings of disaffection to the Government established by law in British India, shall be punishable with transportation of life... to three years to which fine may be added. For further reading on this section, Aravind Ganachari, "Evolution of the Law of 'Sedition' In The Context of Indian Freedom Struggle : 1837-1918". First presented in the Conference on "New Trends In the History of Modern Maharashtra", University of Bombay, 24-26 February 1994. Mariam Dossal and Ruby Malony (ed.), *State Intervention and Popular Response: Western India in the Nineteenth Century*, Popular Prakashan, Mumbai, 1998, pp.147- 171; In the amendment carried out in 1898, the words "hatred and contempt" were inserted along with the term "disaffection". The last word was made inclusive of "disloyalty and all feelings of enmity". Further, three new sections were inserted into *Cr. PC*, namely Section 153-A, 505, and 108. These amendments were to be taken conjointly with Section 124-A of *IPC*.

13. Walter Russell Donogh, *The History and Law of Sedition and Cognate Offences In British India*, Thacker, Spink & Co., Calcutta, 1914, 2nd ed. pp. 46-50.

14. *Ibid.* Appendix-D, pp.30-1. *The Indian Nation* of Calcutta reproduced it in September 1897.

15. Aravind Ganachari, "The Contribution of Marathi Theatre to the Growth of Nationalism", *Proceedings of the Indian History Congress*, 54th Session, Mysore, 1995

16. In the wake of Muzzafarpur Bomb incident, the *Kesari* wrote two articles –"The Country's Misfortune" (May 12, 1908) and "These remedies are not lasting" (June 10, 1908).

17. K.P. Khadilkar, was the Deputy editor of *Kesari* and was secretly involved with the revolutionaries. He was also a famous Marathi dramatist.

18. Tilak told the judge, "there are higher powers that rule the destinies of men and nations and I think it may be the will of the Providence that the cause I represent may be benefited more by my suffering than my tongue and pen". Emperor Versus B.G. Tilak, *The Bombay Law Reporter*, Vol. X, pp. 848-903; The full case was immediately published in Marathi with a view to spread Tilak's message. S.K. Damle, *Tilak Yânchyâvaril Râjdrohâchâ Khatalâ (1908)*, National Publishing, Bombay, 1908, This book was later proscribed.

19. Sumit Sarkar, *Modern India 1885-1947*, Macmillan India Ltd, Delhi, 1984 Reprint, Pp.134-5.

20. Emperor v. B.G.Tilak, *The Bombay Law Reporter*, (1916) Vol. XIX, pp.211-73

21. Though there is no clear evidence about Tilak direct involvement with the armed revolutionaries, from the available records it can be inferred that their activities had his blessings. For an excellent account of this concealed connection, Y.D. Phadke, *Lokmanya Tilak Ani Krântikârak*, Sri Vidya Prakashan, Pune, 1985. The revolutionaries and the Government perceived in their own way Tilak's *Gitâ-rahasya* as justification of the means of violence.

22. M.K. Gandhi, *The Law and Lawyers*, Navajivan Publishing House, Ahmedabad, 1962, pp.77-82. In the first case the judge ordered him to leave the country in 48 hours; in 1908, the judge expressed his duty to pass the lowest sentence, namely, two months simple imprisonment; and in 1913, the then judge called it a "painful duty" and sentenced him 20 pounds of fine, but Gandhi elected to go to jail than to pay.

23. "Triumph of Truth", *Indian Opinion*, February 8, 1908. In *Moral and Political Writings of Mahatma Gandhi*,(hereinafter *MPWMG*) Raghavan Iyer (ed.), Vol. III, Clarendon Press, Oxford, 1987, pp.28-30.

24. *Ibid.* July 27, 1916, Pp.40-43.

25. Judith M. Brown, *Gandhi's Rise to Power- Indian politics 1915- 20,* Cambridge University Press, 1972, p.27., Pp.52-83. In her work, she has tasted the approach of Cambridge South Asian school. This school has fallen into an analogous error of an over schematic and artificial approach. Her book is full of such observations calculated to undermine the importance of Gandhi and over-emphasize the role of British administration.

26. *Ibid.*, pp.52-83, In her work, she has adhered to the approach of Cambridge South Asian School. This School has fallen into an analogous error of an over schematic and artificial approach. Her book is full of such observations calculated to undermine the importance of Gandhi and over-emphasise the role of British administration.

27. *MPWMG.*, 'Statement Before the Court', *The Leader*, April 22, 1917.

4

British Official View of Bhagwat Gita as "Text-Book for the Mental Training of Revolutionary Recruits"

The Sedition Committee Report of 1918 described the *Bhagwat Gita* as "text-book .for the mental training of revolutionary recruits..."[1] Until the emergence of Lokmanya Bal Gangadhar Tilak to political leadership and his interpretation of the *Gita*, the officials perceived the *Bhagwat Gita* only as a religious and philosophical treatise. This article attempts to show that the British official view of *Bhagwat Gita* was deeply influenced by their appraisal of Lokmanya Tilak as an irreconcilable foe of the Raj. When more and more newspapers came to be prosecuted on the charge of sedition after 1905, the nationalists used many devices for mass mobilization. The preaching of *Bhagwat Gita* was one such method, which was considered by the officials as causing greater mischief than even the more reckless Extremist newspapers. With the increase in repressive measures of the Government, this treatise came to be used by the revolutionaries for promoting their cult. The Government perceived the usage of *Bhagwat Gita* as ideological justification to the revolutionary activities. Realising the danger, the administration kept a close watch on leaders of the extremist party and the "political Sadhus" including *Kirtankars, Puran readers,* the members of the Ramkrishna Mission and Arya Samaj, and minutely scrutinized any commentary written on the *Gita.* The article shows that this official view of *Bhagwat Gita* continued until the beginning of Gandhian era, when Gandhi gave his own interpretation of the *Gita,* namely *"Shatham Pratyapi Satyam"* (Unmindful of any cheating, I shall not leave the path of Truth) in place of Tilak's from *Gitârahasya - "Yé Yathâ Mâm Prapadyanté Tantast - thaiva Bhajâm mahyam"* (I shall act in the same manner in which others behave with me).

The article is based on the *Bombay Presidency Police Abstracts of Intelligence, the Sedition Committee Report of 1918, the Bombay Law Reporter*, and other official records.

The *Bhagwat Gita* was the main inspiration and the main spring of Tilak's action. He was introduced to *Bhagwat Gita* during his father illness in 1872,[2] As he progressed in his study of *Gita*, he came to realise that in it are to be found answers to many of the questions on religion, philosophy, and life in general which perplexed him. He came more and more to believe that religion can act as a cementing and integrating force, holding together the diverse elements in Indian society. By 1902, after serious reading of various earlier commentaries on *Bhagwat Gita,* he came to realise that the main message it embodied was not of renunciation but one of action.[3]

Tilak first used the *Bhagwat Gita* to express his political philosophy in 1897. In the early 1890's Tilak began mobilizing and canalizing all existing patriotic forces by introducing the Sarvajanik Ganesh festival and Shivaji birth Anniversary festival. The events of 1896-97 and the moderate policy of 'political mendicancy' were responsible for Tilak's growing popularity as a leader. Against this background Tilak mooted the idea of celebrating Shivaji's coronation ceremony in 1897 since Shivaji *Jayanti* [birth anniversary] could not be celebrated due to the plague epidemic. The function took place on June 12, 1897 amid *mela* songs, lectures and *Puranas*, The report of this function appeared in *Kesari* on June 15. It contained speeches in which Shivaji was compared with other historical figures such as Caesar, Napoleon and Mazzini. Prof. S.G. Jinsiwale's justification of Shivaji's murder of Afzal Khan was also reported. Tilak who presided over the function, asked, "Did Shivaji commit a sin in killing Afzal Khan?" He said, "the answer to that question can be found in the Mahabharat itself. Srimat Krishna's advice in the *Gita* is to kill even our own teachers and our kinsmen. No blame attaches to any person if he is doing deeds without being actuated by a desire to reap the fruits of his deeds... Do not circumscribe your vision like a frog in a well, get out of the Penal Code and enter the extremely high atmosphere of the *Srimat Bhagwat Gita* and consider the actions of great men". Immediately on June 22, 1897, the Plague Commissioner Rand and Lt. Ayerst were murdered by Chapekar brothers. The venomous campaign against Tilak in the Anglo-Indian press, notably by the *Times of India* and *Bombay Gazette*, precipitated legal proceedings against him on charges of sedition.[4] Justice Strachey upheld the contention of the prosecution that Tilak's speech influenced Damodar

Chapeker in committing the murders. Tilak's interpretation of *Bhagwat Gita* was viewed as exhorting the people to take to the cult of violence.[5]

Between 1900 and 1905, one does not find any references in the Police Intelligence Abstracts to the use of *Bhagwat Gita* by the nationalists. During this period, Tilak was closely associated with the revolutionaries. Many of his close associates were involved in raising secret societies and also in the manufacture of weapons. The unsuccessful Nepal adventure of K.P. Khadilkar, deputy editor of *Kesari* and well known Marathi dramatist. and Damodar Hari Joshi of the Shivaji Club of Kolhapur is quite well-known to be repeated.[6] Tilak also seemed to have been in contact with Aurobindo Ghosh, who was then in the service of the Baroda State as Vice-Principal and one who was organizing revolutionary activities in Bengal through his brother Barindra Kumar Ghosh and Jatindra Banerjee.[7] These activities escaped official notice until 1908.

The partition of Bengal in 1905, the Barisal affair, the victory of Japan over Russia, the spread of teachings of Swami Vivekananda, and such other factors provided great stimulus to nationalist agitation especially in Bengal and Maharashtra. The reaction to the Government repressive measures came in the form of *Swadeshi*, boycott, national education and anti-temperance movement. The criticism of the repressive measures led to the prosecution of many nationalist newspapers during the *Swadeshi* movement. As a result, the nationalists particularly in Maharashtra, employed various devices for mass mobilization such as the use of Marathi theatre, *mela* songs, public lectures, *Kirtans* and *Pravachans*. It was through these methods that the nationalists cleverly introduced the *Swadeshi* spirit to the masses in the form of the message of *Bhagwat Gita*, which Tilak described as "*Bahishkar Yoga*" in *Kesari*[8] and Aurobindo justified the similar content in the article "The Morality of Boycott" in *Bande Matram.*[9]

The Bombay Presidency Police Abstracts of Intelligence, (hereinafter *BPPAI)* show many instances of how *Bhagwat Gita* was 'used by the nationalist to convey *Swadeshism*. In 1907, Keshav Krishnaji Damle, father of the celebrated Marathi poet *Keshavsut* and an intimate friend of Tilak, lectured on *Bhagwat Gita* at various places with particular reference to Krishna's advice to Arjun. Though the Sub-Inspector of Belgaum reported that the lecture was of a purely religious character,[10] the District Magistrate significantly added, "the lecture was very effective. He preached rebellion with such cleverness that it is doubtful whether the Penal Code can touch him".[11] In 1910, K.K. Damle was charged with sedition under Section 124-

A of Indian Penal Code, for authoring, *Ekshlokigita,* which was in the opinion of the Justice N.G. Chandavarkar and Justice Heaton of the Bombay High Court, interspersed with seditious matter. K.K. Damle was sentenced to one year's imprisonment.[12] Even Shankar Shrikrishna Dev, the publisher and whose name always figured in the *BPPAI* in the list of 'Dangerous political agitators', was sentenced to two months' imprisonment.[13] Tilak himself[14] and his close associates like K.P.Khadilkar, Prof. Shivram Mahadev Paranjape, editor of *Kal*[15] G.S.Khaparde,[16] Shripad Raghunath Bhingarkar,[17] Vithal Balkrishna Joshi alias V.B. Rahalkarshashtri,[18] S.B.Bhate, and even fairly unknown persons such as Ramachandra Bhao Shirwadkar of Satara. Keshav Bhikajl Kelkar of Sangli,[19] and many others used *Bhagwat Gita* : Krishna's advice to Arjun to get the message of Swadeshi across to the people. These people used different occasions and places such as Poona Summer Lecture series, Shivaji Commemoration movement, and temples to lecture and travelled to distant places in Maharashtra.

The events of 1905-7, enhanced the political stature of Lal-Bal-Pal, and the Surat split marked the triumph of Extremism. With the prosecution of L.B. Bhopatkat, editor of *Bhala,* in1906, Tilak's Sedition Trial in 1908 and consequent deportation, the trial of S.M. Paranjape of *Kal* in 1908 and enacting of new repressive acts such as Seditious Meeting Act of 1908, Newspapers (Incitement of offenses) Act of 1908, the movement got intensified.

In Bengal, the spurt in revolutionary activity after the Partition of Bengal (1905) was essentially due to the efforts of Arabindo and Barindra Kumar Ghosh, Jatin Banerjee and their associates. The police intelligence noted that "the doing of the Anarchist Society formed by Arabindo and Barindra in Maniktola Garden, Calcutta,...was of religious character and the persons who frequented the garden combined the study of the *Bhagwat Gita* with the preparation of bombs- and explosives".[20] How much Aurobindo valued *Bhagwat Gita,* can be found from the articles which he wrote between April 11 and 23, 1907, which clearly spell out his philosophy. He wrote in the last article – "the Morality of Boycott":

> Politics is concerned with masses of mankind and not with individuals. To ask masses of mankind to act as saints, to rise to the height of divine love and practice it in relation to their adversaries or oppressors is to ignore human nature. It is to set a premium on injustice and violence by paralyzing the hand of deliverer when raised to strike. *The Gita is the best answer* to *those who shrink from battle as* a *sin, and aggression as a lowering of morality...* The sword of the warrior,

> as necessary to the fulfillment of justice and righteousness as the holiness of the saint Ramdas is not complete without Shivaji... Therefore, says Shri Krishna in *Mahabharata* 'God created battle and armours, the sword, the bow and the dagger.... (Italics are mine)[21]

This article was submitted as one of the exhibits in the Alipore Bomb Case in 1908. The Comment of Sir Valentine Chirol in *Indian Unrest*, representing the administration's view, is most significant in this respect:

> "The new school represented, perhaps most conspicuously by Mr. Aurobindo Ghosh... whose mysticism found in the sacred story of *Bhagwat Gita* is not only the Charter of Indian Independence but the sanctification of the most violent means for the overthrow of an alien rule".[22]

The same view is recorded in the *Sedition Committee Report of 1918*: "text-book for the mental training of revolutionary recruits", through a so-called moral class.[23]

There was a difference in the position of Aurobindo and Tilak with regard to revolutionary terrorism. While Arabindo believed in armed revolution and terrorism, Tilak supported preparation of an armed conflict but was opposed to terrorism. Though Tilak admired revolutionaries for their self-sacrifice, he felt that time was not ripe for any armed insurrection. Therefore, the thought that a broad based mass agitation can alone lead to *Swarajya.*

The Bombay administration became most vigilant when they learnt in June 1908 of the existence of revolutionary movement in Maharashtra. Intensive police search led to the unearthing of secret societies such as Shivaji Club, Khed Club, Belapur Swami Math Club, Pen Club and Abhinava Bharat. The Government found that many Sadhus were using *Bhagwat Gita* for nationalist purpose. The following note of Director of Criminal Intelligence, Shimla, addressed to the district officials and published in *BPPAI,* explains Government's concern against the "political Sadhus" using *Bhagwat Gita* :

> The *Kirtan Buwas* and the *Puran* readers are the most dangerous of the lot. These men are invariably Brahmins and being of the superior intellect, they know how to win the people to their cause by touching their susceptibilities. I am firmly of the opinion that these men play more substantial mischief than the more reckless Extremist newspapers. What they generally do is this - they select a single passage or verse from some *Puranas*, more especially from the *Bhagwat Gita* for their

> theme. . . (and impress) the advise given by Shri Krishna to Arjun that it is no sin to destroy the enemy, that the destruction of the material or physical body is not the destruction of the *Atma*, of the person destroyed. . . as *Atma* is immortal, that the destinies of human beings are governed by *karmas* or the action of his former life that God alone is the destroyer of the world and everything in it, and the actual perpetrator of the deed is a mere instrument to carry out His Will. Then they carefully twist the subject and apply these principles to the present day politics ... and try to create in the minds of the audience a belief that the Europeans are their enemies and that their presence in India is an evil and block to their advancement and attainment of Swarajya. When murders are thus shown to be justified even by the most sacred of the shashtras, it seems to be no wonder that such preachings should turn the heads of irrational youths like the murderers of Sir Curzon Wyllie and Mr. Jackson...[24]

The Government realised that the "travelling Sadhus" are protected from the surveillance of the authorities as they move "under some colourless names such as Paramanand or Anandanand" and ordered a close watch on them to bring to book those who teach sedition under the veil of religion. No wonder Sir Valentine Chirol who represented official view, wrote:

> "real *sanyasis* are frequently the missionaries of sedition, is certain, and the reputed sanctity gives them access to the zenana in Bengal even small boys of so tender an age as still to have the run of zenanas have, I am told, been taught the whole pattern of sedition, and go about *from* house to house dressed up as little *sanyasis* in little yellow robes preaching hatred of the English..."[25]

The police intelligence kept minute details on the "political Sadhus" after 1908. That complete dossiers of all Ṣwamis of the Ramkrishna Math is found in the *BPPAI*,[26] may be perhaps due to Tilak's admiration for Swami Vivekanand and his *Vedant*,[27] Sister Nivedita's contacts with Arabindo and other Bengal revolutionaries.[28] The activities of all the Arya Samajists were also noted in detail. Police used, at times, unconstitutional methods to coerce the parents of the students studying in national schools to withdraw their children. Syllabi of the national schools were checked to find out whether *Bhagwat Gila* was taught in moral class,[29] and these schools were referred to as "Schools for sedition". Dramas which made references to Shri Krishna's advice to Arjun, were banned.[30] Even *Ekshloki-*

gita of Keshav N. Damle and *Tilak-Gita* of Raghunath Krishna Mule were proscribed.[31]

In order to contain sedition, the Government of India finally enacted the Indian Press Act in 1910. In this respect, the comments of Sir Herbert Risley, the Home Secretary, GOI, while introducing the Bill are noteworthy: "the dialogue between Arjun and Krishna in the *Gita,* a book that is to Hindus what the *Imitation of Christ* is to emotional Christians... (is) pressed into the service of inflaming impressionable minds. I can imagine no more wicked description than that the Indian Song of Songs and that a masterpiece of transcendental philosophy and religious ecstasy should be perverted to the base uses of preaching political murder."[32] Risley acknowledged the philosophical value of *Bhagwat Gita,* but failed to realize that the way nationalist used it was basically a reaction to the British "terror of law", in particular to avoid prosecution under Section 124-A of IPC.

This British official view of *Bhagwat Gita* continued until the beginning of Gandhian era. The differences in the political views of the Lokmanya Tilak and Mahatma Gandhi became an issue of public controversy when a fortnight after the Amritsar Congress. Gandhi wrote in *Young India :*

> "Tilak represents a definite school of thought of which he makes no secret. He considers that everything is fair in politics. We consider that political life of the country will become thoroughly corrupt if we import western tactics and methods. We believe that nothing but the strictest adherence to honesty, fair play, and charity can advance the true interests of the country."[33]

It naturally provoked the Lokmanya to write a strong worded retort to Gandhi. Tilak wrote :

"Politics is a game of worldly people and not of Sadhus, and instead of the maxim "*akkodhenajine Krodham*" (Conquer anger by non-anger) as preached by Buddha, I prefer to rely on the maxim of Shri Krishna "*Ye yatha mam prapadyante tantst-thaiva bhajammayaham.*" That explains the whole difference and also the meaning of my phrase "responsive co-operation". Both methods are equally honest and righteous but the one is more suited to this world than the other. Any further explanation about the difference will be found in my *Gita-rahasya.*[34]

Gandhi replied to him saying that the means are as important as the end, therefore, the true law was *"Shatham Pratyapi Satyam".* This perception of *Bhagwat Gita* in the Gandhian period changed the British official view from the one held by them earlier.

References

1. *The Sedition Committee Report of* 1918. New Age Publishers Private Ltd.. Calcutta. 1973 (New Print). p. 23.

2. Bal Gangadhar Tilak : *Srimad Bhagwat-Gitarahasya Athawâ Karmayogshashtra,* Karnatak Printing Press, Mumbai. 4th ed., 1923, p.15.

3. *Ibid.,* pp. 23-25.

4. The legal proceedings against Tilak were hastened by a campaign by *The Times* and *Bombay Gazette.* The other Anglo-Indian papers echoed in chorus. Not only the letters of 'Justice' and 'Shackles' but also the editorials of the *Times* charged Tilak's articles in *Kesarl* as seditious and faulted the Government for allowing such a man to be on the Governor's Executive Council. On June 28, 1897. 'Shackles' connected Tilak to Rand's murder and the *Times* urged the Government to prosecute Tilak under Section 124-A or IPC. This prompted Sir E. Ashmead Barlette to question the Secretary of State in the Parliament on June 9, as to how such a man could continue on the Executive Council, Tilak refuted the charges in *Kesari* on June 30. He was arrested on August 27 and Judge Strachey redefined the scope of Sec.124-A to suit the conviction and sentenced Tilak to 18 month's imprisonment. Interestingly Damodar Chapekar wrote nothing about this in his autobiographical essay, published in the *Source Material for* a *History of the Freedom Movement In India (hereinafter SMHFMI),* (Vol.II. pp.1012-13) to implicate Tilak. He, on the contrary, accused Tilak of being neither a thorough going reformer nor thoroughly orthodox. Setlur S.S. and Desphande K.G. (ed.). A *Full and Authentic Report of the Tilak Case* (1897) *at the 4th Criminal sessions.* n.d.

5. The discussion on the Afzal Khan episode began with the reading of a paper on that topic in the Deccan College. Pune.. It was also reported in the *Times oj India.* But the prosecution contended that it was innocent discussion in 1896. This shows how the Government was determined in sending Tilak to jail. In talking about the philosophy of *Bhagwat Gita,* Tilak wanted to awaken the sense of duty among the masses and was in no way justifying the cult of violence.

6. On Nepal adventure, Y.D. Phadke has given an excellent account tn *Lokmanya Tilak ani Krântikârak,* Sri Vidya Praknshan. Pune. 1985. pp.40-51.

7. For Aurobindo Ghosh's activities at Baroda and his Maharashtrian connections, see *Ibid.,* pp. 28-39.

8. S.D. Altekar. *'Bahiskârâchi Chalawal'* in *Kesari-Prabodh,* Golden Jubilee volume published by Kesari-Mahotsaw-Mandal, Pune. 2nd ed., 1931, pp. 127 -30. *Kesari* defended boycott in the editorial "*Rashtriya Bahishkar*" on 22-8-1905 and reiterated the defence in the article "Bahiskar Yoga" on 5-9-1905.

9. Sri Aurobindo, *Bande Matram* - Early Political Writings-I. Pondichery, 1972, pp.124-28.

10. *Bombay Presidency Police Abstracts of Intelligence* (hereinafter BPPAI) 1907/ volume XX/No.I8/ 11 May 1907/ Para 349. The record says that Keshav K. Damle sometimes styled himself as Srimat Parmahansa Sri Sacchidanand Swami.

11. *BPPAI*/XX/NO 21/1st June 1907/Para 413.

12. *SMHFMI,* p. 664.

13. Emperor v. Shankar Shrikrishna Dev, *The Bombay Law Reporter,* Vol.XII, pp. 675-682.

14. *BPPAI*/ 1907/XX/ No. 26/ 6 July 1907/567 (c).

15. *BPPAI*/1907/XX/No.19/18 May 1907/Para 384. Khadilkar gave lecture in the Poona Summer Lecture series. It was presided over by S.M. Paranjape.

16. *BPPAI* /1907/XX/25 May 1907/Para 391 (c): Barrister Khaparde a very close associate of Tilak. His lecture on *Gita* was reported by the District S.P. Nagpur.

17. *BPPAI*/1907/XX/No. 23/15 June 1907/Para 492 (b). Tilak held S.R. Bhingarkar in very high esteem as an authority on *Gitarahasya.* p.16

18. *BPPAI*/XX/No.26/ 6 July 1907/ 567 (a): During 1907-8, Vithal Balkrishna Joshi used to work as a teacher under the name of Rahalkar in the nationalist school called Gananath Vidyalaya founded by Aurobindo Ghosh and his Cambridge friend Bar. K.G. Deshpande. He was one of the accused in the Jackson's murder. For some time he worked as Head Master of school at Ratnagiri, founded by Mama Phadke who was connected with Abhinav Bharat of Savarkar brothers. Y.D. Phadke. *op.cit.,* p.36.

19. *BPPAL*/1907/ XX/ No.19/ 18 May 1907/ para 386.

20. BPPAI/XXII/No.IO/13 March 1909/Para 432: Between 1893-1905, Aurobindo Ghosh worked in the services of Baroda State. first in the revenue department and later as Professor of French and English. In 1893, he wrote a series of articles – "New Lamps for Old" in *Indu Prakash* criticizing the policies adopted by the Congress. In 1898, he was joined by Barrister Keshavrao Deshpande, who had taken service at Baroda, which led to

organizing secret societies. In 1902, he got Jatin Banerjee, who had founded secret society in Bengal, recruited in the Baroda Cavalry for a while. At this time he was also visited by his brother Barindra, who was closely associated with secret societies in Bengal and later he edited *Yugantar.* It was through Jatin and Barindra, Aurobindo kept close contact with leader of the Anushilan Samiti of Calcutta, Pramathanath Mitra. Besides, Aurobindo was in contact with the revolutionaries in Maharashtra. Barindra's teacher who influenced him deeply in patriotism was Sakharam Ganesh Deuskar. The latter was an ardent admirer of Tilak. Deuskar's *Desher Katha* in Bengali became very popular among the revolutionaries. For more details, Karan Singh: *Prophet of Indian Nationalism: A Study of the Political Thought of Sri Aurobindo Ghosh.* London. 1963. pp.50-59. Also Y.D. Phadke : *op.cit.* pp. 28-39.

21. Sri Aurobindo. *op.cit.*, pp.124-8.
22. Valentine Chirol , *Indian Unrest*, London, 1910, p.104.
23. *The Sedition Committee Report of 1918*, p.23 & 32.
24. *BPPAI*/1910/XXIII/No.18/ 7 May 1910/Para 1295(ii).
25. Valentine Chirol, *op.cit.*, p. 104.
26. *BPPAI* / XXII /No. 35/ 4 Sept.1909/ Para 1724.
27. Tilak was a *Vedantin* himself. He had met Vivekanand before the latter went to Chicago and thereafter keenly followed his lectures and reported them in *Mahratta.* In 1899, he wrote. "He (Vivekanand) is a *sanyasin* but not an ascetic of the old type to whom the world is nothing but the *sanyasin* of the new type of the *Bhagwat Gita,* to whom the world is everything and his own country and people more dear than all the world put together." "Swami Vivekanand", *Mahratta.* May 7. 1899.
28. Y.D. Phadke, *op.cit.*, pp.30-31.
29. *BPPAI* / XXII / No.12/27March 1909 /Para 562. This para is on Maharashtra Rashtriya Vidyalaya of Poona; No.18/8 May 1909/ Para 904 is on Samarth Vidyalaya of Talegaon and Bagalkot National School.
30. Aravind Gururao Ganachari, "The Contribution of Marathi Theatre to the Growth of Nationalism 1897- 1913,"*PIHC,* 54th Session (1993), Mysore. pp. 582-590.
31. *BPPAI*/XXIII/No. 27/9 July 1910/ Para 2062.
32. Walter Russell Donogh, *The History and Law of Sedition and Cognate Offences In British India,* Calcutta. Second ed., 1914, p. 23.
33. *Young India.* 14 Jan. 1920. *Collected Works of Mahatma Gandhi,* Vol. 16, Publication Division, Government of India, New Delhi, 1964, p. 484.
34. M.D. Vidwans (ed.) : *Letters of Lokmanya Tilak,* Pune. 1966, pp. 284-85.

5

"White Man's Embarrassement" : The European Vagrancy in the Second Half of the Nineteenth Century Bombay

Almost all colonial schemes begin with an assumption of native backwardness and general inadequacy to be 'independent', 'equal', and 'fit'. In an imperial setting, the English class attitudes were transformed into racial attitudes. The maintenance of a proper distance between the English rulers and the Indian populace seemed to them not only socially appropriate but politically necessary. Those who threatened to bridge that distance aroused great concern and was perceived as an underlying threat to the structure of power and authority. One of the important issues which was thought to disturb that "social distance" , immediately after the Revolt of 1857-58, was of European vagrancy - both male and female - in India and Bombay city in particular. This concern is reflected in the Minute of W.R. Mansfield, the Commander in Chief, written on this problem on 6th June 1862 : **"these facts involved a serious stigma on the character of our government, which must suffer in Native eyes accordingly, and that putting aside the question of charity, we lose in prestige as the dominant race in the country, by permitting such as state of things..."**[1] (Emphasis is mine) It is impossible to over-estimate the harm done to the English name by the conduct of this class, whom the officials called by various names - 'European Pauperism', 'Destitution', 'Distress', 'Loaferism' and 'Vagrancy". The *Report on European Pauperism* of December 1863, thus mentions, "This proposal is respectfully submitted as calculated to discountenance vice, which engenders pauperism, and to encourage the virtues by which alone the prestige of the British name in India can be maintained. The European operatives on the Railway are more constantly and closely connected with the natives than any other class of Europeans, and for this reason their moral condition has an important national significance which cannot be safely over-looked".[2] The fact that the Revolt of 1857 provoked among the British an immediate cry for repression, which was followed by a call for cautious retrenchment, reflected changes in both the social and intellectual conditions of British India. The need for social distancing was now more acutely felt.

Against such a background, this article, based entirely on the sources from the *Maharashtra State Archives* and the contemporary non-official writings, attempts to examine the problem of European vagrancy within the colonial structure of power in the city of Bombay in the second half of the nineteenth century. It endeavors to show how the government sought to alleviate vagrancy by providing liberal funds and enacting the European Vagrancy Act XXI in 1869; the difficulties faced in enforcing the said Act such as the need to define the term "European British subject", the establishment of Workhouse and to amend the Criminal Procedure Code with a view to maintaining 'social apartheid' policy, thus bringing the vagrants only under the jurisdiction of European judges; and later repealing the European Vagrancy Act in 1874, so as to contain this officially maintained parasitic class whom the Christian officials called "neglected sheep of the fold".[3] The article seeks to present the conflict between the State on the one hand and the vested interests of European business class represented in India by the Chamber of Commerce on the other, over the question - the responsibility of deporting the vagrants; and between the legal rights of the 'European British subject' and moral obligation of the colonial State. Also it tries to show the hollowness of the missionary claim of "the civilized Christian versus the uncouth native", and exposes the myths so sedulously circulated by the British of "the basic superiority of the White European Christian male" and of the rhetoric of "White Man's burden".

The history of imperialism and its culture can be studied as neither monolithic nor compartmentalized, separate, distinct, but as a total scheme. It is in that light the problem of European vagrancy in Bombay in the nineteenth century needs to be looked into. Neither British imperialism nor colonialism was a simple act of accumulation and acquisition. Both were supported and perhaps even motivated by impressive ideological formations that included the notions that certain territories and people require and beseech domination as well as forms of knowledge associated with domination : the vocabulary of the nineteenth century imperial culture is plentiful with such words and phrases as "inferior" or "subject races", "subordinate peoples", "white man's burden", "bringing light to the heathen", to cite a few.[4] Much of the rhetoric of "New Order" promulgated by the British rulers in India was redolent with self-congratulations, triumphalism and made serious declaration of responsibility. In time, the imperial culture aggressively differentiated "us" from "them", almost with some degree of xenophobia.

In English literature and thought the list of great names who dealt with and wrote about India is astonishingly impressive, for it includes William Jones(1746-1794), Edmond Burke (1729-1797), William Makepeace Thackeray(1811-1863), Jeremy Bentham (1748-1832), James Mill (1773-1836) and John Stuart Mill (1806-1873), T. B. Macaulay (1800-1859), Harriet Martineau(1802-1876)[5], to name a few, and of course Rudyard Kipling (1865-1936) whose importance in the definition, the imagination, the formulation of what India was to the British Empire is undeniable. By constructing their own identity in the secularized notion of the 'modern' and 'civilized', the British emphasized at once the difference, and inferiority of the non-European races. Disciplines like colonial economics, anthropology, sociology and history were built out of these dicta. European writing on Indian history was also an attempt to create a fresh historical tradition. Uncharitable statements about Hindus made by James Mill in his **History of British India**, written in 1819, were calculated to destroy all sympathy between the rulers and the ruled, and central to it was the notion of Indian barbarity. Even John Stuart Mill, the famed author of **On Liberty** and one who worked in the East India Company's office in London, wrote in his **Representative Government** that this ideally best suited polity was not suited to India. For the rest, he wrote, a "paternal despotism" as against "oriental despotism" was not only appropriate but even necessary.[6] Harriet Martineau, essayist, novelist and the author of **The Positive Philosophy of August Comte**, remarked in 1857 that "The unprepared mind, whether Hindu or Mussalman, developed under Asiatic conditions, cannot be in sympathy, more or less, intellectually or morally, with the Christianized European mind".[7] Even Karl Marx succumbed to thoughts of the changeless Asiatic village, or agriculture or despotism.[8] It was Kipling who gave this point of view a classic expression and added phrases and concepts to the language of imperialist domination, such as "East is East, and West is West" and "Take up the White Man's Burden-...".[9] All such things were repeated with schizophrenic habit.

Since the issue of European vagrancy had come up immediately after the Revolt of 1857-58, the response of the English rulers can only be understood in the light of that tumultuous event. In the years immediately preceding the Revolt, it had become customary to assert that India had been acquired not by a succession of evil crimes of personally accountable individuals, but rather as a part of a 'Providential design' and many British historians saw a "hand of God in History". The Revolt did not change the attitudes of thousands of Englishmen overnight, but it provided the justification for believing what they had already begun to believe some years before and only required an opportunity to find a confident expression.

India by then had entered the general English consciousness through missionary propaganda as the quintessence of depravity. With the paternalistic arrogance of imperialism, the British in India talked of "imperialistic philanthropy", whose intentions included such ideas as "Bringing light to the area of darkness" and "Civilizing mission".

The revolt generated a near obsessive fear of 'savage' Indian men. Exaggerated and at times fabricated tales of systematic rape, torture and mutilation began to circulate among the British before the Revolt had been suppressed. How much this prejudiced the minds even of level-headed British, is well reflected in the expressions of Dr. George Buist, the editor of the *Bombay Times* whose contribution to the improvement of civic life of Bombay is well-known. He wrote:

> It is one of the most dreadful things connected with the Rebellion that it has disclosed to us all at once the facts, that we have for a century been living in a den of wild beasts, without having tamed one atom of their ferocity, and that the feline is absolutely a less treacherous and more animal than the human tiger.[10]

This obsession obviously increased the distance between the two races, distance in every sense of the term.

The Indian nationalist response, particularly in Maharashtra, to such British 'imperialist designs' had two contrasting trends : the one tending to regard it as 'Divine Dispensation', the other looking at it as the 'most bitter curse'.[11] Between these two extreme view-points there were several other shades of opinion on British rule depending upon the individual or group perception of the given political and social reality. The foremost among those who made a severe indictment of the British rule was Bhaskar Pandurang Tarkhadkar who wrote in *Bombay Gazette* in 1841 : "We cannot look upon your Government in any other light than that of the most bitter curse India has ever been visited with".[12] This trend was later represented by the Extremists. The others unleashed their bitter attack not merely on the exploitative nature of the British rule, which had caused the economic ruination of the country, but even criticized the fossilized Indian religious and social tradition. They did not regret Indo-British connection, rather welcomed it for the sake of national reconstruction on higher and more elevating lines which implied equality before law with its natural corollary of human rights and a hope for liberation to the millions of downtrodden.

"Prestige" was the key-stone of the British colonial rule. The first notice of European vagrancy which was seen to erode that prestige is found in the 'Minute' of the Commander in Chief of the Indian Navy, W.R. Mansfield, dated 6th June 1862 :

> I have long been keenly alive to the shame and inconvenience to which we are exposed by the destitution of some of our country-men in India under such circumstances, or worse than those reported in this letter. It would hardly be unfair to say that these facts involve a serious stigma on the character of our Government, which must suffer in Native eyes accordingly, and that putting aside the question of charity, we lose in prestige as the dominant race in this country, by permitting such a state of things. What a denial of the practice and lessons of our Church, what a contradiction of the Missionary is conveyed in the fact, that such things do exist.[13]

It was increasing trade and development of public works, he thought that brought the inflow of lower class European labour on daily wages into India. He felt the desirability of legislation and assistance of the government for their deportation. However he expressed that legislation would not alone remedy the evil of destitution and that much would also depend on the charity of the British community, 'from the rich functionaries to the railway operatives and private soldiers'. On his recommendation, a committee consisting of Reverend W.K. Fletcher, Rev. C.T. Wilson and Mr. Charles Forjett, the police chief of Bombay, was constituted to examine : 1. The extent and growth of the evil of European destitution and mendacity, 2. The machinery that exists to provide relief at the Presidency and other large towns, and 3. To suggest a definite and permanent plan for the relief of European pauperism.[14] This Committee made preliminary suggestions that grants could be given to Sailor's Home which provided some relief to stranded sailors, since public charity would not be forthcoming. But on major issues under investigation it chose to remain silent.

Significantly, Sir Bartle Frere, the then Governor of Bombay (1862-1872), held views similar to that of Mansfield regarding social distance with the Indians, and they are evident in what he called the "Colonial Policy" :

> "By this I understand a policy which puts all real power into the hands of European colonists, and treats the natives as ... to be ruled, taught and perhaps petted, but to be excluded from all real power or influence on the measures of Government, and to be governed, not with reference to their own reason and sense of right and wrong but according to our English latest notions of what is best for them..."[15]

This opinion of Sir Bartle was commonly held by most English officers in India.

It was B.H. Ellis[16], the Police Commissioner, North Division, who again brought to the notice of the Government that :

> "they(European vagrants) go from house to house begging often get intoxicated in the Bazar, and in fact are becoming quite a nuisance. Something should be done to make these men return to Europe, as they bring great disrepute on the European character. Many of these men are old soldiers, who took their discharge when the Indian army was transferred to the Crown... they have become a pest to the community at large."

Thereupon Mansfield wrote a second "Minute". While considering it the State responsibility to pay return passage for soldiers seeking discharge, he firmly believed in the necessity of an enactment by which any Firm, Company, Trading or Banking Corporation, or Individuals, carrying on business could be bound to pay the passage of the discharged European labour to England without making any difference between those Europeans who are sent from England after being selected for a job in India and those taken into some service after getting discharge from their earlier employment in India.[17] Even the Commissioner of Customs, George Inverarity who generally concurred with Mansfield, held that the State should pay for a return passage if dismissal of that employee takes place after the lapse of one year of employment.

Mansfield's strong views brought forth conflict between responsibility of the State and interests of the European business class, which resulted into charges and counter-charges. The Bombay Chamber of Commerce, representing business interests of the European enterprises in India, reacted strongly to Mansfield's 'Minute' and called his measure as "tyrannical in its operation, mischievous in its results, and opposed to all recognized principles of jurisprudence"; dictating "oppressive terms to Firms, Companies and Individuals because its tendency would be to prevent the introduction of European industry and enterprise into India", and at the same time would place "a bar to the employment in India of honest European labour". It also expressed that as in England the Church should provide relief to the destitutes and that the State should own responsibility of providing their return passage.[18] Though it supported an enactment of a legislation for the suppression of European mendicancy in India, but believed that the object ought to be achieved "without violating established systems and without unnecessarily checking private and commercial enterprise."

Mansfield issued a supplementary minute in which he urged the Chamber of Commerce "not to consider the issue as a question of 'supply and demand of labour', which is ultimately adjusted by the market but to be one of social relation and obligation between the masters and the community", and expressed that 'to prevent the wanton production of vagrancy" the manufacturers should "consume their own smoke", namely, "that vagrancy should be consumed by those who produce..." He questioned, "Why should the whole Community or the 'State' contribute for the extinction of an abuse caused by these very Capitalists ?" and further commented, **"I would ask leave to remind those who differ from me in this matter that**

British existence in India is an artificial one, and therefore exceptional as compared with the state of things at home. We are compelled to regulate things out in this Country, which amidst the friction of a great homogeneous community arrange themselves with more or less of success, and of hardship to classes and individuals."[19] (Emphasis is mine)

The Chamber of Commerce refuted the contention of Mansfield and complained that he had unnecessarily come down heavily upon them as a class. It urged that their views be placed before the Governor. Mansfield relentlessly replied the charges seriatim, reiterated his argument that European vagrancy is produced by a certain application of capital and that in the absence of preventive measures, it "cannot fail to be one of the results of large industrial development in India." [20] In this conflict the Government finally conceded in favour of powerful lobby of the European business class. The Government, as a general rule, owned the responsibility of providing return passage to European vagrants.

In December 1863, came the exhaustive and lengthy *Report on European Pauperism* which was submitted by the Committee consisting of Reverend W.K. Fletcher, M. Scott, Charles Forjett and Robert Haines.[21] The findings of the Committee as expressed in the Report are quite revealing. Concern for European vagrancy in an imperial setting is very pronounced. It stated :

> "they who see and examine the circumstances of a destitute man must give when pity prompts them, and if in many instances they be deceived, ***that error is a less injury to society then leaving one brother to die of nakedness and hunger. One such example publicly known would do more harm to justify the hatred and contempt of the natives towards their rulers than a thousand instances of European vagrancy.***" [Emphasis is mine]

The Report outlined the following reasons for the growth of European vagrancy : [a] the daily additions of men discharged from the Railway works; [b] because of some fleeing from distress in Lancashire cotton industry due to stoppage of cotton imports due to Civil War in America; and chiefly [c] as a result "of some Seamen unable to obtain berths consequent on the paying-off from the Indian Navy."

The Railway works - conducted by B.B.C.I and G.I.P.Railway Company - increasingly contributed to this problem in the later years.[22]

With the starting of Civil War in America export of raw cotton to the Lancashire cotton industries virtually stopped and that rendered many lower class Englishmen out of job. Though this phenomenon resulted in economic boom and share mania in Bombay due to heavy demand for Indian cotton, many belonging to lower class Englishmen came to India in search of employment. The addition of this people to the already existing number of vagrants compounded the problem. But the most important factor, the Report pointed out, was of those discharged from Navy and Army. During the Revolt of 1857-58 the Government added 1706 men to the Indian Navy alone and in the next year (1858-59) 3531 men were added. But from 1859 to 1862, 43.2 percent of these men i.e. 2703 men were thrown upon the labour market, being discharged without pension from the Indian Navy and its departments. Though during the Revolt the ratio of European soldiers against the Indian soldiers was raised from 1: 6 to 1: 2, between 1859 and 1861, many soldiers were discharged from the European regiments of the erstwhile East India Company. This was not an occasional cause but one affecting the extent of European destitution in the country. It was pointed out that the employers of European labour were the Mercantile Marine, the Railway Companies, the manufacturing Companies and the Government, and from each of these came the European mendicants.

The machinery for relieving the destitute Europeans in Bombay, between 1863-68, consisted of following societies and institutions : 1. The District Benevolent Society of Bombay, 2. The Bombay Seamen's Friends Association, 3. The European Pensioner's and Widow's Home, 4. The Society for Promoting the Education of Poor, 5. The Indo-British Institution, 6. The Roman Catholic Orphanage, 7. The United Presbyterian Orphanage.[23] In addition to these Societies disbursing the alms, money was collected by subscription from the European community by the Church for distributing it to the needy and relief was also provided by the Police Magistrate (after 1865 this post was called the Commissioner of Police) from the funds at his disposal. However, all this relief was far from adequate to meet the needs of the growing European vagrancy. After 1862, two institutions, which significantly provided relief to the vagrants of the new category, were - the Stranger's Friend Society and the Sailor's Home. Until the establishment of the Workhouse under the European Vagrancy Act of 1869, there are found in the records numerous applications of Richard Key, Secretary of the Stranger's Friend Society, and also from Frank Henry Souter, Commissioner of Police, Bombay and one who acted as the Central relieving officers, requesting the Government to provide liberal grant-in-aid. Nevertheless, the Committee was of the opinion that the evil of vagrancy would be increased by the alms and charities administered by the Clergy and the Magistrates, and hence recommended an enactment of a legislation which could provide deterrent punishment. More than relieving their physical wants, the Committee recommended the need to improve their moral character by appointing Chaplains along the European settlements on railway lines at the State expense and call the vagrants as "neglected sheep of the fold". Interestingly, the Committee explicitly stated in favour of European business class regarding "consuming smoke".

Despite this exhaustive report, no significant change took place in remedying this evil except that the Police Commissioner of Bombay, Frank Henry Souter,[24] was appointed as the Central relieving officer, and in that task he was assisted by the Committee on European Pauperism. One finds several of his applications in the records requesting the BG to sanction additional sum for providing relief, and under his able supervision many vagrants were provided with free passage back home.

This issue resurfaced more prominently in 1866. The concerns of imperial rulers are again reflected in the letter, which appeared in *Bombay Gazette* under the pseudonym, "Foreigner" :

> "(the Vagrants) becoming a perpetual source of annoyance and shame, increasing the difficulties of the Government, and rendering nugatory, in no considerable measure, all the efforts used with the view to impressing on the minds of natives of this country the advantages of the purer faith... The appointments in the public services hitherto filled with considerable credit by Europeans and Eurasians cannot now be regarded as the inheritance of their children, and it is now not an unusual circumstance to see John Brown superseded by Babajee Gopaljee... These classes are more immediately connected with the Christian Church, and I hope they are not destined to become a standing reproach to that Church, or to be exhibited before the eyes of the heathen, as a poverty-stricken and inferior race. Such an exhibition of misery in this land must necessarily lower the prestige of the English nation. Already we find many respectable Europeans and Eurasians living, for want of adequate means, in the midst of filth and

wretchedness, in back streets inhabited formerly by natives only, and which are certainly most improper places for the residence of any European or Christian...."[25]

This letter not only reflects the same imperialist arrogance but also presents the conflict : the fallacy of "the civilized Christian having purer faith" versus the "uncouth native". The author suggested a strict but not rude treatment towards vagrants which might cultivate in them the habits of work, or else he feared that "any kindness shown, is sure to be abused, and... when possessed of the means, they often visit the shops of Bhiccajee Pestonjee and other liquor sellers in the native town." The Acting Chief Magistrate of Bombay, R.B. Barton's letter to the Secretary, JD, BG compounded such writings in newspapers. He complained of European vagrants committing theft, brutal assault and robbery, one of whom brought before him for trial was ordered by him to be flogged, for the murder of three natives. The Coroner J. G. Hewlett brought to the notice of the Governor the murder of three natives - Munna Oodowjee, Noopa Mansing and Ushla Pema - by four European vagrants, which he called "the most unprovoked brutality". Even the European jury expressed a strong desire that this case be brought to the notice of the Governor, so that some corrective measures are taken.[26] The leader in *Bombay Gazette* commented that a tolerably steady and honest European can still find occupation in India, and reminded that as competition would increase and supply of Europeans would grow large, the employers would be more exacting in requirement. The consequence of that could throw more Europeans out of work. Though it condemned the "unchecked outrages and drunken atrocities of idle scoundrels", but urged for moderation, to extract good and render them harmless by punishing them with strictest restraint.

The official Englishman, thus, could not dismiss the vulgar Englishmen with the contempt the aristocracy would have employed at home, for the simple reason that his own pretension rested on the same ground as that of the common soldier. The English nation, in its entirety, was depicted as an aristocracy with respect to India; the whole English nation was "aristocracy of nature". The official Englishman was trapped by the realization that if he sacrificed the vulgar specimen of his countrymen by holding them up to ridicule, he was jeopardizing his own position.[27]

The result of Barton and Hewlett's letters was the new Committee to inquire into the problem of European vagrancy under the Chairmanship of Mangaldas Nathoobhoy.[28] The Committee, in their Report, commended the work of Stranger's Friend Society, and especially of Frank H. Souter, as the Central Relieving Officer, for providing relief to 1406 persons at a cost of Rs. 76,228/-. It requested an annual grant of Rs. 10,000 for Stranger's Friend Society and made following suggestions : [a] the need for an enactment of a Local Vagrancy Act, of which certain sections of Police Act (13 of 1856) and Chapter XIX of Criminal Procedure Code could form a part; (b) that due publicity be given to all the proceedings under the Act, and that the power and responsibility of deporting of the European vagrants to rest with the Government alone. Significantly, the Report touched one subject which no other Committee had earlier dealt with, namely, urging the Government to take up measures for the repression of European prostitutes, by persons of foreign origin, in Bombay. It also recommended "public flogging" for the persons engaged in such flesh trade. Most of the suggestions were recommended for acceptance and the Advocate General was approached to look into the legality of the draft proposals and advise the Government accordingly.

What emerges from the opinion tendered by Lyttleton H. Bayley, the Advocate General [AG] on the draft Bill is the conflict between the legal rights of the British European subjects and the immoral aspect of the European vagrancy.[29] He pointed out that the compulsory deporting of the vagrants would amount to infringement of the personal liberty of natural born subject of the Crown, and that they have the legal right to come to Bombay, as also any other Crown territory, and reside at their own pleasure. Besides, in AG's opinion, neither the Governor of Bombay nor the Governor General of India had legal right under the India Councils Act of 1861 of enacting any law or regulation in connection with the deporting of European vagrants, since their jurisdiction extended up to five miles from the shores of India. If the deported vagrant would jump out of the ship or get down at such place as Aden and return back, the Government had no legal right to stop him. Therefore, any legislation by the Indian Government would affect the provisions of the act of British Parliament. The only way out was, he suggested, to have sanction of the British Parliament permitting the GOI to make a law, which could deport a natural born British subject. What was true of the European vagrants who were natural born British subjects of the Crown, he said, was equally applicable to females, who may be imported for the purpose of prostitution. Perhaps, measures could be taken against those who were engaged in the import of white prostitutes or those who are in charge of dens of such females, thought Bayley. He reminded that white prostitutes cannot be prevented from coming to India, but they can certainly be covered under the proposed Contagious Diseases Act and thereby could be examined in the Lock Hospitals. Bayley also clarified that the word "foreigner" does not apply to Europeans and Americans, only except when their presence is considered objectionable on political grounds. Lastly, he spelt out that only a Mofussil Magistrate being a Justice of Peace, is competent to commit a European British subject, and also that the he could only be tried in Presidency town courts. Thus, Bayley's opinion made clear that the European vagrants could only be arrested and tried by the European judges and need to be committed to only Presidency towns.

The opinion of AG set the effort of BG, to contain the European vagrancy and its appendage, the white prostitution, at naught.[30] Fortunately, persons like W.R. Mansfield had by then become the member of the Governor General's legislative council. Therefore, the GOI urgently recognized the necessity of approaching the Secretary of State for India for a sanction of the Parliament. The GOI sought to impress him that "the prevention of European vagrancy is an object of first importance... and that the deportation of vagrant is an essential part of the measure", and assured that "Indian Legislature will not be over-stepping its powers by passing the proposals [bill regarding vagrancy] into law".[31]

The opinions invited from the Magistrates in Bombay Presidency on the draft Bill are very significant for their forthrightness on the nature of vagrancy. Almost all unanimously supported the need for legislation. John Connon, Acting Chief Magistrate of Police and former editor of the *Bombay Gazette*, felt distressed to comment on the importation of European prostitutes. He wrote, "This vile trade... tends to the exhibition of European races here in a more distressing, degrading and infamous way than any possible form of male vagabondage." Dossabhoy Framjee Karaka, the Third Police Magistrate at Bombay and one who was also Member of the Committee on European Pauperism (1867), regretted that their proposals regarding prostitutes was not embodied in the draft Bill. Arthur Crawford, another member of that Committee, thought that "the somewhat cautious wording of sections appear to convey an impression that the European vagrant is to be feared or is entitled to special consideration." It was useless and also a waste of public money, he remarked, to construct work-houses for these irreclaimable loafers. Nana Moroji, the Third Police Magistrate, Bombay, supported the idea of establishing the workhouse, but felt the need for greater surveillance over the main source of evil, namely, the "numerous dens of imprudence and debauchery, the grog shops and the brothels".[32] These opinions of the Bombay officials did contribute to the passage of the Bill on European vagrancy. Equally important is the fact that except Nana Moroji, Dossabhoy Framjee and Mungaldas Nathoobhoy, are found no comments in the government records from any other Indian, official or non-official.

The petition of the vagrants reveals that they had their own story to tell. One such petition said :

> "We cannot descend to live by theft or plunder and we do not know really what to do with ourselves exposed all to the heat of the Sun and to the dew by night without food on the open green is what suffering humanity cannot along abide... Were we seamen we might have obtained employment in some of the ships but being most of us tradesmen and mechanics we are at a perfect loss.... To compete with the inhabitants, a thing which it is impossible they can expect to do in India, where East-Indian and native can afford to work for wages, on which it would be next to impossible for a European to exist."[33]

Interestingly, the English Parliament was not approached since public opinion in England on this issue was raised so much as to create a panic. With the consent of the Secretary of State for India, the Bill was presented in the Lord Mayo's Council on 11th August 1869, subsequently referred to the Select Committee, and was finally passed into an Act - The European Vagrancy Act XXI of 1869 - on 18th September 1869.[34] The discussion on the Bill in the Viceregal Council and the final passage of the Act XXI, truly reveals the official mind in a colonial set up. The Act defined some important concepts : [a] "Vagrant" means a "person of European extraction found asking for alms when he has sufficient means of subsistence", or "asking for alms in threatening or insolent manner", or "continuing to ask for alms of any person after he has required to desist", or wandering about without any employment or visible means of subsistence. Henry Maine, the Law Member and the one who moved the Bill, clarified that "In India, mere begging without more was not to be, as in England, an offence. Mere begging would only expose the beggar to be declared a vagrant, and to be thereupon dealt with under a process as one of peculiar tenderness." Therefore, the Act further qualified that "asking for alms in a threatening manner, or continuing to ask for alms of any person after he has been required to desist" could be punishable. This was not to be applied to mere begging but only to all persons of European extraction. [b] The Act stated that "persons of European extraction" included even Americans and Australians. [c] "Magistrate" was defined as Magistrate of Police within the limits of the Presidency towns, and in the mofussil, a person exercising powers under the Code of Criminal Procedure, and not less than those of a Subordinate Magistrate of the First Class who was also a Justice of Peace. This certainly eliminated Indians judicial officials from committing the European vagrants. Henry Maine clarified that "Magistrate was not the authority who made declaration of vagrancy but the authority who punished for certain special offences committed by the vagrant class." The admission of Mr. Cockerell during the discussion in the Viceregal Council is interesting for its racial prejudice :

> "We could not disguise from ourselves that, by section 4 of this Bill, we were about to impose upon Native police officers a perilous responsibility, the due discharge of which was likely to be attended with great personal hazard; for the European loafer was unquestionably apt to prove dangerous to deal with when you attempted to exercise what to his apprehension might seem an unwarranted interference with his personal liberty."[35]

It should be remembered that during the colonial period, when an Englishman left his native land and settled himself in a foreign country, he lost imperceptibly his insular peculiarities. And when the country in which he took up his dwelling place happened to be an Asiatic one, the Englishman merged in the European. In India, the Englishman, the German, the American, and even an Australian, became one nation - the European. And in case of need, of trouble, or distress, they acted as brothers. To overcome legal difficulties as raised by the AG, L.H. Bayley, regarding deporting of a vagrant, it was decided under the said Act that a 'voluntary' agreement would be drawn between the Secretary of State for India and the vagrant to be deported with a free passage, so that the vagrant would not anytime complain of his personal liberty being encroached upon. Curiously, as the member of the Viceroy's Executive Council, Sir W.R. Mansfield, the Commander in Chief, raised the question of the responsibility of European business class to provide return passage to the vagrants, but nobody paid any attention. Since it was believed that European vagrants were undergoing privation by being in a hostile geographical environment, the Act was extremely soft on punishment. Also, it sought the creation of Government workhouses for the vagrants. It was stated in the Act that a European vagrant "shall be entitled to an allowance for his subsistence at the rate of eight annas per diem. But significantly, it was mentioned in the Act itself that certain Sections relating to the workhouse would come into operation only after 1st January 1870, while enforcement of many other Sections concerning powers of the police Magistrate and other police officers were indefinitely postponed, and thus creating further problems.

The note of John Jardine, the Under-Secretary, JD, BG, discloses the problems faced by the administration. It says :

> "The vagabond life in India has a great charm for lazy vicious Englishmen. They are very kindly treated and fed by the villagers wherever they go and the distances between stations gives the loafer a zest for the enjoyment of drink which he can easily purchase as, European officers and ladies supply him liberally with funds in order to get rid of importunity... Till the vagrancy act was passed they had virtual impunity which still exists as even the Sections of the Vagrancy Act in force are a dead-letter and the expense of the Government is helping on these men is as great as ever...The Magistrates are under an impression apparently that no one Section of the Act is to be enforced..."[36]

The GOI did not think it fit to start workhouses immediately and thereby incur expenditure. Instead, relief was provided through the Stranger's Friend Society as was done earlier. The dislocation of trade after the share mania (1860-65) and the liquidation of the Bank of Bombay compounded the problem of seeking employment. The vagrants were provided with a batta of 6 to 8 annas per diem. However, the GOI was always slow to release the funds for providing relief. John Jardine put the problems of the BG in his letter to the Secretary,

Home Department (Public), GOI, requesting for release of funds and to sanction an expenditure of Rs. 5000 for providing workhouse:

> "I would beg to notice that the Batta of six annas a day allowed these men is but sufficient to prevent actual starvation, and admits of no provision whatever for clothing, the consequence is they are to be met in all parts of the Town wandering about the streets without shoes to their feet, and otherwise in a most pitiable condition quite revolting to witness...These men from actual want have recourse to every possible device for obtaining relief, and it was only within the last few days *that one of them went through the mockery of being converted to Mahommedanism in order that he might hang about the mosques and be fed and clothed by the Mussalman community of the Town.* I would respectfully submit that such occurrences are to be deplored and are fraught with much harm, and that the rapid increase of European vagrants in Bombay is a subject calling for the early and serious consideration of Government... I am also to remark that the long delay already experienced in receiving assent to the building of a workhouse has prevented this Government placing the legal checks on European vagrancy which the Act was intended to supply and in this way, a large expenditure has already been incurred which might have been obviated in accordance with the intention of the Act."[37] (Emphasis is mine)

The urgency of starting workhouses was thus impressed on the GOI. It was suggested by some officials that the vagrants be deported to some such place as Mauritius or Cape Colony, Australia or San Francisco, but the administration of those respective places opposed any such move to have irreclaimable lazy Europeans. The official records show that hundreds of vagrants were deported to England, and few Europeans deported to their respective countries at the government expense, "a charge upon Indian tax-payers", and even a gratuity of 10 pounds was paid to each of the deported vagrants.[38] Despite initial hesitance the Government Workhouse was opened on 19th April 1872. With it the grant-in-aid to the Stranger's Friends Society was virtually stopped by the GOI, despite protests from the Bombay officials.[39] Rules for the management and the discipline to be maintained therein were framed in April 1871. A resolution attached to these rules, published in the *Government Gazette* rendered further clarifications to some of the clauses to the European Vagrancy Act. It stated that the "persons of foreign extraction" were also to include persons born in Europe, America, West Indies, Australia, and New Zealand; and that term could be applicable to the "legitimate son of a father and grandfather so born." For the arrest and custody of vagrants - European or Eurasians, it said, "European officers shall be employed in preference to Native police officers". To improve the moral character of the inmates of the workhouse, religious services at government expenses were prescribed.[40]

The first report of the Governor of the Workhouse, Major Raitt, regarding its working depicts the actual state of affair. He says, nearly all the inmates were strong, healthy men who could earn a livelihood by manual labour but they seemed to be incorrigibly idle and have depraved habits. Even though employment was sought for them, they hardly bothered to work. Writing about their gross insubordination, he complained that "mere remonstrance with these men is found utter useless", and that "under the existing law and the Rules no provision is made for punishment of those vagrants", consequently they paid no heed to the warnings. Major Raitt wrote:

> "At present the great majority of the vagrants seem to live a life of the lotus eaters, spending their time in unmitigated and unprofitable idleness. Well fed, well housed. And well clothed, with plenty of congenial society, and no work, they remain in the Workhouse until at last the influx of vagabonds into that Loafer's Paradise fill it to overcrowding, and numbers have to be deported to England by Canal Steamers. So attractive indeed is the workhouse to vagrants that many of them refuse to leave its hospitable shelter even when the offer of a free passage home is made to them."

Even W.P. Walshe, who succeeded Major Raitt as the Governor of the Workhouse, also made similar statements, "Anything short of compulsory power will be useless, for many of these men will tell you on your face and unblushingly that so long as they can mock about and pick up a free and easy living in India - a country which suits their habits well - they will not go."[41] The only remedy, both of them urged, was to give them punishment of hard labour and maintenance of strict discipline.[42]

In September 1870, the Government of North-West Provinces submitted certain proposals for the revision of the law relating to the trial of European British born subjects for minor offences and requested that the mofussil Judges be given more powers. The discussion among the officials could be termed as a prelude to the

Ilbert Bill Controversy of 1883. Importantly, the outcome of this discussion had a direct bearing on the European vagrancy in Bombay. Opinions were invited by the GOI on this issue from the High Court Judges. Of the Judges of the Bombay High Court, Justice M. R. Westropp, L.H. Bayley, J. Phillip Green, M. Melville and C. Camball gave a joint opinion against any change in the Criminal Procedure Code, by empowering more powers to the mofussil judges. Only Justice J. Gibbs gave a dissenting opinion. He felt that owing to the Railway constructions and the introduction of other purposes of a large number of European population of the lower classes, an alteration in law was not only advisable but necessary. He favoured the extension of jurisdiction over the British born subjects to competent natives. However, he wrote, "I am perfectly aware that a proposal to do away with the privilege - a European British born subject possess of being tried by the High Court, save for the trivial offences... would raise at all events in Bengal, such a fierce opposition that it is hopeless to expect the Government of India would pass such a law putting European and Native subjects on the same footing and making all alike..."[43] Eventually, amendments to the Criminal Procedure Code were proposed in the Imperial Council in 1872, with regard to two things : [a] extension of power to the Indian judges of having jurisdiction over European British born subjects, and [b] increased power to Magistrates for the punishment of European British offenders. Both these proposals had direct bearing over the issue of European vagrancy.[44] B.H. Ellis, a liberal Jew, in the Imperial Council, initiated the first proposal. But the opinions expressed by other members thereupon unfold the racial prejudice against Indians and show the official struggle to maintain "social distance" at all costs. Ellis' argument was that "if we excluded any Justice of Peace from the exercise of certain powers, we were really casting a stigma on the whole educated Native population of India." Those who supported him were the Viceroy Lord Mayo, the Commander in Chief Lord Napier of Magdala, Richard Temple, but finally the proposal was negatived as majority of the members held views similar to those expressed by most of the Bombay High Court judges. Regarding the second amendment, it was made clear that they were intended only for the repression of the loafer, the troublesome and irrepressible European vagrant. Lord Napier's objection to that proposal was that "an imprisonment for three months in the hot weather was a very serious punishment", and further added, "there are no places in which a European could be imprisoned, without injury to his health, in the hot weather in India." Having worked in Bombay earlier, Ellis clarified, "It was with the loafer, and the unfortunate people who from want of proper means of subsistence had been driven to crime, that we had to deal... The knowledge that punishment would swiftly follow crime was the best deterrent of crime." Sir Richard Temple, another member of the Council, placed the whole question in proper perspective :

> "there was great necessity for those provisions of the Bill which empowered Magistrates to try Europeans for petty offences...[and] those provisions arose out of the necessities of the age, and the progress which we had made in the development of the resources of the country and immense increase of industrial enterprise of Railways all over the country and the immense increase of industrial enterprise had caused the influx of a large number of our countrymen : without any disparagement to them as a body, and it must be admitted that some of them occasionally fell into trouble and into evil ways. The increase of Europeans of what might be called the working classes had been very great : it was one of the necessary circumstances concomitant with some of the greatest improvements of the age."[45]

Although Governor General Lord Mayo supported the argument in general, he felt that "A great deal had been said about the loafer, and a bad name had been given to a class of Europeans who did not always deserve the stigma that had been cast upon them." The motion regarding punishment was carried through with many reservations. However, the speeches of other members reveal every kind of race hatred against Indians. The strong reactions of the Native press on the race impartiality are reflected in the editorial of *The Hindu Reformer*, "The just liberal and reasonable amendment proposed by the Hon'ble Mr. Ellis was lost, only because of our great English law givers could not overcome their caste prejudices, discard the narrow and ignorant prejudices of their own countrymen of the lower order. Thus the illiberal feeling of caste triumphed over the noble feelings of justice and impartiality".[46] In such a vitiated environment, when some European soldiers murdered natives in 1871, the *Indu Prakash* in its editorial censured the English authorities for encouraging these atrocious crimes through the race partiality of the criminals, further commented, "A belief is spreading among the people that the English authorities allow themselves to be improperly swayed by race partiality, even to the sacrifice of justice... The state of things has created a feeling of despair among the natives when they happen to suffer at the hands of Europeans."[47] In an another editorial, *Indu Prakash* wrote, "the people say that the English government, which boasts of its higher civilization, its Christianity and its love of justice, is not a bit superior in the above respects or may be said to be even worse... one cannot help thinking that the trials of the European accused are a mere mockery."[48] The *Native Opinion* criticized the superior privileges enjoyed by a European in India "no matter whether he is an adept in thieving, a reckless spendthrift, a drunkard, a confirmed gambler, a robber or even a murderer" and pointed out that mere accident confers upon him privileges which are denied to Natives. The *Native Opinion* wrote with disgust, " Cases of European soldiers murdering natives too frequently occur, and yet the state takes no measures to remedy, or even to mitigate, this crying evil..."[49] Although the British government did best to protect the interests of this "loafer" class by diligently maintaining the "social distance", but their "prestige" among the Indians was fast eroding. As in the Criminal Procedure Code amendment Bill (1872), similar arguments were advanced and a hue and cry was raised by the Anglo-Indian and European Community when Courtney Ilbert introduced the Ilbert Bill in 1883 under Viceroy Ripon, to empower Indian Judges with the authority to try the loafer class Europeans.[50] It was felt that the Ilbert Bill had suddenly sprung a mine on the European community. The British non-official community was impervious to argument, and was encouraged in its blind fury by British officials. With very few exceptions the entire European judiciary officials expressed their unqualified condemnation. It was a "white revolt" and finally the Ilbert Bill was enacted in an almost unrecognizable form. As in the earlier instance, the European community in India gained a resounding victory and the so-called "Liberalism" for which the English Prime Minister Gladstone and the Indian Viceroy Ripon stood received a severe buffeting. In both these Bills - the Criminal Procedure Amendment Bill (1872) and the Ilbert Bill (1883), the Indian community was vilified beyond measure and class-bitterness and race feeling was intensified to an almost incredible degree.

By 1874, the GOI recognized the urgency to repeal the European Vagrancy Act XXI of 1869 by a new modified Act - No. IX of 1874, which sought to include what was now felt essential. While initiating the Bill L.H. Bayley, former Advocate General and now member of the Executive Council of the Viceroy, commented during the discussion, "It was introduced to meet an evil which had grown almost intolerable

- one which had interfered materially with the police of the country, and which was not only a scandal, but had almost assumed the dimensions of a political embarrassment..." The Lieutenant Governor of Bengal, as one of the member of Viceroy's Council, echoed similar sentiment, "It was the very greatest possible evil that men of the class which this Bill affected should enter and go about this country in the way they did, disgracing their country and disgracing the British name."[51] The new Act IX made certain significant inclusions. To the list of "Persons of European Extraction" were added people from Tasmania, New Zealand, Natal and the Cape Colony. Since some difficulty was felt under the existing definition with regard to persons "who were not of pure British blood, although of legitimate descent", a clause was further added which further clarified that it "does not include persons commonly called Eurasians or East Indians". Thereby it eliminated an important early class that collaborated with the British rulers and limited the privileged class to unmixed white-men only. With a view to enforce discipline in the Government Workhouse, the Act now invested in the Magistrates and the Governors of the Workhouses with power to inflict the punishment of hard labour and solitary confinement not exceeding seven days, on European vagrants. Even Second Class Magistrates were now empowered to try the erring European vagrants.[52]

The Government began the practice of inviting yearly reports on the working of the European Vagrancy Act. From 1883, the practice of recording previous history of the European vagrant was started. However, the Secretary, JD, BG, candidly stated :

> "I have felt bound to observe on the fact that these histories are just the vagrant chooses to tell his own story. - While dishonesty is as occasionally the case and more frequently where drunkenness is the true cause of his poverty and vagrancy, the man is not likely to confess it. He prefers to concoct a more credible tale, and thus the entries made are in very many cases little else than so much of fiction..."[53]

Before 1883, vagrants for whom employment could not be found in other provinces were deported to Bombay. They received free passes from the Government to travel to Bombay. Till June 1885, the vagrants so deported were provided with a police escort. With the discontinuance of this practice, the consequence was that the majority of the vagrants who were provided with free passes would leave the train on way, and fail to reach Bombay, thus defeating the object of either seeking employment for them or deporting them to their country.

The Government incurred considerable losses on account of providing passes for the vagrants from the other Presidency areas to Bombay.[54] However, one finds the Bombay Government protesting against the importing of European vagrants to Bombay from other Presidencies, as it did lay considerable economic strain on the Government. On the other hand, it asked the respective Presidency Government to defray the cost of maintaining the vagrant brought from their presidency or deporting them to their respective country.

The yearly reports on the working of the European Vagrancy Act make conflicting claims, on one hand it expressed deep anxiety and alarm about the increasing nature of this evil; and on other hand makes claims of saving money by decreasing expenditure on this account. These statements often appear to be fabricated to suit the liking of the higher authorities. There are plenty of applications in the official records for seeking permission to deport European vagrants at state's cost. One finds innumerable cases of desertions from the workhouse. W.P. Walshe, the Governor of the Workhouse at Bombay, year after year keeps repeating in his report the evil character of this problem. In 1883, the Government also started a Female Workhouse.[55] Curiously, there are no files on Indian vagrants.[56]

The discriminatory imperial culture as evident in the case of the European vagrancy in India, expressed itself in every day affairs. Wilfred Scaven Blunt, who has authored the book – *India under Ripon*, narrates in the article "Ideas about India : Race Hatred" about racial arrogance of the Europeans : "Railway traveling is notoriously dangerous for them (Indians) in this respect and native acquaintances had tales tell of abuses from English fellow passengers, and of having been turned out of their places by the guards to accommodate these, and now and then been personally ill-treated and knocked about..."[57] Even a person of the stature of Justice M.G. Ranade had to face such ignominy at the hands of arrogant Europeans. At the root of such behaviour lay the belief in the inherent superiority of even a low-class, "White European Christian", be he a loafer, or vagabond or vagrant.

Furthermore, advocates of "imperial difference" made ludicrous arguments while opposing the Ilbert Bill, that it would place white woman "at the mercy of lascivious native male judge".[58] With the gradual spread of liberal ideas among the English educated Indians the realization of such distinction became quite distinct.

Advocates of the view that India was fundamentally different from Europe and hence the need for maintaining "the distance" was Sir James Fitzjames Stephen, a so-called liberal and utilitarian Law Member of the Viceroy's Council. It was the Tory, Ellis Ashmead-Bartlette, who echoed the same theme more fully in the House of Commons in 1883, a line which was toed by most of the officials as well as non-official Europeans with varying degrees. He said : "It is not the force alone that British rule in India is maintained... It is the repute, the ***Prestige*** , the innate sense of superiority that makes the little band of soldiers and administrators respected and obeyed by the masses around them. If an Indian were to see an Englishman tried and sentenced by one of his own race, he would soon lose the natural respect which at present is felt for Englishman, and will begin a course of encroachment which can only end in trouble and mutiny."[59]

Trouble, the colonial government did experience when Lokmanya B.G. Tilak did challenge their superiority in the last decade of the nineteenth century and early twentieth century, by exposing the myth of their "rule of law", the universal character of English law and legal system in India.[60] Not mutiny, but a revolution in thought and approach that Mahatma Gandhi brought about, not by deriding the "white", but by seeking to alleviate the poor, rustic Indian from dust to human dignity, blunted the edge of European aparthied policy. Thus, the problem of European vagrancy in nineteenth century India and Bombay in particular, indeed became **"White-man's Embarrassment"**.

References

1. *Maharashtra State Archives (MSA)/ Judicial Department (JD)/* 1862/ Vol. 13 / Compilation No. 607.

2. *MSA/ JD/* 1867/ Vol. 13/ 140, *REPORT ON EUROPEAN PAUPERISM*, December 1863. P.19.

3. *Ibid.* p.23.

4. Edward W. Said, *Culture and Imperialism*, Vintage ed., 1994, p.8.

5. Sir William Jones (1746-1794) was a British Orientalist, whose *Grammar of Persian Language*(1771) is very authoritative. Edmond Burke, author of *Reflections on the Revolution in France* and famed for his speeches in parliament against Warren Hastings Case. W.M. Thackeray, novelist, who wrote *Vanity Fair* and The *History of Henry*

Esmond. Jeremy Bentham, famous Utilitarian and one who wrote on law and jurisprudence. James Mill, a close colleague of Bentham and a Utilitarian, Harriet Martineau, essayist, novelist, and economic and historical writer, she was known for her liberal Utilitarianism. Rudyard Kipling, English short-story writer, poet and novelist, chiefly remembered for his celebration of British imperialism and his tales and poems of British soldiers in India.

6. John Stuart Mill, *Considerations on Representative Government,* George Routledge and Sons, London, Second impression in "The New Universal Library" 1905, Pp.329-331.

7. Cited by Edward Said, *Ibid.* p.244.

8. *Ibid.* p. 183.

9. Frances G. Hutchins, *The Illusion of Permanence - British Imperialism in India,* Princeton University Press, New Jersey, 1967, p.41.

10. Aroon Tikekar, "Dr. George Buist of the Bombay Times : A study of the self-proclaimed Messianism of an Anglo - Indian Editor, 1840-57" in N. K. Wagle (ed.) *Writers, Editors & Reformers, - Social and Political Transformation of Maharashtra 1830 - 1930,* Manohar, New Delhi, 1999, p.108.

11. For a detailed study of the concept of "Divine Providence" see J.V. Naik, "Perceptions of British Rule in Maharashtra : A Selective Study" in Ahsan Jan Qaisar and Som Prakash Verma (ed.) *Art and Culture - Endeavours in Interpretation,* Abhinav Prakashan, New Delhi, 1996, pp. 107-117.

12. For a detailed study of Bhaskar Pandurang Tarkhadkar's severe criticism of the British rule, see J.V.Naik, "An Early Appraisal of the British Colonial Policy", *Journal of the Bombay University,* Vol. XLV (N.S.), No. 81-82, 1975-76, pp.243-270.

13. Minute by His Excellency the Commander in Chief, Lt. Gen. William Rose Mansfield, dated 6th June 1862.*MSA/ JD* / 1862/ Vol. 13/ 607.; By virtue of being the Commander in Chief he was the member of the Governor's legislative Council on 18th May 1860. He became the member of Viceroy's legislative council in 1865 and soon became Baron Sandhurst.; The Minute was written because of the letter of William Crawford, Senior Magistrate of Police, who forwarded the letter of 2nd Magistrate of Police, N. Oliver to the Governor, which sought immediate grant of funds for the relief of European destitutes and sailors.

14. Raymond West to H. Brook, Secretary to the Chamber of Commerce, No. 2204, 27 June 1862, *Ibid.*

15. John Martinue, *Life and Correspondence of Sir Bartle Frere*, London, 1895, Vol. II, pp.345-46.

16. B. H. Ellis, Police Commissioner. N.D. to A.D. Robertson, Chief Secretary, Bombay Government (BG), No. 1232, 12 August 1862, also No. 1470, 3 October 1862, *Ibid.* Sir Barrow Herbert Ellis (1823-1887),. ICS, son of S. Herbert Ellis, a leading member of the Jewish community. Educated at University College School, London University and Hailybury; he came to Bombay in 1843, acting for some time during Sir Bartle Frere's absence as Chief Commissioner in Sindh, was Chief Secretary to BG and member of Council Bombay(April1865- May 69), Member of the Supreme Council of Governor General 1869-75, and later became Member of the India Council 1875-85. He died on June 20, 1887. Even E.W. Ravenscroft, Acting Magistrate of Surat reporting to Ellis, echoed similar concern : "The number of destitute is so great in Surat... they were penniless and almost starving. The great majority of these were persons who had been dismissed on account of ill health or misconduct from the employment of the Bombay Baroda and Central India Railway..." *MSA/ JD/* 1862 / Vol. 28/ 1146.

17. 'Minute' (Second) by His Excellency Sir William Mansfield on European Vagrants, 27th October 1862, *Ibid.*

18. H. Brook, Secretary, the Chamber of Commerce, Bombay, to W.H. Havelock, Acting Secretary, JD, BG, 24 November 1862. *MSA/JD/* 1863/ Vol. 14/ Comp. 9.

19. A further 'Minute' by His Excellency the Commander-in-Chief on Vagrancy, dated 23rd December 1862. *Ibid.*

20. Minute by His Excellency Sir William Mansfield, the same being an answer to a letter from the Chamber of Commerce dated February 10th 1863, on European Vagrancy, *Ibid.*; This is a very long minute and it seeks to refute the claims of the Chamber of Commerce point-wise.

21. *Report on European Pauperism*, dated 15th December 1863, *MSA/JD/* 1867/ Vol. 13/ Comp.140.

22. Even the Great Indian Peninsula Railway Company which did very good work between 1862 and 1866, like all other firms in Bombay, suffered considerable loss when the share mania declined; and in 1866-67 its finances sunk so low that it was forced to apply to Government for assistance. At this juncture the government of Seymore Fitzgerald strongly urged upon the Government of India the importance of buying out the Company, and thus regaining possession of harbour foreshore.

This proposal was sanctioned by the Secretary of State in 1869, and the Company went into voluntary liquidation in 1870. After May 1870, thus came the Port Trust. Added to the above problems was the aftermath of the Share mania, namely, the collapse of Bank of Bombay.

23. The District Benevolent Society was founded in 1830 at the instance of Bishop Turner of Calcutta and was named Friend-in-Need Society. Sir Jamshetjee Jeejeebhoy built a Dharmashala and placed it under this Society, endowed it with the annual sum of Rs. 3600. The Bombay Seamen's Fund Association was founded in 1835 go provide relief to the seamen of shipwrecks. *Report on European Pauperism*, December 1863, *Ibid.*

24. Sir Frank Henry Souter (1831 ? - 1888) Served as Volunteer against the rebels in the Nizam's dominion in 1850; appointed as Superintendent of Police at Dharwar in 1854; In the Revolt of 1857, captured the Nargoond Maratha Chief; suppressed Bhil brigands in the North Deccan in 1859; Commissioner of Police, Bombay 1864-1888. Knighted at Bombay in 1875, and died at the Nilgiris on June 5th 1888. C. E. Buckland, *Dictionary of Indian Biography*, Indological Book House, Indian ed. 1971, p.397.

25. Letter to the Editor by "Foreigner", *Bombay Gazette*, 18 September 1866 and also on 20 September 1866.

26. *MSA / JD /* Vol. 13/ 140.; No. 419 of 1866. 10th December 1866.

27. Francis G. Hutchins, *The Illusions of Permanence - British Imperialism in India*, Princeton University Press, New Jersey, 1967, p. 111.

28. The changes in the Constitution of the Committee had to be effected due to the reason that Rev. W.K. Fletcher, A.R. Scoble, M.H. Scott and Gumpert left India. Major Henderson was transferred to Poona and Mr. Barton resigned. The new Committee consisted of 1. Mangaldas Nathoobhoy, prominent Indian businessman and Member of the Governor's Council. 2. A.T. Crawford, 3. Dossabhoy Framjee Karaka, 4. J.P. Green, and 5. Frank H. Souter, the Commissioner of Police, Bombay. *MSA /JD /* 1868 / Vol. 25/ 1049/ 1058/ 458; Report of the Committee on European Pauperism, dated 31st July 1867. Dossabhoy Framjee retired after 27 years of service as Second Presidency Magistrate in 1887.

29. Opinion of L.H.Bayley, No. 69 of 1867, dated 25th November 1867,*Ibid.*, and No. 67 of 1867, dated 7 November 1867, *MSA / JD/* 1868/ Vol.62/ 1232.

30. Note on Advocate General's opinion by William Wedderburn, dated 2 December 1867, *MSA/JD/*1868/ Vol. 25/ 1049/ 1058/ 458.

31. To Sir Stafford H. Northcote, Secretary of State for India, signed by Sir John Lawrence, the Viceroy, W. R. Mansfield, the Commander in Chief, Henry S. Maine, the Law Member, and other Members of the Executive Council, i.e. G.N.Taylor, John Strachey, Richard Temple, General H. W. Norman. No.13 of 1868, Home Department (Legislative), dated 25 September 1868. *Ibid.*

32. John Connon, the Chief Magistrate of Police to the Secretary, JD, BG. 15th September 1868; Dossabhoy Framjee, 29th January 1869; Nana Moroji, 17th September 1868, Arthur Crawford, 2nd Feb. 1869; *MSA / JD/* 1869/ Vol. 19/ Comp. 394.

33. *MSA / JD/* 1869/ Vol.19/ 394 and *JD* / 1870/ Vol. 40/ 159.

34. The members present were : The Viceroy Lord Mayo, the Commander in Chief W.R. Mansfield, Major General Sir H.M. Durrand, the Law Member Henry Sumner Maine, John Strachey, Barrow Herbert Ellis, F. R. Cockrell, and Colonel Richard Strachey. *ABSTRACT OF THE PROCEEDINGS OF THE COUNCIL OF THE GOVERNOR GENERAL OF INDIA* (hereinafter *APCGGI*), 1869, Vol. VIII, The European Vagrancy Bill; *A Bill to Provide against European Vagrancy, along with a 'Statement of Objectives and Reasons'* prepared by Henry Maine, is found in *MSA/ JD/* 1868/ Vol.25. The Act No. XXI of 1869 is found in *MSA/ JD/* 1869/ Vol.19 / 394.

35. *APCGGI*, Vol. VIII, p. 301.

36. *MSA/JD/* 1870/Vol. 40/ 159, pp.205-6.

37. No. 4873 of 1870, JD, BG, *MSA/JD/* 1871/ Vol. 47/ 9.

38. From the Governor of the Committee of Management, Government Workhouse to its President, No. W-23/448, 18th February 1874, *MSA/ JD/*Vol. 59/ 725.

39. Frank Souter, the Commissioner of Police, Bombay, writing to the Secretary, JD, BG, No. 114 of 1870 & No. 1544 of 1870, *MSA/JD/* 1871/ Vol. 41/ 273.

40. *The Bombay Government Gazette*, No.16, 20th April 1871, *MSA/JD/* 1871/Vol. 47/ 9

41. *MSA/JD/* 1874/Vol. 59/ 725.

42. No.1899 of 1872, 26th April 1872, JD, BG, All these comments of Major Raitt were conveyed by letter to the GOI, *MSA/JD/* Vol.45 / 9.

43. *MSA/JD/* 1870/ Vol.41 / 1221.

44. *ABSTRACT OF PROCEEDINGS OF THE COUNCIL OF THE GOVERNOR GENERAL OF INDIA*, 1872, Vol. IX, pp. 392-435.

45. *Ibid*, p.433.

46. *The Hindu Reformer*, in the *Report on Native Papers*, 4th May 1872, *MSA/GD*/1872 / Vol.49/ 26.

47. *Indu Prakash*, 27th March1871, *Report on Native Papers*, 1st April 1871. *MSA/GD*/ 1871/ Vol.45/ 58.

48. *Indu Prakash*, 17th July, *Report on Native Papers*, 22nd July 1871, *MSA/GD*/ Vol.45/ 48.

49. *Native Opinion*, 7th May, *Report on Native Papers*, 13th May 1871, *Ibid*, & 10th December 1871, *RNP*, 16th December 1871, *MSA/GD*/ 1872 / Vol.49 /26.

50. In February 1883, the Law Member, Sir Courtney Ilbert, introduced a bill abolishing the principle of jurisdiction on the basis of race. For details see, S. Gopal, *British Policy In India*. Orient Longman, Reprint 1992, pp. 148-150.

51. APCGGI, 1874, Vol.XIII, The European Vagrancy Bill. Pp.92-93.

52. *Bombay Government Gazette*, 16th April 1874, in *MSA/JD*/ Vol. 88/ 669/ 1441.

53. *MSA/JD*/ 1883/ Vol. 72/ 141.

54. *MSA/JD*/ 1891 / Vol.114/ 801. No. 3101 of 1891, dt. June 9th 1891.

55. The Female workhouse was started on 30th January 1885. Prior to that a few of the female vagrants were sent to House of Hope, a private organization. *MSA/JD*/ 1886 /Vol. 47 / 723.

56. The reason could be that the Indian vagrants were treated under the Indian Penal Code and sent to jail. The files on European vagrants are found because they needed special treatment and enjoyed special status in a colonial setting.

57. Wilfred Scaven Blunt, "Ideas about India II : Race Hatred", *The Fortnightly Review*, 1st October 1884, No. CCXIV, NS.

58. Thomas R. Metcalf, *Ideologies of the Raj*, Cambridge University Press.1998, p.121.

59. *Hansards Parliamentary Debates*, 22 August 1883, col. 1684, Quoted by Thomas Metcalf, *Ibid.*, pp.210-11.

60. Many modern 'European' scholars do circulate the myth that "the law the British raj was universalistic, in principle treating all men as equal before it", creating a more "uniform system of law based on codes, with cautious and selective legislation that it incorporated into Indian personal law English conception of morality and liberty...." For example, read Lloyd I. Rudolph, Susanne Hoeber Rudolph, *The Modernity of Tradition – Political development in India*, Orient Longman, 1967, pp.279-293.; For a detailed analysis of how Tilak used the sedition cases proceeded against him, for mass mobilization, see Aravind Ganachari, "Evolution of the Law of 'Sedition' in the Context of the Indian Freedom Struggle 1837-1922", in Mariam Dossal, Ruby Malony (ed.) *State Intervention and Popular Response – Western India in the Nineteenth Century*, Popular Prakashan, 1998, pp.147-171.

6

"Two Indian Revolutionary Associations Abroad : Some New Light on the Pan-Aryan Association and the Indo-Japanese Association

The Pan-Aryan Association in the United States of America and the Indo-Japanese Association in Japan are the two earliest political associations started by Indians in those respective countries. While the existing works on Indian revolutionaries abroad make passing reference to the Pan Aryan Association of U.S.A., there is hardly any account of the Indian revolutionary activity in Japan prior to the activities of Rash Behari Bose. This article, which is primarily based on the *Bombay Presidency Police Abstracts of Intelligence,* seeks to throw some new light on these Indian revolutionary associations and evaluate their contribution to India's freedom struggle.

I

The Pan-Aryan Association was the earliest known Indian political association founded, in September 1906, in America by two India's revolutionaries — Samual Lucas Joshi (1878-1940) and Mohammad Barkatulla (b. ? D. 1928).[1] It was started in New York on the lines of Indian Home Rule League[2], with the purpose of making a common cause with the similar movement in Ireland. This was one of the first Indo-Irish endeavors for attaining their *swaraj.*[3] About the same time, Joshi attended a meeting of the United Irish League delegated on 21. October 1906, to enlist the support of the Irish leaders. Further evidence of this is the fact that President of the Pan-Aryan Association was an Irishman named A.S. Dulin. Joshi became the Secretary of this Association. It seems, Joshi was assisted in this effort by George Fitzerald 'Freeman', who edited the *Gaelic American,* a mouth-piece of Irish revolutionaries and which espoused the cause of Indian independence[4], and John Devoy of *Clan-na-Gael.*[5]

The first public meeting of the Pan-Aryan Association took place at the Hotel 'Martha Washington', N.Y., on 11 February 1907, which was presided over by A.S. Dulin and speeches were delivered by S.L. Joshi, Mohd. Barkatulla and Indu Bhushan Dey Mazumdar[6] in which they emphasized British oppression and the new industrial movement in India. The report of this meeting and the prospectus of the Association were published by the *Gaelic American* in its issue of 2 March 1907. The aims and objectives of this Association could be thus summarized —

1. To secure Home Rule for India.
2. To carry on propaganda in the United States with a view to attain the same. and to bring India and America in closer contact.
3. To spread among the people of India a knowledge of the advantages of freedom and national unity.
4. To help the students *from* India, to educate and send them back. so that they may spread the message of liberal education and industrialism.

For achieving closer co-operation with the Irish leaders, S.L. Joshi attended a meeting of United Irish League in New York on 26 October 1906, in which Mr. Bulmer Hobson of Belfast was the principal speaker. The meeting was stated to have been attended by over 2500 people including every active Irish and Indian nationalists in New York. After Bulmer Hobson spoke on "the Aim, Methods and Working of the Sinn Fein Movement",[7] Joshi spoke on the *Swadeshi* movement in India. Joshi pointed out that it was similar to the one mentioned by Hobson, started for the purpose of achieving emancipation—political and economic from a common enemy, the English. He also pointed out the economic ruin that was wrought by the English rule in India. And said, "We feel that Ireland's cause is our own and our hearts are knit with the hearts of Ireland".[8] At the close of the meeting a resolution was passed of which contents were as follows:

> "We extend to the people of India our sympathy and good-will in their struggle for the recovery of their independence and we congratulate them on the splendid progress they have made through the *Swadeshi*

movement in the revival of industries which have been destroyed by England, and which are a necessity in the national life. We hope and pray that India and Ireland may march side by side to complete in absolute freedom".

Joshi and Barkatulla's close contacts, with Shyamji Krishna Verma, Mrs. Bhikaji Rustom K.R. Cama and the India Home Rule League of London, can be understood from the report of the second Annual General Meeting of the Indian Home Rule League, held on 23 February 1907. This Report was published by Shyamji Krishna Verma in *Indian Sociologist.* The report applauded the establishment of the Pan Aryan Association by their friends and sympathizers.[9]

In October 1907, Mrs. Cama, the well known Indian revolutionary abroad, arrived in New York. She was put up in the Hotel 'Martha Washington', from where the Pan-Aryan Association functioned. Her interview was published in New York *Sun* of 20 October 1907, in which she exposed the British oppression in India. It also mentions that S.L. Joshi was present at that time. Mrs. Cama's lectures were arranged under the auspices of the Pan-Aryan Association[10]

It must be noted here that Myron H. Phelps, an Irish American, also organized two organizations — Indo-American National Association on 5 September 1907 and Society for the Advancement of India in November 1907, in New York, for similar purposes[11] It seems, Phelps' effort to unite his Association with the Pan-Aryan Association, did not succeed. In the opinion of police report it was because Joshi and Barkatulla were jealous of Phelps' position and influence rather than any divergence of political views.[12] Interestingly, a letter signed by six Bengali students, which appeared in the *Bande Matram* of Calcutta in its issue of 11 April 1908, regretted Phelps' arbitrary manner in running his Society with-out desiring the active cooperation of any of their representative leaders and expressed their intention of joining the Pan-Aryan Association.[13] This disseminated influence of the Pan-Aryan Association among Indian students studying in America. The biographical sketch of Samuel Lucas Joshi and Mohd. Barkatulla is very scant. A few facts about them, culled from the Police 'secret' files and the contemporary records, may be briefly stated. S.L. Joshi[14] was born in 1874, at Buldhana, in Maharashtra (then in Berar). His father, Rev. Lucas Mahoba Joshi was connected with the Church Mission Society for more than forty years. S.L. Joshi lived at Nasik from 1876 to 1888. He completed High School education at Aurangbad. From 1890 to 1895, he studied for B.A. degree at the Nizam College, Hyderabad. During most of this time, he lived with the Rev. M.G. Goldsmith of Church Mission Society. After taking his degree, he went to Bombay in 1896 and was employed in the Bombay Government secretariat. Later, he joined the office of the Bombay Presidency Magistrates' court, while studying law in the Bombay Government Law School. In 1899, he was appointed Head Master of the Church Mission Society's High Master at Hyderabad, Sind. In 1900, he went to Amballa as the Head Master of a High School. There, he received an offer of a lecturership in Indian Languages in an American institution for training for people desiring to be missionaries. He left for America in August 1902. The institution where Joshi was working in America having changed hands, he came to New York where he made his living by lecturing on India for the New York Board of Education and also as representative of the Foreign Missions Industrial Association. In this capacity, he lectured extensively on the need for reviving Indian industries on modern scientific lines.

When the work of this mission was given up for want of funds, Joshi turned to research work at Columbia University where he took his M.A. degree in 1905. It was during his lecturing on Indian industries that Joshi seems to have become interested in revolutionary activities. Very little is known about Mohd. Barkatulla's early life and also about his family. He was probably born around 1870.[15] He went to U.S.A. towards the end of 19th century and gradually became involved in the incipient Indian revolutionary movement over there. He, more than Joshi, seems to have been in close contact with the Indian revolutionaries like Shyamji Krishna Verma, Mrs. Cama, Sardar Rewasingji Rana and others. In 1908, Surendra Mohan Bose, who had come from Japan, with Gurudatta Kumar and Tarak Nath Das, had started publishing *Free Hindustan* a bi-monthly journal from Vancouver, British Canada, which was a close imitation of *Indian Sociologist* of S.K. Verma. Due to pressure of British administration there, it was moved to Seattle in Autumn 1908 and then to New York. George Freeman, S.L. Joshi and Barkatulla are said to have played a major role in having *Free Hindustan* published from New York. However, its publication abruptly ended in 1910.

The activities of the Pan-Aryan Association came to an end around February 1909. Even Phelps had to close down his Association and India House in New York around the same time. Perhaps, the reason for this closure could be advanced was that William Jenning Bryan, who was Governor of Nebraska and later became Woodrow Wilson's Secretary of State in 1916, castigated the British rule in India by comparing it with

Czarist rule in Russia. The British Foreign Office showed total displeasure to the US administration at such utterances of Bryan. It was with a view to achieve US-British friendship, President Theodore Roosevelt countered Bryan's views on India[16] and the U.S. administration suppressed all kinds of pro- Indian activities in New York, at the instance of British Government.[17]

While Mohd. Barkatulla left for Tokyo in March 1909, S .L. Joshi took up a teaching assignment in Maharaja College in Baroda State. When the Government of India objected to this appointment through the Political Resident, Joshi disclaimed his earlier association with Mrs. Cama and others, and thereafter, the political intelligence did not keep a track of his activities. After some years he was allowed to take up Carnegie Exchange Professorship in America. During 1926- 1936, he was the Head of the Department for Comparative Religions and Indian Philosophy at Dartmouth College. He died on 16 June 1940 at Chicago.[18] During this period, he helped many Indian students who went to America for higher education.

II

The striking and pre-eminent position which Japan had attained as one of the foremost nations of modern times, not only evoked admiration but stimulated the newly awakened Indian national sentiment and the spirit of industrial revival, during the extremist phase of Indian national movement. Maharashtra's connection with Japan began in the closing years of 19th century. B.G. Tilak's close associate Vasukaka Joshi, proprietor of the Chitrashala Press, had wished to establish contacts with Japan through Nepal Government, and even visited Japan himself.[19] Perhaps, it may be because of his efforts that Japanese Government agreed to give financial help to the draught stricken people in Maharashtra in 1900. The native newspapers in Maharashtra followed the Russo-Japanese War with unabated interest. It was *Kesari,* who in return to Japanese help earlier undertook the task of giving pecuniary aid to the families of Japanese soldiers rendered destitute in the war. 'One rupee' contribution was collected in the Deccan and Rs. 2000/- were sent to the Yokohama Specie Bank.[20]

One of the earliest who went to Japan in 1899, was Krishnaji Dadaji alias Kedba Kulkarni, a member of the secret society named Shivaji Club of Kolhapur, in Maharashtra. While most of these used to go to Japan to learn match-box or glass manufacturing, a few of them acquired the knowledge of bomb-making[21] and on their return used to secretly help the armed revolutionaries.

Many students, mostly from Maharashtra. Bengal. Baroda. Madras and Mysore, followed K.D. Kulkarni. Around 1906, there were as many as 50 of them in Tokyo alone. Most of them were students of Tokyo Higher Technological School, the Tokyo and Kyoto Imperial Universities and the Sapparo Agricultural College.

A few other Indian students acquired knowledge different kinds at a variety of factories. Their Japanese colleagues respected them for their intelligence. The mutual advantages of a closer connection between the two countries, especially in the field of commercial, industrial and educational activity was realised and need for a properly organized agency was felt by these students. They had the good fortune of enlisting the warm sympathies of the frontline leaders of modern Japan including such celebrities as Count Okuma, one of the four 'elder-statesmen'(the *Genro);* the founders of industrial enterprise in Japan, i.e., Mr. Kondo, President of the Nippon Yusen Kaisha, and Baron Takahashi, President of the Yokohama Specie Bank. The result was the establishment of the Indo-Japanese Association in Tokyo.[22] One of the chief supporters of this cause was H.D. Tata. The aims and objectives of this Association were:

1. To guide and help every possible way Indian students and others, proceeding to Japan for study or business.
2. To provide a building for the accommodation of Indian students for housing a suitably equipped library.
3. To create and foster in the intelligent classes of Japan, interest in Indian students, esp. in Indian commerce and industries, and to devise means for developing commerce and industry in India.
4. To spread the knowledge of Indian vernaculars among the educated class of Japan.
5. To encourage intercourse between the two countries so as to bring the people into closer contact[23].

One of those students who played a large part in .the establishment of this Association was Govind Narayan Potdar[24]. He had gone to Japan in 1903 and had remained till December 1908, to study Applied Chemistry. He along with other students, started India House in Tokyo, similar to the one at London[25] and branches were opened in Kyoto, Osaka, and in almost all industrial cities. Among other prontinent students were : Surendra Mohan Bose, who later went to America, K.D. Kulkarni, L. Barthakur, S.C.

Ray. S.C. Ghosh, J.J. Sawant, S.C. Bose, J.B. Bidyant, B.H. Khatao. Besides, many Indian business, firms in Japan seem to have lent all kinds of support to the activities of Indian students.[26] Many of these after their return to India started *Swadeshi* industries[27] and some of them actively connected with the armed revolutionaries.

The arrival of Mohd. Barkatulla in February 1909, gave a shot in the arm to the anti-British political activities at India House. He took up the assignment of teaching Urdu at the Tokyo School for Foreign Languages. The statement given to the police after much interrogation by one Nananal Pranshankar alias Kanchan Kumar, who had visited India House at Tokyo and other places in Japan, reveals the influence that Mohd. Barkatulla wielded.

"He (Barkatulla) is a good and spirited speaker. He speaks against the British Government, a man of strong political views...From my travels through Japan, I came to the conclusion that in Tokyo Indian politics were freely discussed and that the Japanese took a lot of interest in them. I understood that Barkatulla was a great favourite of the Indians and the Japanese, and commanded immense influence... He told me that the Japanese who were present for my lecture at the India House were the sons of military men. He said that India would regain her liberty one day through the combined assistance of China and Japan... In my opinion, Barkatulla is the Shyamji Krishna Verma of Japan. He is friendly with the Captains of the Japanese steamers coming to and fro from India. Barkatulla carried on correspondence in cipher... Savant, Gokhale and Mukherji know Japanese and are friends of Barkatulla."[28]

There is an interesting report from the D.C.I. Simla : "It has since been suggested that the arms which are being smuggled into India by the Japanese include rifles which are sent out in parts packed separately in merchandize".[29]

It should be noted that before the First World War, a Japanese secret society named *Shina Ronin.* with its leader Toyama Mitsura, was actively supporting Indian revolutionaries. It also had the financial backing of Japanese Government.[30] Because of the growing anti-British and pro-Pan-Aryan sentiment, the obvious self-interest of some Japanese commercial houses and seamen could be easily blended with their new imperialist ideals, and a substantial part of the illicit arms and ammunitions secured by the revolutionaries in India used to come from Kobe and Yokohama.[31]

On 1st August 1912, the Viceroy of India appealed to the Secretary of State to request the Japanese Government to put an end to the publication of the *Islamic Fraternity*, which Barkatulla edited from Tokyo.[32] The governments of Gombie Yamamoto and Shigenobu Okuma wanted good relations with Britain, and so it was not possible for Indians in Japan to carry on an effective anti-British agitation, until the activities of Rash Behari Bose. Barkatulla left for San Francisco on 6 May 1914.[33] The Indo-Japanese Association which had become centre of anti-British political activity until 1914, again became apolitical organization.

References

1. *Bombay Presidency Abstracts* of *Intelligence* (hereinafter *BPPAI)*. Year 1910 / Vol. XXIII / No.11 /19 March / Para-758.

2. The Indian Home Rule Society was formed by about twenty Indians under the leadership of Shyamji Krishna Verma on 18 February 1905, in London on lines of Irish Home Rule League Society. For details see. Indulal Yajnik , *Shyamji Krishna Verma.* Bombay. 1950. 130-133.

3. One of the earliest links between Irish and Indian patriots was that an Indian student named Camille F. Saldhana was helped. in May 1906. by the *Clan-na-Gael* to go to Dublin to establish contacts with the Sinn Fein leaders. Arun Kumar Bose, *Indian Revolutionaries Abroad. 1905-1922.* Patna. 1971. p. 38.

4. George Freeman and John Devoy seem to have been in touch with Mrs. Cama in Paris regarding smuggling of arms. DCI on 9 March 1915. Home-Political. 1915 - April. 412-15 B. source quoted by Arun Kumar Bose. *Ibid.* p. 48.

5. Clan-na-Gael was a revolutionary society established by a group of Irish Americans called Fenians in the second half of the 19th century. This Society under John Devoy had proclaimed its political alliance with Indian revolutionaries. The *Gaelic American* was banned by the Government of India in 1907.

6. *BPPAI* I 1910 / XXIII I No.11 I Para 758; A letter from Mrs. Cama to Indu Bhushan Dey, which the police intercepted, made them interrogate him and check his luggage on his arrival at Bombay in 1910. He gave following information about himself to the police. He was studying in Cornell University and had shared similar tendencies with many other Indians abroad, and that he has now given up such ideas. He travelled some time with Prince Victor of Cooch Bihar and undertook his last trip to America, Egypt and Turkey at the expense of the Cooch Bihar State. The correspondence found with him revealed

his association with Mrs. Cama. Barkatulla, Myron H. Phelps and other extremists. A photo of S.L. Joshi and a group photo with Myron Phelps was also found. *BPPAI* / 1910 / XXIII / *No.9/5* March/ Para 596.

7. *Sinn Fein.* meaning "We Our-self". Irish nationalist party founded by Arther Griffith (1872-1922) in 1905. It was extremist outfit, later became the political wing of Irish Republican Party.

8. *BPPAI* / XXIII / No.4 7 / 3 Dec. / Para 758.

9. *Ibid.*

10. *Ibid.*

11. Aravind Gururao Ganachari. "Myron H. Phelps (1856-1916) : An Early American Advocate of India's Freedom", *PIHC,* 52nd Session, New Delhi. 1991-92. pp.650-661.

12. *BPPAI* / 1910 / XXIII / No.4 7 / 3 December / Para-3197.

13. *BPPAI* / 1910 / XXIII / No.24 / 18 June / Para-1820.

14. *BPPAI* / 1910 / XXIII / No.47 / 3 December / Para-3197. History-sheet of S.L. Joshi. Photograph of S.L. Joshi in *BPPAI* / 1909. 758.

15. Arun Kumar Bose. *op.cit.*, p. 253.

16. President Theodore Roosevelt countered Bryan's views on India, in his speech delivered at the Metropolitan Memorial Methodist Church at Washington on 18 January 1908.

17. At this time, the India Office in London as well as the Government of India were extremely watchful of the activities of the Indian revolutionaries and their foreign collaborators abroad. Dunlop Smith, who was a close confidant of Lord Minto in the India Office, then headed by Lord Morley, made discreet inquiries whether any Irish society or any other organisation was supporting Indian revolutionaries. *Minto Papers,* Correspondence - Eng. & Ind.. L & T. Vol. II, No.7. Dunlop Smith to Lord Minto, dt. 12 July 1907. Quoted by M.N. Das. *India Under Morley and Minto.* London. 1963. pp.115-16.

18. *The Times* of *India,* 17 June 1940; Also, V.S. Joshi, *Agnipathâvaril Parâgandhâ* (Marathi), 1987, pp. 156-7.

19. For details see, Y.D. Phadke, *Lokmanya Tilak Ani Krantikarak* (Marathi), Pune, 1985, pp. 48-49. Their hopes of having help of Nepal Government were dashed as that government was not ready to incur the displeasure of British Government in India.

20. *Maharashtra* State *Archives / Political Department / Confidential 'A' Proceedings for May 1905,* No.10 of 1905, dated 14 April 1905, pp. 371-73.

21. K.D. alias Kedba Kulkarni, was an active member of the Shivaji Club. On his return to India by the end of 1906, he joined the services of Gwalior State, but was dismissed in 1907. It was he who introduced Krishnaji Damodar Limaye, another member of the Shivaji Club, to G.N. Potdar to learn bomb making. From 1913, Kulkarni evaded warrant for arrest but was eventually arrested in 1918 and sentenced to 7 years imprisonment. For details see Phadke, *op.cit.*, p. 49.

22. Printed note of the Indo-Japanese Association given by R.D. Tata to the police. In *BPPAI* / 1909 / XXII / N0.49 / 11 December / Para-232-I.

23. *Ibid.*

24. *BPPAI* / 1910 / XXIII / No 17 / 30 April / Para-1194: The History sheet of G.N. Potdar describes him as an extremist and a protégé of Dr. Moreshwar Gopal Deshmukh, Hon. Secretary of the Hindu Educational Fund of Bombay. Potdar was from Akalkot in Sholapur Distrct and studied in Nizam College. Hyderabad. He was graduated from University of Madras in 1903. The police described that Potdar learnt bomb-making in Japan and was close to revolutionaries from Bengal and Maharashtra. He was in close contact with Waman Baji Ruikar, who was connected to Belapur Swami Club and Hotilal Verma, one who was arrested in Bengal for revolutionary activities. Potdar, later started a monthly called *India House Magazine*, published from Bombay.

25. *BPPAI* / 1910 / XXIII / N0. 49 / 11 December / Para-2321.

26. *Ibid.* The police report gives the list of 27 Indian firms in Tokyo and Yokohama alone. Of these 11 were in Kobe, and 7 in other industrial cities. Both the India House and these firms also gave loans to the students. The firms also helped the Indian visitors to Japan in providing lodging and boarding.

27. Potdar started manufacture of sulphuric acid at Mahim and also helped the Talegaon Glass Factory. Balkrishna Hari Khatao started Belgaum Match Factory. Both were given financial help from the Paisa Fund started by Tilak.

28. *BPPAI* / 1914 / XXVII / No.22 / 6 June / Para-1058.

29. *BPPAI* / 1914 / XXVII/No.3 / 24 January / Para-121.

30. Don Dignan, *Indian Revolutionary Problem In British Diplomacy-1914-1919*, New Delhi. p.97.

31. R.P. Dua, *The Impact of the Russo-Japanese (1905) War on Indian Politics*, Delhi. 1966. p.67-68.

32. The *Islamic Fraternity* edited by Barkatulla tried to unite the Islamic people of Turkey to make a common cause and to fight the British. According to the Police, this monthly was a fanatically Pan-Islamic. But in the wider context it does not seem to be true. Before the Director of Foreign Languages and the

Japanese Government warned Barkatulla, the publication of this paper had ceased on 12 Oct. 1912. He also wrote two revolutionary pamphlets. *Akher al-Helal Saif* in Urdu and *Proclamation of Liberty* in English. For Barkatulla's later life see *Dictionary* of *National Biography*. Vol. I, edited by S.P. Sen. Calcutta. 1972. 130-140. Photograph of Barkatulla in *BPPAI* / 1913. p. 915. Group photo of India House in *BPPAI* / 1910. p. 748 does not give any information of Barkatulla's contribution to "German Connection". Also see Nirode K. Barooha, "Har Dayal and the German Connection", in *IHR*, Vol. VII, July 1980-Jan. 1981. Nos. 1-2, pp.184-211.

33. R.P. Dua, *op.cit.*

7

An Early American Contributor to India's Struggle For Freedom : Myron H. Phelps (1856-1916)

Myron H. Phelps(1856-1916) was one of the earliest American champions of India's struggle for freedom. None of the existing works on American contribution to India's independence takes any note of Phelps' pioneering effort in promoting India's cause in the United States.[1] This article which is mainly based on *Bombay Presidency Police Abstracts of Intelligence*, seeks to evaluate Phelps' contribution to India's freedom struggle.

The biographical information about Phelps is very scanty. A few facts about him, culled from the Police 'secret' files and contemporary records, may be first briefly stated. The Phelpses were Irish immigrants to United States. Myron H. Phelps was born in Illinois, USA, on April 2nd, 1856. He graduated from the Yale University in 1876 and took law degree from Law School, California in 1885. He owned a farm in New Jersey and practiced legal profession. He was connected with the legal section of the Rubber Goods Manufacturing Company in the USA. As their representative, he is said to have stayed in Colombo for more than a year and also visited India. On his return to America, he carried on correspondence with friends in Colombo and in India. There is some evidence to suggest that Swami Vivekanand, when he visited America to attend Parliament of Religions, had stayed with him at New York in 1895.[2] Phelps seems to have visited Egypt in around 1902-3. There, he was impressed by the religion of the Bahai's. He authored a book called *The Life and Teachings of Abbas Effendi.*[3] It concerned with the religion of the Babis or Behai's, founded by the Persian Bab and his successor Behaullha and Abbas Effendi. Phelps' Irish background and personal experience of British imperialism in India and elsewhere made him very critical of British rule. He was active in everything hostile to England and was particularly so during the Boer War.

On September 5, 1907, he organised "Indo-American National Association" at Maine. Dadabhai Naoroji was made Honorary President of the Association. The chief aim of the Association were:

1. To assist Indian students in America.
2. To present Indian questions in American press.
3. To secure facilities for Indian visiting America and for Americans visiting India.
4. To convey the sympathy of Americans to the people of India through the Indian press, and to help to secure for them from the British Government a measure of self-rule.[4]

In November of the same year, Phelps started in New York a "Society for the Advancement of India".[5] The objective of this Society were similar to that of the Indo- American National Association. In May 1908, two branches of the society were opened at Detroit and Chicago.[6] 6 The proceedings of the meetings of the Society, showed that it received a number of letters from the *Swadeshi* agitators of India, mostly connected with newspapers. They gave a harrowing picture of general poverty and wide-spread famine in India. One of the most well informed persons at these meetings was Rev. Dr. Cuthbert Hall. A committee of three Phelps, Dr. Hall and John DeWitt Werner, - was formed in to consider as to how the Society should be organised in order to carry out its objectives.

At this time the India Office in London as well as the Government of India were extremely watchful of the activities of the Indian revolutionaries and their foreign collaborators abroad. Dunlop Smith, who was a close confident of Viceroy Lord Minto in the India Office, then headed by Lord Morley, made discrete inquiries whether *Clan-na-Gael*,[7] the revolutionary Irish society or any other organisation in America was supporting the Indian revolutionaries. It should be noted that the *Clan-na-Gael* under John Devoy, had openly proclaimed it political alliance with the Indian revolutionaries abroad. Smith also reported to the authorities in India that "a lawyer in New York named Phipps (the correct name was Phelps and not 'Phipps') had started an "India House" ostensibly to help Indian students, but really to inculcate sedition. He did not help them with money but did a lot of harm in other ways."[8] Since then Myron Phelps was closely watched, and a detailed diary of his day to day movements and activities was kept by the Intelligence Department. The police records thus kept, reveal Myron Phelps' connection with India in her quest for freedom.

Phelps first attracted attention as a writer of a series of eight "Letters to the Indian People", the first of which appeared in the *Gaelic American*[9] On 10th August 1907 and the last in January 1908. These long letters were reproduced in the *Hindu* of Madras, with whose editorial staff Phelps regularly corresponded. These 'Letters' reflected his ideas on Indian freedom struggle. In the first 'Letter', while conveying the sympathies of Americans to the people of India "in their present trials", Phelps drew a parallel between the history of

American colonies of Great Britain, and that of India. Keeping in mind the then prevailing *Swadeshi* movement in India, he showed that the boycott of English goods in America preceded the Revolution. He claimed that the *Swadeshi* was an American institution before it was used in India, and hoped that it would produce similar results in India.

The second 'Letter' described "America's Struggle for Swaraj". In that Phelps gave an account of the trial of John Peter Zenger, editor of *New York Weekly Journal* that took place in 1734-3. John Zenger's (1697-1746) paper opposed the policies of the colonial Governor William Cosby. He brought independent spirit to New York journalism. Although many of the articles were contributed by his more learned colleagues and supporters - Lewis Morris, James Alexander and William Smith, Zenger was still held legally for their content as editor and publisher. For a year the paper continued its scathing attack on Cosby until, on November 17, 1734, Zenger was arrested for allegedly libelous statements in the Journal. The trial continued for two years. Disregarding the judge's admonition due to bias, to the acclaim of the general public and the spectators, the colonial jury acquitted Zenger on the ground that such charges were based on fact - a key consideration in libel cases since that time. This was the first major victory for the freedom of press in the American colonies. The account of the trial was published as - *A Brief Narrative of the Case and Trial of John Peter Zenger* (1736)[10], which aroused great interest in America and Britain. Perhaps, Phelps wished to draw an analogy with the prosecution of many an editor in India at that time and suggested that like Zenger Trial which fired the cause of liberty in American colonies, trials in India like the one of Lokmanya Tilak would have similar effect on the Indian fteedom struggle.[11] The third 'Letter' was entitled - "the Struggle and the Ideal", in which he urged the people of India to unite. In a postscript to this letter, he asked his Indian correspondents to send letters which would enable to 'prepare vivid description for the American press and thus excite American interest and sympathy'. The Government of India viewed this as a positive evidence of Phelps' 'malafides' and recorded that "a more than usual astute journalist on the look-out for copy".

The forth 'Letter' announced the formation of Indo-American National Association. It concluded with a request for interesting, readable and informative articles, and assured that he would negotiate for the authors a good price for their contributions. The fifth was headed 'Union in *Swadeshi* - the Salvation of India'. In this, after describing the drain of Indian wealth to England, he made a long presentation of economic aspect of *Swadeshi.* In the sixth 'Letter', he discussed - "Educational Opportunities for Self-supporting Students in America" He pointed out that it would be possible for Indian students to earn and learn in America. The seventh 'Letter' described the economic decline of England. Phelps also made it clear that all these were his personal opinions and did not commit any Societies with which he was connected.

The last 'Letter' appeared in January 1908. It was addressed to the "Mohammodans of India", mainly to attract their attention and to bring them also into the national agitation. Aware of British policy of 'divide and rule', Phelps, perhaps intended to suggest that if Muslims would join Swadeshi movement whole-heartedly, it would have tremendous impact on the British government. In this letter, he announced the establishment of 'India House' in New York, where Indian students could find 'warm welcome and a comfortable home at a moderate cost'. These letters were favourably viewed both in India and America.

However, it seems that Myron Phelps did not create a favourable impression on some of the Indian students who came in contact with him. This is evident from 'An Open Letter to Myron Phelps' written by six Bengali students from New York. This letter was also published in the *Bande Matram* of Calcutta on April 11, 1908.[12] The signatories accused Phelps of conducting affairs of the Society in an arbitrary manner without consulting Indian representatives. They also complained that he did not do anything for the Indian students to 'earn their way through American colleges', and that 'India House' was meant only for Hindu students. The accusation of he being favourable to Hindus seems to be a canard, for he admired 'Vedanta' of Swami Vivekanand as much as the Behai's faith of the Muslims.

The Pan-Aryan Association of Samuel Lucas Joshi (1878-1940) and Maulvi Mohammad Barkatulla (b.? d. 1928)[13] and the two associations founded by Phelps held divergent views on the conduct of activities for furthering the cause of India's freedom. Prior to the establishment of his associations, Phelps had been in close contact with them. He was also in communication with Shymji Krishna Verma an S.C.K. Rutnam. He also attended the meetings of Madam Bhikaiji Rustom K.R.Cama.[14] Despite Phelps' endeavour to make a common cause with the Pan-Aryan Association, the latter always remained hostile to him, for he did not openly identify himself with radical character of the anti-British Irish agitators or the Indian revolutionaries in America. The chief objective of Phelps' work, as stated by him, was to arouse the masses in America, India, England and Ireland, and make a combined demand for justice in favour of the oppressed people in India and the British dependencies. Should the oppression continue, he warned, it would lead to open revolution in India to throw off the foreign yoke. The main ideological difference between Phelps and the leaders of Pan-Aryan Association was that, whereas the former supported Swadeshi movement of the Indian Extremists to bring the British to their heels, the latter wanted to overthrow the British by armed revolution. The difference is well brought out in a police report on S.L. Joshi.[15] It states:

> "It may be put down to Joshi's credit that he was antagonistic to Phelps and his India House and it is known that the Pan-Aryan Association did not unite with Phelps' Society for the Advancement of India in spite of the endeavours made by the latter, but our information is that Joshi and Barkatulla were jealous of Phelps' position and influence and it is likely that antagonism was as much due to this as to any divergence in their political views"

Phelps' Society corresponded with difterent sections of people in all parts of India. It received inquiries mainly regarding technical and trade education in America. Of these, a number of those who had requisite qualifications and the adequate finances were encouraged to come to America. The negotiations for such Indians going to U.S. were conducted through the Scientific and Industrial Association of Calcutta. The Society also endeavoured to find employment for them but with not much success.[16]

In early 1908, Phelps succeeded in getting from several colleges in United States other than New York, offers of free education and reduced fees for the Indian students. However, owing to financial difficulties, Phelps' India House could not make much progress. Writing to the Congress paper *India* of London,[17] he said,

"On the whole I would say that American feeling in regard to India is of a piece with American feeling with regard to all else,... With the exception of a handful, comparatively, of public spirited men and women, the great majority are not interested in matters so remote; and even when informed, are not disposed to tamper with what may eventuate to their material advantage, especially when such tampering takes them perforce against the sluggish current of the 'dead level'. But 'God and one make majority', and we are not discouraged."

Despite opposition from the rival Indian organisation, financial difficulties and the general American apathy, Phelps continued to run India House. As a way out, he requested Bipin Chandra Pal to make a lecture tour of America which could motivate the Americans to lend financial support to India House. B.C. Pal acknowledgingly thanked Phelps for his efforts to arrange his lecture series, but could not make the trip.[18] In a letter addressed to the Indian newspapers on March 16, 1909, Phelps painfully announced the closure of India House.[19]

In 1906, William Jenning Bryan, who was Governor of Nebraska and was one who later became President Woodrow Wilson's Secretary of State, castigated the British rule in India, comparing it with Czarist rule in Russia. The British foreign office showed total displeasure to the U.S. administration at such utterances of Mr. Bryan. It was with a view to achieving US- British friendship; the American President Theodore Roosevelt countered Bryan's views on India in 1908. He made a speech in praise of the British rule in India?[20] Thereupon, Phelps convened a meeting of the members of the Society for the Advancement of India on February 11, 1908, to consider a draft of an 'Open Letter' to President Roosevelt refuting his utterances regarding India. Phelps was chiefly instrumental in having it prepared along with Rev. J. T. Sunderland. At the outset, the signatories made it clear that they neither had any bias towards the President and his administration nor against England. They regretted that the President had allowed himself to speak without 'adequate information, to the detriment of a helpless people held in political subjection...' While appreciating the regenerative role of England in the colonial America, they expressed desire that, "some day her eyes will be opened and she will do a like justice to India, transforming a slave empire into a self-governing nation of freemen." They lamented that as the President of the erstwhile English colonies, "he should be willing to give to the world an utterances which can but postpone the coming of such a day" for India. The signatories lauded the efforts of Indian leaders such as Dadabhai Naoroji,

G.K. Gokhale, RC. Dutt, Lala Lajpatrai and the radical members of Labour Party in England, in giving authentic and unbiased information on Indian affairs.

The burden of their argument was that India was deprived of any meaningful responsibility in her administration, despite Lord Morley's liberalism; that the British rule was a 'system of pure absolutism : from the Viceroy downwards and as autocratic as that of the Czar of Russia'; that the : freedom of press was extremely curtailed, many editors were imprisoned on the charge of 'sedition' and sent to unknown jails; and that the objections to India's self-government were same as the one raised by the supporters of Lord North's government regarding colonial America: "If left to their descretion they would speedily fall into mutual strife, anarchy and ruin." The "Open Letter" contradicted the President's claim that England does not draw a penny from India, and called the Englishmen in India as "carpet-baggers" and "birds of prey". They showed how India was drained of her wealth, salt was taxed 2000 percent of its cost price, rail-road policy was controlled by the prospect of strategic value and financial return to England, and that there was shameful neglect of irrigation. "Reform in India is England's great and pressing duty and cannot be much longer evaded or deferred" they concluded.[21] This 'Open Letter' was widely published in America and elsewhere, and it made considerable impact.

On March 27, 1909, Phelps sailed from Boston to England. On his way he visited Vienna and Paris. In Paris, at the instance of British Foreign Office, the Ministry of French Foreign Office turned down his application for permission to visit India. At London, Phelps was thrown out of the Waldorf Hotel for being a political agitator.[22] Probably, it was the publication of his 'last will' that earned him permission to visit India.[23] On way to India, he visited Egypt, may be to reacquaint himself with the faith of the Behai's.

Phelps arrived in India in March 1910. Here he travelled widely throughout India. He concerned himself with the philanthropic activities connected to education, and lectured on various topics. He met many reformers and political leaders like Dr. R. G.Bhandarkar, Dhondo Keshav Karve, N.C.Kelkar, G.S. Khaparde, Kaulgikar, Veer Vamanrao Joshi, and others.[24] Through out, the Police followed his movements. On September 8, 1911, he complained to the Police Commissioner of Central Provinces that people had been warned not to attend his lectures on the ground that he was 'connected with anarchy'. He denied having any connection with the revolutionary parties in America, England or India, and informed that the purpose of his visit to India was to "investigate for himself the conditions of the British rule... and wished to get the views of all classes, official and non-official, about Indian problems of administration". The information he tried to seek concerned the issues like the 'excessive expenditure on the army, cotton and excise duties, the liquor traffic, and want of intercourse between Indians and Europeans.[25] At Allahabad, he called on the Commissioner of Police who found him 'mild mannered, quite, unassuming and unassertive old man". The Commissioner then reported to the Director of Criminal Intelligence, Simla, that Phelps was aware of being tailed by the police, and that, "the present system of espionage in his case has only been to throw him into the arms of extremists, who are the only people not afraid to have him, even the moderates won't see him or have anything to do with him as a rule". He felt, Phelps was 'harmless'.[26] Finally, the DM, Simla, instructed that "his (Phelps') extreme opinions have gone a considerable change and the cm officers need hot give any special attention.[27] In April 1912, Phelps went to Calcutta. He visited Ratindranath Tagore's (Ravindranath Tagore's son) farm and complimented him for using advance technology in agriculture?[28] He also seems to have met many nationalists leaders of Bengal including Bipin Chandra Pal.

Phelps was an admiter of Indian culture and philosophy. He made an unsuccessful attempt to translate *Bhagwat Gita?*[29] He took to Indian dress and visited many pilgrimage centres. He also acquainted himself with the Ramkrishna Mission, the Arya Samaj and was deeply influenced by the Radhaswami Cult.[30] Phelps died on 30th December 1916, at Dr. Y.N. Bhajekar's Hospital in Girgoan, Bombay. Interestingly, it is not a coincidence that Phelps went to Dr. Bhajekar's hospital and not to the hospital meant for Europeans, for Dr. Bhajekar himself was an ardent nationalist and used to treat nationalist agitators free of cost.[31]

Myron H. Phelps, was thus one of the early Americans[32] to zealously espouse the cause of India. Through the Indo-American National Association and Society for the Advancement of India, he made pioneering efforts to promote the cause of India in America. He was aware of the inadequacies of his endeavours but he sincerely tried to create a favourable opinion for India in America and to help the Indian students. If he differed from other Indian revolutionaries in America, it was a difference only in degree and not in kind. He firmly believed in the Extremist method of political agitation and fully supported Swadeshi movement. He deserves a place in the ranks of non-Indians who espoused the cause of India's freedom.

References

1. Aroon Coomar Bose, *Indian Revolutionaries Abroad* 1905-1922, Bharati Bhavan, Patna, 1971. Bose makes a passing reference to Myron Phelps, p.41; A large portion of the "Open Letter to the President Roosevelt" has been published in *Source Material For A History of the Freedom Movement In India*, Vol. II, Government Central Press, Bombay, 1958, pp.547-51.

2. *South Indian Mail* of Madura, 28th March 1910, Quoted in History-sheet of Myron Phelps, *Bombay Presidency Police Abstracts of Intelligence* (hereinafter *BPPAI* /1910 /No. XXIII/No. 24/ Para 1820; A letter of Swami Vivekanand bears the address of Phelps : 42, Greenacre, Maine, *Letters of Swami Vivekanand*, Adwait Ashram, Almora, 3m edition, 1944, p. 108.

3. The book was published by G.P Putnam's Sons, N.Y., VII + XXX + 243 pps. 1903; The second edition came out in 1912 when Phelps was at Calcutta. An introduction to this book is written by Edward Granwille Browne, Fellow of Pembroke College, Sir Adanls Professor of Arabic, and sometime Lecturer in the Persian in Cambridge University.

4. *BPPAI*/ No.24 of 1910, *op.cit.*

5. It was incorporated under the state law. Its Directors were - Myron Phelps, Mary A. Phillips, Eugene Kremer, Joseph C. Pumpelly and John Milton Scott. Phelps was its Corresponding Secretary and Acting Treasurer. The yearly subscription was one dollar. The official monthly meetings of the Society were normally held in the New York Bar Association Club and subsequently at India House. *Ibid.*

6. Of the Detroit Branch, Mrs Charles Funke was the President, Miss Alma Knapp, Elizabeth and John Street were Secretaries. Charles H. Aldrich, former Solicitor General was the President of the Chicago branch and Mrs Lucy Adams was the Secretary.

7. *Clan-na-Gael* was a Society established by a group of Irish Americans called Fenians in the latter half of the 19th Century. They fought for Irish independence, adopted revolutionary method" and evinced keen interest in India's fight against British colonialism.

8. *Minto Papers*, Correspondence - England and Abroad, L & T, VoUl, No.7, Dunlop Smith to Lord Minto, Dated 12th July 1907, Quoted by M.N.Das *in India Under Morley and Minto*, George Allen and Unwin Ltd., London, 1963, pp.115-116.

9. The *Gaelic American* under the editorship of George Fitzrald "Freeman" had been openly espousing the cause of Indian independence and attempted to incite Indians, especially soldiers to revolt. 'Freeman' was an Irish American and his paper was a mouth piece of Irish revolutionaries. Note by B. Duff

(Army Department) on 5th June 1907, H.P., 1907, Aug. 234-250-A, as quoted by Aroon Coomar Bose in *Indian Revolutionaries Abroad, op.cit,* p.39.

10. *Concise Dictionary of American Biography,* Charles Scribner's Sons, N.Y., 1964, p.1271.

11. The Indian government prosecuted Lokmanya Tilak, Bhupendranath Dutt of *Yugantar*, Aurobindo Ghosh of *Bande Matram*, a paper started by Bipin Chandra Pal, L.B.Bhopatkar of *Bhala*, R.N.Mandlik of *Vihari*, and S.M. Parañjape of *Kal* to name a few.

12. *Bande Matram*, 11 April 1908, Quoted in No.240fl91O, *BPPAI, op.cit.*

13. For details see, Aravind Ganachari, "Two Indian Revolutionary Associations-Abroad: Some New Light on the Pan-Aryan Association and Indo-Japanese Association", *Proceedings of the Indian History Congress.* 57th Session. Chennai, 1996, pp.789-798. Samuel Lucas Joshi, son of Rev. Lucas Maloba Joshi of Church Mission Society of Nasik, was the Secretary of the Pan-Aryan Association. He was working at that time as the Lecturer in Oriental Languages. Maulvi Barkatulla was originally an inhabitant of Bhopal, went to U.S.A. towards the end of the century and gradually became involved with the incipient revolutionary movement there. Later, he was responsible for establishment of India House at Tokyo.

14. *BPPAI*/ 1910/ Vol. XXIII! No 46/ para 2170.

15. *BPPAI*/ 191O/Vol. XXIII/No.47/para 3197, 3rd Oct. 1910.

16. The Report of Society for 1908 gave a few examples of employment arranged by him, including that of Prabhakar Sadashiv Shilotri, father of famed Hindi film actress of the yesteryears - Shobhna Samarth. Shilotri got a doctorate from the Cornell University, one who wrote a book on bank nationalisation in 1919 and founded the Shilotri Bank. After his return to India in 1916, he financially supported the revolutionaries. He was an ardent nationalist.

17. *India* of London, 20lh November 1908, Quoted in *BPPAI*, No. 24 of 1910.

18. A pamphlet published in December 1908, announcing the forthcoming issue of the *Swarajya* magazine, there is a printed letter from B.C.Pal to Phelps, in which *the former* thanks the latter 'for the trouble you are taking to secure some engagements for me in the cause of my countrymen before the enlightened public of America and indirectly through them before the civilized world at large". *Ibid.*

19. The Criminal Intelligence Department quote without giving the exact reference. He wrote – "I find myself under the necessity of making an announcement particularly painful to me to some extent, I fear, disappointing to Indian students who intend coming to America. The financial support for India

House from the American public has not been forthcoming and the Society for the Advancement of India has decided it wise not to endeavour to continue it." *Ibid.*

20. The speech was delivered at the Metropolitan Memorial Methodist Episcopal Church, Washington on 18th January 1908. He said, "The mass of the people have been and are far better off than ever before, and far better than they would be now if English control were withdrawn from India, or overthrown. .. If English control were withdrawn from India, the peninsula would become a chaos of bloodshed and violence; all weaker peoples, the most industrious and law-abiding, would be plundered and forced to submit to indescribable wrong and oppression, the only beneficiaries among the natives would be the lawless, violent, and bloodthirsty." *Ibid.*

21. Lord Morley stated in the House of Commons: "If it could be said that this chapter of reforms led directly and necessarily up to a parliamentary system for India. .. a parliamentary system in India is not the goal to which I for one moment, would aspire." Morley talked of self-rule as the ultimate goal for India. *BPPAI*/ Vol. XXIII/ Appendix / p.728.

22. The Manager of the Hotel gave the following explanation to the press on 21st June 1909: "We have nothing against Phelps personally, but do not wish to create a clientele of that kind; nor do we wish Waldorf to become a resort for political agitators". *BPPAI*/No.24 of 1910, *op.cit.*

23. When he was refused the permission to visit India, he publicly reiterated his wish and published a "Last Will". In that "Will" he stated that should something untoward happen to his life while attempting to visit India despite official refusal, $ 10,000 has been kept to investigate the true cause of his death.

24. At Poona, he visited Fergusson, Deccan and Agricultural Colleges, D.K.Karve's Widow Home, called on Dr. R.G. Bhandarkar, and stayed with the then *Kesari editor N.C. Kelkar, BPPAI*/ 1910/ Vol.XXIV/ No 33/ 19 August 1910/ para 1705; In the Police records, there is a photograph of Phelps with N.C.Kelkar, taken at the *Kesari* Office. *BPPAI*/Vol.XXIV, p.891; At Vadnera, he stayed with G.S. Khaparde, a close associate of Tilak and Bipin Chandra Pal, and met many others. *BPPAI/Vol.XXIVI* No.381 23 Sept.1911. Kaulgikar of Sholapur was an ardent follower of Tilak, so was Veer Vamanrao Joshi of Amraoti.

25. Note by the Commissioner of Police, Central Provinces, *BPPAI*/1911/ Vol. XXIV/ No 38/ 23 Sept.1911.

26. *BPPAI*/ 1911/ Vol.XXIV/ No.39/ 30th Sept/para 2037.

27. *BPPAI*/1911/ Vol. XXIV/ No.49/ 9th December / para 2613.

28. M.V. Kamat, *The United States and India 1776-1976.* The Embassy of India, Washington D.C., 1976, p.162.

29. His change of dress to Indian style is mentioned in the *BPPAI*/ No.33 of 1911/ Vol.XXIV/ 19 August /para 1704; No.37 of 1911/16th Sept/ para 1923; His attempt to translate *Bhagwat Gita* is mentioned in No.30 of 1910/Vol. XXIII/ 30th July / para2288.

30. "While in Calcutta, he had acquired a partiality for the Radhaswami doctrines, as he has since given himself out to be a convert to the Radhaswami faith". Phelps hired a house at Allahabad and employed a person to teach him Hindi. *BPPAI* / Vol. XXVI No. 21/25th May / para 867.; His interest in Radhaswami faith can be judged from the fact that a book called - *Notes of Discourse on Radhasoami Faith Delivered by Babuji Maharai in 1913-14 As Taken By A Satsangi Mr. Myron H. Phelps,* Agra, 1947, has beep published.

31. *BPPAI* /1917/ Vol. XXXI No.21 13th January / para 52.

32. Among the early advocates of India's freedom were: Rev. J.T. Sutherland (1842-1936), a Canadian Unitarian Minister, who became naturalized American. He wrote - *The Causes of Famine in India* (1900) and *India in Bondage* (1924). He was among Lala Lajpatrai's chief workers; William Jenning Bryan; John Haynes Holmes, an American evangel of Mahatma Gandhi since 1920; B.W. Huebsch, publisher of Lala Lajpatrai's books in America; Roger N.Baldwin, Director of American Civil Liberties Union; Professor Robert Morse Lovette, one of the editors of *The New Republic* and Professor of English at the University of Chicago. See Haridas T.Majumdar, *America's Contribution to India's Freedom*, Central Book Depot, Allahabad, 1962, pp.6-8.

8

"Surveying Repressed Sex : The Infanticide of Illegitimate Children : The Vijiya Lakshmi Case (1881)

The Age of Consent Controversy (1884-1891) began with the publication of "Notes" on "Infant Marriage in India" and "Enforced Widowhood" by Beheramji Merwanji Malabari on 15th August 1884. This controversy virtually divided the Indian opinion on the question of social reform concerning women's emancipation.

This article, which is mainly based on the archival source material (Maharashtra State Archives) and the contemporary writings, seeks to argue that the "Considerations On the Crime of Infanticide and Punishment in India" published in May 1876 by Sir T. Madhav Rao, the Diwan of Baroda, in the *Journal of National Indian Association*, in which he argued that child marriage and caste-rules prohibiting widow marriages as the main reasons for infanticide, both of the illegitimate children and also of females[1], and demanded an amendment to the Indian Penal Code (IPC), was a perfect prelude to the "Notes" published by B.M. Malabari which paved way for a major social legislation of historical importance.[2] The Government of India (GOI) thought fit to enquire into the issues raised by Sir Madhav Rao. It is in this context, the article attempts to discuss the social significance of the Vijia Lakhsmi Case (1881). The social discourse that this case brought forth was heavily loaded against women, as the widow alone was held responsible for maintaining individual morality and social ethics, not her male counter-part. The popular verdict undoubtedly was that murder being committed during a paroxysm of pain and shame, merited less than the death penalty, and also less than transportation for life. The judgment delivered in this case received wide press coverage and provoked strong public reaction mostly favourable to Vijia Lakshmi, the accused. The Sarvajanik Sabha of Pune also sent a memorial to the Bombay Government (BG) to mitigate her sufferings. Importantly, judgment seriously raised the question of validity of the theory and practice of the British legal system in India. The notion of repressed sex is not, therefore, a theoretical matter. Indeed, the cases which involved the infanticide of the illegitimate children reveal how women were rigorously subjugated.

The facts of the Vijia Lakshmi Case (1881) may be briefly stated. Vijia was twenty-four years old brahmin widow of late Kashibhai Pranlal, from Olpad village near Surat. Perhaps, unable to control biological urge in the prime of her life, she gave in to passion at a critical moment. In order to save herself from shame of delivering an illegitimate child in widowhood allegedly murdered it at its birth. She confessed the crime to the Chief Constable of the place who kept a strict watch on her, and also repeated it before the second-class magistrate. However, before the Session Judge Mr. S. Hammick, though she admitted having given birth to a child, pleaded that it was still-born. She retracted her earlier statement confessing the crime and stated that she was induced into making a false confession by the importunity of the Chief Constable. Not accepting her subsequent statement, the Session Judge Mr. Hammick held that the alleged confession formed the most important part of the evidence for the prosecution, and therefore, found Vijia Lakshmi guilty of murder. He sentenced her to death on 3rd May 1881.[3]

The case came up in appeal in the High Court of Bombay before Mr. Justice Raymond West and Justice J. Pinhey. Mr. Shantaram Narayan,[4] a noted social reformer, appeared for the accused and Vishwanth Narayan Mandlik,[5] a social conservative, represented the Crown. The learned Judges in their carefully elaborated judgment, confirmed the conviction, but thought it proper to commute the capital sentence to transportation for life. Significantly, the Judges did not think that Vijia Lakshmi deserves any special consideration and declined to refer the matter to the Government for and mitigation as was done earlier in similar cases.[6]

The capital punishment given by the Session Court came in for severe criticism in the press. *The Times of India* was in the forefront demanding leniency, and published a number of letters in support of

Vijia Lakshmi in particular and widow remarriage movement in general.[7] The *Indu Prakash* demanded abolition of capital punishment in the case of such hapless widows as Vijia Lakshmi and wrote,

> "A less severe punishment will effect all that the legislature requires and this course has been long ago recommended by no less an authority than Sir T. Madhav Rao, the present Diwan of Baroda..."[8]

Similarly, the *Mahratta* too urged for a favourable review of the suggestions made by Sir Madhav Rao.[9]

It was in May 1876, that Sir T. Madhav Rao, who was the Diwan of Baroda seems to have come across many cases of infanticide of new-born illegitimate children in Gujarat, published a note entitled – "Considerations on the Crime of Infanticide and Its Punishment In India", in the *Journal of National Indian Association,* and also submitted a Memorandum to the Government of India on this subject on 24th July 1876,[10] in which he advocated abolition of capital punishment for widows committing infanticide, since he believed that the punishment was excessive and cruel. He felt that the milder punishment in the cases of infanticide would not increase its number, and that the circumstances in which the infanticide occurs needs to be seriously looked into. He attributed the causes of infanticide to infant marriages and enforced widowhood while yet in the vigour of health, compounded by caste-rules prohibiting widow re-marriages. In some cases overpowered by passions in weak moments, the widow commits the offence of infanticide. Out of shame and the fear of social opinion, the widow commits the offence of infanticide. The motive is not pleasure or profit in this crime but only the dread of public exposure of her frailty. Sir Madhav Rao held that the Indian Penal Code which provides punishment of transportation for life as an alternative to that of death, was equally excessive and cruel, and hence needed an urgent amendment to IPC. Such an amendment, he thought, would leave as little a scope as possible for frequent exercise of prerogative of mercy by the Government to mitigate the sentence and thus interfere in the judicial process. In sum, Sir Madhav Rao's suggestion was that the punishment for the offence of infanticide be reduced from murder to **"culpable homicide not amounting to murder"**.[11]

Acting upon these suggestions, the GOI solicited information on the cases of infanticide from all Session Judges, the High Court Judges, and concerned police officers, of all presidencies.[12] The statistical information so collected was : "out of 381 cases of women charged with having killed their illegitimate children, sentence of death was passed in 18 cases and carried out in only 3 cases; sentence of transportation for life was finally passed in 152 cases and regarding the remainder, the accused were either acquitted for want of evidence or sentenced to imprisonment for varying terms from 3 years to 10 years."[13] The GOI thus surmised that : 1. almost all authorities consulted were of the opinion that the working of the law of infanticide is not attended with the evils referred to by Sir Madhav Rao. 2. The 'minor' punishment of transportation for life, is normally, mitigated by Government. From imprisonment, the convicted widow returned to society as tainted outcast; but "by transportation she would be placed in a new sphere, where, if she again gives away to her instincts, there will be no inducement to kill her child", for she can settle down in the community of prisoners with the convict spouse. 3. As the sense of shame constitutes a strong temptation to infanticide, it should, in accordance with the principles of Jeremy Bentham which permeate IPC, be met by the counteracting dread of a severe and certain punishment. Hence, any modifications in Indian Penal Code concerning law of infanticide, as suggested by Sir Madhav Rao, was ruled out.[14]

It should be noted that while the Government boasted of modern principles of justice based on the principles of 'reformative law', their own statistics vindicated Sir Madhav Rao's arguments. The judicial authorities, almost totally European, generally held sharp bias against Hindu widows and were oblivious to the Indian social situation in which the widows were placed. These issues prominently resurfaced again in the Vijia Lakshmi Case in 1881.

In response to Sir Madhav Rao's Notes and Memorandum, the "Minutes" recorded by the High Court Judges of Bombay, namely, Justice Maxwell Melvill, Justice Kemball, and Justice Raymond West in 1877, make an interesting study. Justice Melvill, who was known for being liberal and considerate to the plight of widows, concurred with Sir Madhav Rao, but did not think that the legislature could do anything further. His comment shows only lip sympathy but refuses to take any positive steps towards mitigating widow's plight. He wrote :

> "...It is impossible not to feel with Sir Madhav Rao that in the generality of such cases as he describes, a term of imprisonment would be adequate sentence... I should be very glad if any section could be

drafted which, without indicating disregard of the sacredness of human life, would yet permit a mitigated sentence in the cases contemplated by Sir Madhav Rao and exclude it in all others. But I do not think that any change in the law could be made which would not be open to more objections than it removed...."[15]

Justice Kemball felt that the question of punishment was difficult, however felt that "reducing the punishment imposed by law would not diminish the crime". Justice Raymond West's line of argument was the one which was finally accepted by the GOI. Although he posed to be an upholder of high principles of justice and promoter of high human values, his comments apparently logical though, were indeed harsh in tone and devoid of any sympathy for young widows, who were consigned to a life of unending misery due to hostile social environment in which she was placed :

"...Conceding so much in pity to human frailty as not to put them to death, the Government should, in all ordinary cases, rid society of their baneful presence as promptly and completely as possible. A claim of indulgence to these infanticidal women which goes beyond what is now allowed, however agreeable to mere sentiment, is opposed to all sound principles of penal law. ***The sense of shame, the dread of popular censure which impels a woman to murder her offspring while it is impotent to restrain the indulgence of her lust, rests on a perverse and distorted sensibility which the legislature ought not to encourage. In so far as this feeling constitutes a strong temptation to infanticide, it should be met by the counter-acting dread of a severe and certain punishment...*** The punishment of infanticide forms part of a general system designated for the protection of human life by throwing round it, in every stage and condition, associations of sacredness which may form the central core of the popular consciousness on that subject. No deviation from the system should be allowed except for reasons of extreme necessity or public expediency. No such reasons appear to exist in this case...."[16] (Emphasis is mine)

The judgment given by Messers Justice West and Pinhey, later in 1881 in the case of Vijia Lakshmi, was fundamentally an affirmation of the above quoted 'Minute' Justice West had submitted to the GOI. The judgment was widely regarded by the press as unduly harsh and inequitable.

Interestingly, Justice West did not accept the defence counsel's argument that the confession was extorted from Vijia Lakshmi under severe police pressure and that the child was still-born. Any rationalization of the act of infanticide in the name of guarding her own honour and protecting from shame, Justice West thought, was to lend justification to the killing of 'unwanted' humans, and that the courts established to guard against such danger must endeavour to instill a wholesome fear under such circumstances; or else the crime would increase in number. The fact that four cases of similar type came up before the Court that week, might have led Justice West to infer that "the leniency that had been exercised was bearing fruit in an increased number of crimes of this kind, and it was time that the mercy should be stopped..." Justice West and his colleagues declined to take an enlightened view of this matter, repudiated State responsibility in protecting widows from social repression by the orthodox Hindu society. Not only they disowned State responsibility, on the contrary held that it was the responsibility of the society, in its own interest, to look into the question of remarriages of widows and caste rules dispassionately and judiciously. He, in contravention of earlier practice, even declined to refer this case to the Government for mercy and mitigation.[17] Such an argument was a classic example of hypocrisy of the so-called liberal Englishmen with their halting and fractured logic.

The judgment given by Justice West and Pinhey provoked strong reaction in the press, both Anglo-Indian and vernacular. *The Times of India* urged that the Governor should reconsider the sentence of the High Court with a view to mitigation, notwithstanding that the court itself refused to recommend it, and offered a lengthy rebuttal to Justice West's arguments. On Justice West's comment that the remedy ought to be found by society itself, the *Times of India* pointed out that "That is just what the community is trying to do; it recognizes the evils of prohibiting widows from marrying again, and it has found in the Lakshmi Case a current instance to point the moral. The Brahmin widow, it is true, is very far from being blameless, but it is her very guilt which gives point to the agitation in her favour. Prevented by the laws of caste from remarrying, neither natural propensities permitted her, nor such religious culture as Brahmins think it worth while to impart to women sufficed to preserve her chastity. For this Mr. Justice West holds her to be wholly inexcusable, on the ground that, having been married, her cravings for maternity ought to have been satisfied, overlooking the fact that her brief married experience left her more than ever a woman, while her widowhood, without any of those moral safeguards which surrounds a European woman in a similar case, doomed her to a life of degradation, drudgery and temptation...Under the tyranny of caste laws and customs, the Hindu widow is now as much dead to the world as if she had cremated herself on her husband's funeral pyre. It must not be supposed that in saying that we have said we in the least justify the murder of her offspring by the woman Lakshmi... Surely Mr. Justice West is indiscreet in going so far as to suggest that the murder was premeditated and the time of its execution was pre-arranged...."[18] The *Bombay Gazette* also expressed similar sentiment.[19] Suggestions were made in the Anglo-Indian press for seeking State intervention in the matter of Hindu widow's remarriage.

A letter entitled – "The Curse of Vijia Lakshmi" in the *Gujrati*, criticised the Hindu society for its heinous customs and called Justice West's judgment as a reproach and disgrace of British justice and their respect for fair sex.[20] The *Rast Goftar* lauded the assistance given earlier by the Government, especially by Sir Frank Souter in Cutch, to Dahibai, the first Bhatia widow who ventured to remarry, and in the present case demanded an enactment of law "for the protection, support and relief of suffering widows".[21] Others who shared similar opinion were *Yazdan Parast*, *Jame Jamshed*, *Bombay Samachar*, *Shamsher Bahaddur*, and *Hitechhu* of Ahmedabad.[22] However, a few newspapers such as *Bombay Chronicle* of the Christian missionaries, *Native Opinion* of V.N. Mandlik, who was the State counsel, and diehard orthodox paper *Pune Vaibhav* hailed the judgment and supported the orthodox view. The *Indian Spectator* made a significant observation :

> "Time has come when Government may be expected to look closely into the vagaries of caste. A mere protest against the marriage of a widow may be passed over. But the ex-communication of the parties and their supporters is simply intolerable... When the British Government put a stop to Sutee, it ought to have taken thought of the future of those unhappy creatures, weak and unprotected, whom they snatched from the unholy flames... Are not the heads of the caste so many conspirators when they punish a second marriage with ex-communication? Why should Government hesitate to resist the aggressiveness of Caste. If Sutee was a heinous crime, enforced widowhood is four times more heinous... It is certainly not dignified

of a mighty Government to be debarred in remedying this huge national evil by the obstinacy of a handful of bigots."[23]

B.M. Malabari reiterated his stand in his famous "*Notes on Infant Marriage and Enforced Widowhood*" published on 15th August 1884, which virtually divided the entire public opinion in India.

The Sarvajanik Sabha of Pune, which did not approve of the High Court decision, submitted to the BG, a memorial[24] pointing out that the Vijia Lakshmi Case is representative of a large number of similar cases, in which the present state of the law for infanticide too often conflicts with the national sense of justice which is opposed to widow marriage and inflicts harsh and unbearable social disabilities upon widows. It urged that a difference be made between the crimes committed in wantonness and deliberation, and those committed from a sense of shame and under a temporary insanity, and demanded that immediately an amendment to the existing law be effected to bring the desired change. It expressed that "**banishing the unfortunate woman to a penal settlement without any hope of amendment will be one continuous torture to the victim far more horrible to be borne than the sudden pang of death.**" (emphasis is mine) What the Anglo-Indian and indigenous press pointed out to the government was that the initiative for change has come from the enlightened section of the natives. However, judiciary worked more as a disguised hand of the government which was most reluctant to enact social legislation since the time of Revolt of 1857, so as not to jeopardize their political interests.

Eventually, the BG did take note of this Memorial and press reaction. The Government examined the entire correspondence that had taken place earlier in response to Sir Madhav Rao's 'Note'. It was also noted that the High Court almost as a matter of course, referred such cases to the Government for mitigation. Justice West's argument that the leniency exercised in the cases of infanticide was 'bearing fruit' was considered hastily drawn conclusion. Importantly, C.G. Macpherson, Under Secretary, Judicial Department, BG, in his observations quoted what Mr. James Gibbs[25] had recorded in a 'Minute' on a case of infanticide (1874) referred by the Session Judge of Kaladghee, Satyendra Nath Tagore :

"In England even, cases of this kind are leniently dealt with – I have always felt great pity for uneducated Hindu widows whose law is supposed to prevent their remarriage, and whose religion as they understand places a very slight moral restraint on their action."

Before initiating any definite action in this matter the Government thought it advisable to invite the opinions of the judges who tried the Vijia Lakshmi Case.[26]

Justice West strongly reiterated his stand again and felt that mitigating a sentence in such a case "would be virtually to repeal the law and to introduce the uncertainty which is the most effective encouragement of crime". The other judge of the Bench, Justice Pinhey too concurred with Justice West. He blamed the press for blowing this case out of proportion and wrote :

"they had no right to have the case discussed for weeks in the newspapers during the period that elapsed between the trial before the court at Session at Surat and the consideration by the High Court. It is not desirable that trial by newspaper should be substituted for trial by the legally constituted tribunals. Nor is it desirable that the sympathies of the public should be excited and attempts be made prejudice the minds of the judges (for judges read newspapers like the other members of the public)..."[27]

The Chief Secretary, BG, finally noted : "the separate opinion of Mr. Justice West appears to me to deal with the case without an appreciation of the circumstances of a Hindu widow and rather from an abstract point of view. Moreover, the learned Judge appears to hold views on the subject which differs from the other Judges who have of late tried similar cases. I do not see how Mr. Justice Pinhey's complaints of the public discussion of this case affects it. [sic] on what grounds he charges the friends of the prisoner with carrying it on. It appears to have been done by theoretical partisans and are consecrated by Sir Madhav Rao and M. G. Ranade..." Finally, the Governor in Council was pleased to reduce the prison sentence to five years.[28] It must be noted that the Government did not wish to effect any long term changes by amending the Indian Penal Code as desired by Sir T. Madhav Rao in 1876, and thereby tended to the likes of the orthodox section of Hindu society, instead it chose the short route to mitigate the sufferings of the widows by commuting the sentence.

Ever since, the BG regularly invited six monthly reports on such kind of infanticide.[29] Even the High Court Judges decided as a rule, to send all such cases to Government for mitigation of sentence.[30] It was statistically shown that leniency had not increased frequency of the crime.[31] Eventually this issue got submerged in the Age of Consent Controversy (1884-1891).

Curiously, through out the deliberation of this case and the reaction that followed, as in other cases of infanticide, no body ever bothered to inquire about the responsibility of the person who fathered the child. This is also reflected in the official records of similar cases which were reported in the six monthly reports. In other words, conventionally the male was free from social responsibility or stigma in all such cases and responsibility of maintaining social morality was thus thrust only upon womenfolk.

The social significance of this case may be gauged from the reference made by an earliest feminist contemporary writer Tarabai Shinde in her ***StreePurush- Tulana*** (1882) to Sir Madhav Rao's suggestions, the Vijia Lakshmi Case and the vituperation of *Pune Vaibhav* against State interference in matters of social legislation.[32] By citing this case she not only pointed out the gender discrimination prevalent in the then contemporary Hindu society but also indifferent attitude of British Indian administration towards repressed sex by disclaiming their responsibility. The Case also shows how the British Indian legal system, which was regarded, in terms of its underlying principles, as the harbinger of modernity, but in actual practice was compromised by the colonial judicial authorities. The colonial administrators, by and large, could hardly understand the intricacies and complexities of the conventions and customs governing Hindu family, and indeed their entire social life. It is baffling that officials such as Justice Raymond West, who were known for being considerate to natives' aspirations, and Justice Pinhey, who is so much lauded for his judgment in favour of Rakhmabai in the Dadaji-Rakhmabai Case regarding restitution of conjugal rights, should have based their judgment in Vijia Lakshmi Case on theoretical assumption in total disregard to the existing Indian social reality.

What this Case reflects is not altogether lack of understanding of Indian social reality on the part of colonial rulers but their deliberate reluctance to support a just cause for fear of jeopardizing their economic and political interests. No wonder the British Indian government waited for seven years to pass legislation regarding the Age of Consent since the publication of the "Notes" by Malabari in August 1884. In this context it may be pertinent to quote what M.G.

Ranade wrote to *The Times of India*, on 22 August 1884, in reply to B.M.Malabari's 'Notes' :

> "... A small community like yours does not present to you much difficulties; but even with you the reformers are working without the renovated heart which alone furnishes the necessary impulse. The European nations are not aware of this difficulty; they have passed through the metaphysical stage, and the considerations of positive good and evil here below have with them a force which suffices to them through, when a majority is secured on the side of change. It is this conviction of the hard conditions of the problem which retards our progress. People find fault with us, even abuse us for half-heartedness, for our apparent want of fire or enthusiasm. God only knows that in our households we are perpetually at war with our dearest and nearest, we struggle and strive to do our best and have perforce to stop at many points when we fear the strain will cause a rupture. This is our present situation.... I have had something to do with the guidance of the remarriage movement in this Presidency, and I feel confident that we have made good progress during the last fifteen years and more. It is a very delicate subject. When the victim of cruelty welcomes the disgrace and effacement, it is not to be expected that startling results will be achieved soon. We are slowly touching the consciousness of the people, disarming the opposition of the terror of ex-communication and teaching the female sex to rebel and protest...."[33]

Malabari could seek backing of the Government because of comparatively liberal character of the administration under Lord Ripon, and his officials such as Mr. James Gibbs, Mr. Courtney Ilbert, and Sir Stuart Bayley. Malabari's fervour to take up the issue of Vijia Lakshmi in his columns of *Indian Spectator*, is certainly reflected again in the second 'Note' on "Enforced Widowhood" (1884).[34]

References

1. The infanticide which Sir T. Madhav Rao referred to was regarding killing of new-born illegitimate children by the widows and not female infanticide which was so very prevalent in Gujarat, in particular in Kathiawar. For female infanticide see John Wilson, *Suppression of Infanticide in Western India*, American Mission Press, Bombay, 1855; Also Dr. Bhau Daji Lad, "Essay on Infanticide", in *Writings and Speeches*

of Bhau Daji , T.G. Mainkar (ed.), Bombay University Press, Bombay, 1974, pp.257-277. Both the works refer to the practice of female infanticide among the Jadejas and in Kathiawar and other places of Gujarat.

2. For more details on the Age of Consent Controversy, see Charles H. Heimsath, "The Origin and Enactment of the Indian Age of Consent Bill, 1891", *The Journal of Asian Studies*, Vol. XXI, No. 4, August 1962, pp.491-504; Also Richard P. Tucker, *Ranade and the Roots of Indian Nationalism*, Popular Prakashan, Bombay, First Indian Edition, 1977, pp. 207-238. The Age of Consent raised the marriage age of girls from 10 to 12.

3. *Maharashtra State Archives* (*MSA*), *Judicial Department (JD)*, Volume 46, Compilation No. 1036. Full report of the Surat Infanticide Case is reported in *The Times of India*, 27th May 1881, and also Petition from Vijia Lakshmi, May 1881, No.726 of 1881, pp. 259-270. She became a widow at the age of 18 and the crime was committed at the age of 24

4. Shantaram Narayan was son of Narayan Vasudev Dhabholkar. Both father and son were renowned persons among the Indian circle in Bombay. See Anant Kakba Priyolkar, *Dr. Bhau Daji –Vyakti, Kal Ani Kartutwa* (Marathi), Mumbai Marathi Sahitya Sangh, Mumbai, 1971, p.430.

5. There is no mention of this Case in, Ganesh Ramkrishna Havaldar, *Raosaheb Vishwanath Narayan Mandlik Yanche Charitra* (Marathi), Part 1 & 2, Mumbai Vaibhav Press, 1927, First edition. Mandlik (1833-1889) was a "Conservative" social reformer in the mould of Edmond Burke. In matters of social reform, 'Conservatism' advocates a gradual change and places a strong belief in religion and ancient institutions since they are the very foundation of culture. Mandlik shunned any kind of state interference in social matters including any social legislation. He was a Member of the Bombay Legislative Council during 1874-1884, and was Member of the Viceroy's Legislative Council during 1884-1886.

6. *MSA /JD* / 1881/ Vol. 46 / 1036, "Judgment in the Case of Imperatix Vs. Vijia Lakshmi, widow of Kashibhai", 25th May 1881, by Justice Raymond West and Justice J. Pinhey, pp. 315-341.

7. *The Times of India* (*TOI*) , Editorial Note, 16th May 1881; Letters : "Infanticide and Hindu Widowhood" by K.M. Shroff, 17th May 1881; "The Case of Vijia Lakshmi" by 'X' & 'Y', 20th May 1881; A letter dated 19th May 1881, written under pseudonym ***PRO BONO PUBLICO*** from Surat wrote that he was present at the time of the Case, and that, "the confession was an apparent desperate expedient 'in a paroxysm of

agony and shame' to put an end to her 'absolutely unbearable life". It was owing to this that the assessor unanimously found her not guilty.

8. *MSA/JD/* Vol.100/ *Report on Native Papers*, for the week ending 28th May 1881.

9. *Mahratta*, 22nd May 1881.

10. *MSA/JD/* Vol. 65/ 1002, pp. 119-154 & *MSA/JD/* 1879/ Vol. 87/ 1002, pp. 293-96. This note – "*CONSIDERATION ON THE CRIME OF INFANTICIDE AND ITS PUNISHMENT IN INDIA*" is perhaps the earliest native demand presented to the British Indian Government for a social legislation, not only demanding an amendment to the Indian Penal Code but urging them to be very sympathetic to Indian social reality. No reference to this 'Note' is found in any of the historical researches on social history. However it is baffling that Sir T. Madhav Rao, as the Diwan of Baroda State, with his reputation as "Nestor of Indian Statesman" and who was so radical in submitting such a Note (1876) and a Memorandum (1878) demanding state intervention in social matters, became a social "Conservative" and went on to oppose the younger generation politicians whom he regarded as harsh critics of Government. He was accused of being guilty of political opportunism. R. Suntharalingam, *Politics and Nationalist Awakening in South India*, Rawat Publication, Delhi, 1980, pp. 100-103.

11. *Ibid.* He also urged the Legislative Department of the Government to take a review of the cases that have come to the British court in the last ten years. The GOI did act upon, sent his Note to the provincial & district officials and asked for relevant details.

12. *Ibid.*, No. 564, William Stokes, Secretary to the GOI to E.H. Ravenscroft, Acting Chief Secretary to the Government of Bombay, dated 31st August 1876; Also Resolution of the *JD, BG*, NO. 5736 of 1876, dated 29th September 1876.

13. *MSA/JD/* Vol. 87/ 1001, No. 6242 of 1879, dated 15th October 1879, p. 295. Information regarding such cases of infanticide of illegitimate children from all presidencies is separately given; *MSA/JD/* 1877/ Vol.75 /(B)/ 785, Information sent to the GOI by the BG, NO. 4532 of 1877, dated 25th July 1877, along with "*Statement showing Cases of Women Killing Their Illegitimate Children directly after Birth, which have come before the Session Judge's Court in the Last Five Years 1871-1884*,

14. *Ibid.*

15. *MSA/JD/* 1877/Vol. 75 (B)/ 785, pp. 301-307. Sir Maxwell Melvill (1834-1887), ICS, Judicial Commissioner in Sindh, Puisne Judge of the High Court Bombay from 1869-1884, Member of the Bombay Legislative

Council from 1884 till his death at Poona on August 5th, 1887. C.E. Buckland, *Dictionary of Indian Biography*, Indological Book House, Delhi, 1971, Reprint, p. 285.

16 *Ibid.*, pp. 311-319. Justice Raymond West (1832-1912) became Judge of the Bombay High Court in 1873 and remained on that post up to 1886. He was Vice-Chancellor of the Bombay University during the period 1878-1886. In the later life, he came to be known as the supporter of the Indian cause. He died on 8th September 1912.

17. *MSA/JD/* Vol.46/ 1036, pp. 315-342.

18. *The Times of India*, 27th May 1881.

19. *Bombay Gazette*, 27th May 1881.

20. *MSA/JD/* Vol.100/ Report on Native Papers/ for the week ending 11 June. From this date onwards the *Report on the Native Papers* covered this entire controversy under the title – "The Vijia Lakshmi Case and Hindu Widow Remarriage"; *Gujrati*, 5th June 1881. A sentiment was expressed by *Gujrat Mitra* and *Samsher Bahaddur.*

21. *Ibid., RNP/* 25th June 1881, *Rast Goftar* of 12th June. Sir Frank Souter, was later the Commissioner of Police in Bombay and was known for his fair sense of justice.

22. *Ibid., RNP/* 18 & 23rd June. *Yazdan Parasht* of June 12, also pointed out the boldness of the Jamnagar ruler in making a law regarding remarriage of widows of Khawas Caste in his State.

23. *Ibid., RNP/* 18th June 1881.

24. MSA/JD/1881/Vol.46/1036, Memorial of the Sarvajanik Sabha of Poona, No. 31 of 1881, 5th June 1881. Also *Abstracts of Proceedings (AP)/ Government of Bombay(BG) / JD/* 1881/ p. 588, No. 4298/1586; Vijia Lakshmi also sent two petitions demanding mercy on 10th and 21st June 1881.

25. Mr. Justice James Gibbs (1825-1886) ICS, Puisne Judge of the High Court, Bombay (1864-1874), Member of the Bombay Legislative Council (1874-1879), Member of the Viceroy's Legislative Council (1880-1885), Vice Chancellor of the Bombay University 1870-1879. C.E. Buckland, *op.cit.*, p.164. The 'Minute' which he recorded was with the full concurrence of Sir Philip Wodehouse (1811-1887), the then Governor of Bombay from 1872-1877; Macpherson's Note in *MSA/ JD/* 1881/ 46/ 1036. His opinion was concurred by E. H. Ravenscroft, the Secretary, *JD, BG*, and the Governor of Bombay, James Fergusson.

26. *MSA/JD/* 1881/ 46/1036. pp. 271-285; In the said case the convict was sentenced to seven years of imprisonment.

27. *Ibid.*, Minutes recorded by Hon'ble Justice West and Justice Pinhey, pp. 343-349.

28. *Ibid.*, Note by the Governor, pp. 353-355; Sentence commuted to five years, vide No. 4645 of 1881, dated 18th July 1881; Two more Memorials were submitted – one from Kasilal Mithalal and the other from members of the Motala Brahmin Community. They were informed that neither the sentence can be further reduced , nor the BG would forward it to the GOI for commutation. *MSA/ AP/ JD/* August 1881/ No. 5425/ Sr. No. 1996, pp. 739-40; Also, *MSA/ JD/* 1882/ Vol. 52/ 122.

29. *MSA/ JD/* 1882/ Vol. 86/ 499; *JD/* 1884/ Vol. 308; and *JD/* 1885/ Vol. 53/ 305 & 601.

30. *MSA/JD/* 1882/Vol.86/ 977/ pp.196-7. Letter from E.M.H. Fulton, Registrar of High Court to C. Gowne, Chief Secretary to *BG*, *JD*, 12th August 1882.

31. *Ibid.*

32. Tarabai Shinde, *Stree Purush –Tulana* (Marathi), 1882, S.G.Malashe (ed.), Mumbai Marathi Granthsangrahalaya, Mumbai, 1980, pp. 10-11 & 34.

33. *The Times of India*, 22 August 1884.

34. *MSA/ General Department/* 1885/ Vol. 72/ 379, pp. 143-144; Dayaram Gidumal, *Beheramji M. Malabari : A Biographical Sketch*, T. Fisher Unwin, London, 1892.

9

Mary Carpenter and the Reform Movement in Western India

Mary Carpenter (1807 - 1877), celebrated English social reformer and penologist, daughter or Dr. Lant Carpenter with whom Raja Ram Mohan Roy stayed at Bristol, was the one who authored the book - *Last Days of Raja Ram Mohan Roy* - the person whom she both loved and admired. It was he who drew her attention to the socio-religious problems, especially of destitute children, which resulted in her taking keen interest in the regeneration of India.

Because of her social and humanitarian work, and her concern for the people of India, she was respected and admired by the reformers in Western India such as Dr. Bhau Daji Lad, Dr. Atmaram *Pandurang, Lokhitwadi* Gopal Hari Deshmukh, Mahipatram Roopram and even social Conservative, *a la Burke,* like Vishwanath Narayan Mandlik.

This article, which is primarily based on the archival *(Maharashtra State Archives)* source material and the contemporary literature, attempts to examine Mary Carpenter's influence on the social reformers of Western India, during her visits to India between 1867-1876, and discuss the issues she took up, such as the establishment of Female normal school for training female teachers, reformatory and industrial schools for juvenile delinquents and the prison reforms. The paper also seeks to bring out how she exerted to impress her ideas upon the bureaucracy, both in India and England, with a view to bringing about the desired social change. She served, as the catalyst in the establishment of the Prathana Samaj in 1867. She was the progenitor of many reform movements in Western India.

Before we discuss her work in India, it would be useful to recapitulate a few salient features of her illustrious life. Born in Exter,

England, on 3rd April 1807, She was the daughter of - Dr. Lant Carpenter, Unitarian Minister and educationist. Mary was given an unusually liberal education. At the age of ten her family moved to Bristol, which became her home for most of the rest of her life. In August 1829, she began with her mother a girls' school at Bristol. Immediate stimulus for her taking keen interest in socio-religious problems of India, and extending her sympathy for the urchins at home and abroad, was provided by the visit of Raja Ram Mohan Roy and Joseph Tuckerman, the Boston philanthropist, both of whom were friends of her father, to Bristol in 1833. In 1846, she opened the first Ragged School in Lewin's Mead section, one of the nasty localities of Bristol and became increasingly interested in investigating the causes of juvenile crime. She made careful reports to the authorities on all issues she took up for investigation, and saw to it that many of her suggestions were accepted and implemented. The books she wrote reveal her social thought and the kind of social reformer that she was. In the first, which was published in 1851 -*Reformatory Schools for the Children of the Perishing and Dangerous Classes, and for Juvenile Offenders* - she drew the classical Victorian distinction between the deserving and the undeserving poor, but with the warning that if the children of the deserving were not assisted by society, they would be recruited into the ranks of undeserving. She put her theories into practice by devoting her personal fortune to setting up a reformatory school in Bristol in 1852. In the following year, she published the book, *Juvenile Delinquents, Their Condition and Treatment,* in which she insisted that juvenile offenders should be treated differently from adults. Her findings provided the basis for the provisions of the Juvenile Offender's Act (1854). In recognition of her work she was often consulted by the British parliament in matters relating to education and treatment of juvenile offenders.[1]

Her interest in India was further aroused by her association with two young Bengalis - Satyendra Nath Tagore and M. Ghosh- who were then studying for I.C.S examination in England. Perhaps, it was from them that she learned details about the condition of women in India, which convinced her that there was a vast field social work awaiting for anyone who wished to serve the oppressed and depressed without any prejudices or preconceived ideas. Before leaving for India, she wrote to a Hindu gentleman in England, : "I am going only as a token of warm sympathy in your work, your countrywomen, to gain such comprehension of the position as may enable me to be future use, and to do anything I can...."[2] She thus desired to see and judge for herself; her first purpose, therefore, was not to teach but to learn.

Mary Carpenter's first visit to India lasted for about six months from 5th October 1866 to 20th March 1867.[3] Thereafter, she came to India five more times between 1868 to 1876. Being a social reformer of note, she brought with her introductory letters form Lord Cranborne, the then Secretary of State for India, Miss Florence Nightingale and other high dignitaries, but her friends in India had already communicated with Sir Bartle Frere, the then Governor of Bombay Presidency, whose kindness at once secured for her more abundant help then she had ever looked for. During her stay in India, she visited Bombay, Ahmedabad, Surat, Madras, and Calcutta, and met not only important leaders of the Indian community, but also many high officials including the Viceroy, Sir John Lawrence.

Having surveyed educational scene in India, Mary Carpenter soon realised that the movement to promote female education in Bombay, differed from that in the other Presidency capitals; in the sense that it was largely originated by the narrative inhabitants themselves. Despite the monetary crisis Bombay faced after the end of share mania in 1865, she felt that the natives were very generous in supporting Girls' schools. Here, she was much impressed by the work done by the Students' Literary and Scientific Society *(SLSS)*, with regard to the female education.[4] This Society was founded by the students and professors of Elphinstone College in 1848, and soon was joined by almost all the enlightened natives of Bombay. Members of *SSLS*, who discussed many questions of immediate interest and of practical importance, started eight schools for girls and in which initially they voluntarily worked as teachers. When Mary Carpenter met President Dr. Bhau Daji (1824-1874) and Secretary Vishwanath Narayan Mandlik (18331889) and visited these schools in 1867, She was all praise for their gallant effort. Among other manifold reformist activities, Dr. Bhau Daji was a supporter of the cause of female education. He was connected with many political and social institution of his time and Mary Carpenter held him in high esteem. He was the first native President (1863-73) of *SLSS*.[5]

Mary Carpenter was also impressed by the new way Alexandra Girls' School was conducted, in which not only Parsees and a few Hindu girls received liberal English education but even employed lady teachers. This was the first Girls' school, which owed its existence to the philanthropic efforts of Manickjee Cursetji (1808-1887)[6] judge of the Small Causes Court and the first Indian to be enrolled as the member of the Bombay Branch of Royal Asiatic Society.

Mary Carpenter had a special attraction for Ahmedabad. It was here that the lines of her future work were first laid down. S.N. Tagore, the first Indian ICS and the one who held the post of Assistant Judge at Ahmedabad, with whom she was much acquainted since his England days, put her in contact with both prominent local leaders and the sympathetic officials such as Collector J .E. Oliphants. Discussions with natives made her aware of the difficulties which stood in the way of female education in India, such as, the general unwillingness of the masses to take any step which hurt the religious susceptibilities of the people. The universal practice of early marriage placed an almost insuperable bar to further education. She realised that the trained female teachers was the need of the hour. Special effort had to be made to awaken the public opinion in favour of female education and for that the creation of a cadre of trained female teachers was essential. This was to be attained through the establishment of Normal Schools. In *Lokahitadi* Gopal Hari Deshmukh, Judge of the Small Causes Court at Ahmedabad, and more importantly known for his scathing attack, in his celebrated *Shatapatre,* on outdated Hindu customs and social obscurantism, Mary Carpenter found a sympathetic ally in the cause for the establishment of Female Normal Schools. The address presented to her by *Lokahitwadi* and others, speaks volumes of the interest she evoked in the cause of female education:

> "Your visit to India particularly for the furtherance of native female education, your travel to several Presidencies for the purpose of learning the causes which keep it back, and determining some remedies for its advancement, and your free intercourse with us, happily evince an uncommon interest in the welfare of the natives of this country - namely such interest as has scarcely been hitherto taken by any European gentleman or lady... We therefore feel in no small degree obliged for the self-sacrifice which your aims and labour involve, and beg publicity to convey to you this expression of gratitude....[7]

In Female Normal School, how *Lokahitwadi* saw a remedy in mitigating the condition of the suffering widows, can be found from the letter he wrote to Mary Carpenter in 1868[8] :

> The schools in this city (Ahmedabad) have been in existence for the last fifteen years, but they have not produced one girl who is able teach. The girls leave as soon a~ they are of marriageable age (at latest between ten and eleven), and thus forget what they have learnt. If God will bless your endeavour, the fruits of them may soon be perceived. There is a vast material in India. There are thousands of widows under the vow that they shall never remarry. It is only necessary to utilize these unfortunate widows, and what is now felt as a curse will be a blessing... Until there is a Normal School, with the professed object of sending out competent teachers, no plan side of India looking very anxiously for the success of your appeal, and also for your return."

At Ahmedabad, she also visited Normal Training School for male teachers, with its Principal Mahipatram Roopam,[9] a noted social reformer and biographer of Durgaram Mancharam (1809- 1876), one of the founders of the Dharma Sabha (1844). Mahipatram had visited England to study the educational institutions and had returned full of admiration for the method of training teachers used by Mary Carpenter and tried to introduce them here later. She was in full praise for his institution.

The result of all these efforts of Mary Carpenter, at Ahmedabad, was the Memorial sent to the Government demanding Female Normal Schools by Collector J.R. Oliphants and other Europeans, and also Premabhai Hemabhai (1815.-1887), a member of the Legislative Council, and his Nâgar community members. Curiously, the Memorial bears signatures of all lady members of Premabhai's family.[10]

In Bombay, memorials were sent by two groups, one headed by V.N. Mandlik[11], and the other by Mangaldas Nathubhai demanding female Normal Schools.[12] Mary Carpenter too, independently sent a Memorial[13], in which she pointed out that she had the support of the enlightened Hindus, and that "the work will require the greatest wisdom, judgment, and freedom from low and narrow prejudices...." While she admitted that the difficulties encountered in starting Female Normal School were much greater than those in Male Normal Schools, she did not think the impediments were not insurmountable. She observed that the female boarding school in Bombay under the supervision of Mrs. Nesbit, and in Poona under that of Mr. and Mrs. Gardiner, produced remarkable female instructors.[14] However, considering their zeal for conversion, Mary Carpenter clearly emphasized that the instruction in girls' schools must be strictly secular as was in Boys' school, and demanded that, "in these proposed Institutions the Government principles of non-interference in religious matters is to be strictly adhered to. While the personal religious liberty of every inmate of the Institution is to be respected, no one, while in it, is to attempt any religious proselytism." [15] She also felt that such Normal Schools be put under the care of a European lady teacher. She suggested that they must study both English and vernacular languages, which would prepare them to play a constructive role in the society.

Sir Alexander Grant, the Director of Public Instruction, while giving his opinion, which became the basis for government action, paid a rich compliment to Mary Carpenter for her "earnest and authoritative exposition of her views", and for stirring up the question "without any ulterior views" among the influential natives both in Bombay and Ahmedabad. He concurred with her views on most of the matters but pointed out that the principle of non-interference and to place the proposed institution in a Christian family circle were contradictory. He voiced his trepidation : "I do not think it could be carried out, at present, without the risk of drawing upon Government the imputation of attempting an interference with social ideas." But for Mary Carpenter, in normal circumstances such a proposal would not have been entertained. Sir Alexander carried discussions with the local leaders of both Bombay and Ahmedabad, and suggested that besides secular character there should be "an honorary committee of five native gentlemen, interested in Female Education, to be appointed for each School."[16] The Government of India finally sanctioned half the amount of Rs. 1,55,200/- a year for five years on an experimental basis with the condition that an equal amount will be provided by the Native Community. [17]

The movement for Female Normal School made progress, though slowly. A Female Normal School was established at Bombay, where Miss Richmond who was sent from England by the Secretary of State, had been employed. While on her second visit to India, Mary Carpenter set up a Female Normal School at Ahmedabad and worked for some time as the Head mistress till illness made her leave India.

Later, this school made good progress under Miss Chamberlain. In Western India, unlike in Bengal, there was no dearth of public support for this scheme. Many philanthropists like Jagannath Shankerseth, Dr. Bhau Daji, Mangaldas Nathubhai came forward to provide funds for stipend to female scholars. The Bombay Female Normal School, later in November 1870, was shifted to Poona due to economic reason.[18] For Poona, the Government secured the services of Mrs. Mitchell, former Head mistress of the Alexandra Girls' School. The female students of the Bombay School were pained at this government decision and they memorialized to the authorities against such an action. They argued that in the first place they had to encounter serious difficulties in procuring consent of their guardians, and now the said government action only intensified the trouble and virtually sealed their fate. The Ahmedabad School started by Mary Carpenter and Mahipatram Roopram in 1869 came to be known as Mahalakshmi Female Training College after 1874. Particularly in Western India, Mary Carpenter's idea of Female Normal School was certainly a success.

The second issue which Mary Carpenter took up, in India was of the reformatory Schools and Industrial Schools, a project in which she had attained great success, by establishing Ragged School in Bristol. Visits to the jails at Ahmedabad and other places revealed to Miss Carpenter the principle that jails are not adapted to youthful criminals, and therefore, the necessity of establishing Reformatory schools and Industrial Schools, as the best means of reforming juvenile offenders, and of arresting incipient crime. What she advocated was that, the juvenile section be separately delineated from, prisons as it exists in the present, and separate reformatories be established in districts, where the offenders are taught trade with a view to make him respectable member of the society. She thought that the initiative ought to be taken by the Government. Hence Carpenter sent Memorials to the concerned authorities, to that effect.[19]

In this regard, she was pleasantly surprised to find a proto-type of the Ragged School - The David Sassoon Industrial and Reformatory Institution [DSIRI] - already in operation in Bombay, which she visited. Once Mary Carpenter reported about this institution, enquiries were made by the Secretary of State for India regarding its history and working. This institution owed its existence to Dr. George Buist in 1843 and got the name of David Sassoon, noted Jewish merchant and philanthropist, who made the munificent donation on 27 March 1857.[20]

One finds differing perceptions of this issue among the officials of executive arm of the government on this one hand, and the members of Judiciary. The former felt that there were more pressing issues wanting expenditure than this, the latter voiced an express need for establishing separate juvenile reformatories and not as previously attached to the prisons.[21] The Government invited from time to time progress reports of DSIRI and magistrates were instructed that they should send juvenile delinquents to that institution[22] as the Act V of 1876 or The Reformatory School Act of 1876,[23] and establishment of Juvenile reformatories at Bombay, Poona, Dharwar, Ahmedabad and Hyderabad in Sindh were proposed.[24] The credit for this enactment goes to Mary Carpenter for her incessant correspondence on this subject with the concerned officials in India and England.

The third issue which formed the part of the same Memorial sent by Mary Carpenter was prison discipline. She proposed that punishments such as "Iron on their legs" be done away with; that classification of offenders ought to be done as -male and females, convicts and under-trials, adults and juveniles - that under-trials be put in a separate cell; that female convicts be provided a female warder; that moral instruction be provided so as to reform them, and finally, that industrial activity among the prisoners be inculcated.[25] These proposals of Mary Carpenter reflect Benthamite idea of prison reform. The attitude of the officials was one of apathy and any talk of change was turned down on the ground of economic expediency. Though no significant improvement was achieved, yet her proposals formed the agenda of the meetings and conferences of jail officials. Mary Carpenter's observations on jails are similar to those personally experienced by noted reformer of Maharashtra, Gopal Ganesh Agarkar (1856-95) as recorded in his prison memoirs *Dongrichyâ Turungatil Amche 101 Diwas* [1882].

In one respect Mary Carpenter's contribution to socio-religious reform movement in Western India may be considered unique. She, in her own confession, became a catalyst in the establishment of the Prarthana Samaj in 1876.[26] It must be noted that Ramchandra Balkrishna Jayakar, the President of the Paramahansa Sabha, which was a precursor of the Prarthana Samaj, had close interaction with Mary Carpenter while in England during 1863-65.[27] Ramchandra

Balkrishna held high government post of Assistant Commissioner of Customs and was a leading social reformer without any dichotomy in thought and practice. He was also a prominent member of the Student's Literary and Scientific Society in 1851. He had educated his daughters in Alexandra Girls' School. Mary Carpenter was, in fact, to stay with Ramchandra Balkrishna, but for his untimely death. Perhaps, it was through him that Dr. Atmaram Pandurang Tarkhadkar, brother of the celebrated social thinker Dadoba Pandurang, had known Mary Carpenter even before her arrival in Bombay. Dr. Atmaram was also intimately known to Satyendra Nath Tagore. Dr. Atmaram Pandurang, along with Ramchandra Balkrishna's daughter met Mary Carpenter to the latter's delight immediately on her arrival in Bombay.[28] Dr. Atmaram Pandurang was one of the leading lights of the day. Following account given by her confirms her contribution:

> "On several occasions Dr. Atmaram Pandurang assembled at his residence a number of native gentlemen - his wife and daughter, with some other ladies, being occasionally present - to hold friendly conference on the topics which had occupied my attention. What I heard from them confirmed my opinion which I had already formed, that the educated Hindus have no belief in the idolatry and superstitious ceremonies, to which the uneducated so strongly adhere; but that these are so interwoven with all their domestic and social habits, that cannot at present emancipate themselves from them. The enlightened appear to be pure theists, and many are of a very religious and devotional spirit, though they fell unable to embrace Christianity. As they appear to converse on the subject, and pleased to find that I recognised with them the great truth that we have all one common Father in Heaven, I ventured to urge upon them to act up to their own convictions, and to unite together in a pure social worship of their own. On the Sunday after my departure this was commenced. At the house of the Doctor, all who desired assembled Sunday evening for a prayer-meeting without distinction of sex or age - the first attempt of the kind in India."[29]

Mary Carpenter later wrote to Dr. Atmaram Pandurang : "Your letter filled me with joy, for I trusted that quietly and most ostentiously a work was beginning of the greatest importance in India in the little service which you have established in your small circle...." She wished for their spiritual success.[30]

Mary Carpenter was an ardent admirer of Karsondas Mulji, Gujrati social reformer, whom she had met in England with Ramchandra Balkrishna. She lauded his role in Maharaja Libel Case and even quoted Justice Sir Joseph Arnold's elaborate and learned judgment in that famous case, in her Indian memoirs. She was also responsible for the establishment of the Bombay Social Science Association, along with Justice Gibbs, Sir Alexander Grant, Maneckjee Cursetji, and Dr. Bhau Daji.[31]

The contribution of Mary Carpenter's untiring and secular efforts to the reform movement in Western India can be gauged from the address presented to her, byDr. Bhau Daji, V.N. Mandlik, and others on behalf of Students' Literary and Scientific Society, at a Public function held on 13 March 1867 :

> "The record of your fame a sincere, zealous, and disinterested friend and active well-wisher of mankind had traveled to this land before your arrival. To the truly noble and self-sacrificing order of British womanhood, to which you belong, India owes order of a debt of gratitude;....Our task thus remains only partially accomplished; but the Divine blessing, we intend to preserve our humble effort, and cannot but feel that such devoted friends of our Sacred cause as yourself, by their love and sympathy, zeal knowledge and experience, in pointing out such remedies as the comparison of our condition with that of other countries might suggest, afford us a sure ground of hope for the success of our labor...."[32]

References

1. She also wrote the book *Our Convicts* (1864) suggesting prison reforms. For further details see J. Estlin Carpenter, *The Life and Work of Mary Carpenter,* Macmillan and Co., London, 1881, Second edition.

2. *Ibid.*, p. 253.

3. Mary Carpenter published the account of her first visit in *Six Months in India,* (hereinafter *SMI)* in two volumes, Longman, Green and Co., London, 1868. The book is dedicated to the memory of "the Rajah Rammohun Roy", and she further writes "the Great

Reformer of India, who first excited in the author's mind a desire to benefit his country".

4. The Students' Literature and Scientific Society was founder on 13th January 1848 by the students and professors of Elphinstone College, for the purpose of affording its members an opportunity of improving in reasoning and composition, and opportunity of improving in reasoning and literature, scientific and general subjects. Professor Patton was elected the first President, with Professor Reid and Sinclair as Secretaries. and Mr. Dadabhai Naoroji as Treasurer. The first four Reports of the Society are not available. But the later Reports reveal that almost all the educated natives of Bombay of that time, who sought to bring social change, were its members. They undertook reading and discussion of English essays, published many schoolbooks. There were Branch Societies: 1) Gujrati Dnyan-Prasarak Mandali. 2) Marathi Dnyan-Prasarak Sabha, and 3) Buddhi-vardhak Hindu Sabha. When Mary Carpenter visited their schools, they had eight Girls' schools under their care. Dr. Bhau Daji Girls' School, Jagannath Shankarshet Girls School, Bhagwandas Purshootam Girls' School, and two Girls' schools patronized by Seth Mangaldas Nathubhai. There were three Marathi and four Gujrati schools for girls. *Report of the Students' Literary & Scientific Society for the session of 1866-6 7*, Pp. 24-25.

5. For an account of Dr. Bhau Daji Lad's activities concerning female education see Anant Kakba Priyolkar, Dr. *Bhau Daji-Vyakti Kal va Kartutwa(Marathi)* Mumbai Marathi Sahitya Sangh, 1971, pp.184-195; How Mary Carpenter held him in high esteem is found in- Mary Carpenter, *SMI.* Vol. II, *op.cit,* 9-10., Dr. Bhau Daji was the first Secretary of the Bombay Association.

6. Manickjee Cursetji, was one of the earliest Indians to go to England. He was well versed in English language and was known as "Byron of the East". He was one of the earliest to get the position of judge of the Small Causes Court. He opened the first Girls' School, employed an English lady teacher and enlisted his daughters as assistant teachers under her. In 1863, the School was named after Princess Alexandra of Denmark, when she married Prince of Wales. Manickjee was appointed as Sheriff of Bombay in 1853 and 1863. A.K. Priyolkar, *Doctor Bhau Daji. op.cit.*, pp.108-117.

7. *SMI, op.cit.*, Vol. II, pp. 39-40.

8. Gopal Hari Deshmukh to Mary Carpenter, 3 March 1868, cited in J. Estlin Carpenter, *op.cit.*, pp.282-283.

9. *SMI*, pp. 47 & 58.; For details about Mahipatram Roopam as a social reformer see, R.L. Rawal, *Socio-Religious Reform Movements in Gujrat during the Nineteenth century.* Ess Ess Ppublication, New Delhi, 1987, pp.127-134.

10. Maharashtra State Archieves (MSA), Education Department (ED)/ 1866/ Vol. 31 /Compilation 234. It is dated November 1866.

11. G.R. Havaldar,Raosaheb *Vishwanath Narayan Mandlik Yanche Charitra,* (Marathi), Mumbai. Vol. I, p.287; Also cited by H. V. Mote, *Vishrabdha Shâradâ* (Marathi), Vol. I, 1817-1947, H.V. Mote Prakashan, Mumbai, 2nd edition, 1993, p.99.

12. *SMI. op.cit.*, p.11.

13. *MSA/ ED/1866/* Vol.3 / Comp.212. The topics in the Memorial concerned Female Normal Schools, Reformatory and Industrial School and Prison discipline. It is dated 1st January 1867. A similar Memorial was addressed to the Governor General of India. dated 12 December 1866. *MSA/ ED/ 1867/* Vol. 2/ Comp.12.

14. *MSA/ ED/*1866/ Vol.3/ Comp. 212.

15. *MSA / ED/*1867/ Vol. 2/ Comp.12. p.134. She also emphasized a separate boarding for non-Christian native girls.

16. *Ibid.*, Sir Alexander Grant, Director of Public Instruction, to C. Gonne, Secretary to Bombay Government, No.234 of 1867-68, dated 23 April 1867.

17. *Ibid.*, No.2017, The D.P.I. to C. Gonne, Secretary to the Bombay. Government. The proposal also received sanction from the GOI and the Secretary of State.

18. *MSA/ED/1870/* Vol.3/ Comp.5; The entire scheme ran in rough waters when the GOI reduced the grant by Rs.I000/- per annum; but after repeated requests restored to the original amount. The Bombay Female Normal School was shifted to Poona because of the high rent for building and higher salary to be paid to European Lady teacher.

19. *MSA/Judicial Department* [JD]1868/Vol. 34/Comp.1194 & 129; Also in *MSA/ED/* 1866 Vol.3/ Comp. 212.

20. *"Historical Resume of the Origin and Progress of the David Sassoon Industrial and Reformatory Institution"*, Education Society's Press, Byculla, 1868, attached in *MSA/JD* /1867/ Vol. 3-A. There is no compilation number; A nucleus of the Juvenile Reformatory was first formed in Bombay in 1843, through the efforts of the late Dr. George Buist. Finding that destitute orphans and vagrants numbering from 200 to 300 boys were yearly taken by the police of Bombay, Dr. Buist established in that year what may be termed a Ragged School at Sewree, supported by private contributions with the express object of affording for such orphans and vagrants an asylum, where they:)bight not only be fed but trained to some useful trade, which might enable them in after-life to earn their bread by honest industry, and thus constitute them useful members of society. On the repeated and urgent representions of Dr. Buist to secure for the School the benefit professional superintendence, the late Court of Directors allowed in i850 the services of second class Engineers, as Superintendent and instructor. Under the Government Engineer, the school received for the first time a regular organisation with a definite object. The institution bears the name of David Sassoon, a highly respectable Jewish merchant of Bombay, because of the munificent donation of Rs.30,000 and a house with premises, he made on 27th March 1857, on the condition that the Government must annually contribute an equal amount of interest of Rs.30,000, and that salary of the permanent Engineer would be paid by them. This offer had been preceded by that of Mr. Jagannath Shankerseth who offered to grant a site for the school, and Seth Mangaldas Nathubhai offered interest on a fixed deposit of Rs. 17,000/-.

21. *MSA/JD/* 1870/ Vol.83/ Reformatories.

22 *MSA/JD/* Vol.55/907; *MSA/ JD/* Vol. 17/ Comp.908 & 984. 23. *MSA/ JD/* Vol.30-A

23. *MSA/JD/* Vol. 30- A.

24. *MSA/JD/* Vol. 130/ Compo 130.

25. *MSA/JD* /1868/ Vol. 34/ Comp. 1194.

26. J. Masselos, *Towards Nationalism - Group affiliations and the Politics of public associations in nineteenth century Western India*, Popular Prakashan, Bombay, 1974, p.82.

27. *Dwarakanath Govind Vaidya, Prarthana Samajacha Itihas* (Marathi), Mumbai, 1927, *Charitratmak lekh: Dr. Atmaram Pandurang.* p.14.

28. Mary Carpenter, *op.cit.* Vol. I, p.22. Mary Carpenter gives the date 25th September 1866.

29. *Ibid.*, Vol. II, pp. 20-21.

30. J. Estlin Carpenter, *op.cit.*, pp. 277-278.

31. *SMI*, Vol. II, pp. 33-34.

32. *Report of the Students' Literary & Scientific Society for the session of 1866-67*, pp. 24-25.

10

Dilemma of a Convert : Pandita Ramabai's Confrontation with Apologists - Hindu and Christian

Pandita Ramabai (1858-1922),[1] the extremely erudite high caste Hindu woman, who entered into Christian faith, via Brahmoism, on the advice of Father Nehemiah Goreh in 1883.[2] She never identified religion with nationality, and on her conversion she did not cease to be a staunch nationalist that she has ever been. Her approach to religion and social reforms, was rational and humanitarian, just as that of Raja Rammohun Roy whom she greatly admired.[3] She also had much in common with the religious and social philosophy of Theodore Parker (1810-1860), the American rebellious Unitarian priest, abolitionist and social reformer. She believed that her new faith was to be non-sectarian, non-authoritarian and universal in character, which would bring her religious peace and enable her to pursue her cherished goal which was "**to do away with all kinds of prejudices which deprive a woman in India of her proper place in society**".[4]

But as a convert she soon discovered that Christianity, as it was practiced by different sects, did not grant freedom of conscience, nor was it free from priest-craft and its attendant evils; and that, in some respects, it was even more dogmatic and more rigid than the faith in which she was born. If she found the champions of Hindu orthodoxy obnoxious, the Christian missionaries, with whom she was closely associated, were equally unreasonable and therefore intolerable. She thus had to wage struggle on two fronts to maintain her own in matters religious and social. This article attempts to bring out the nature and content of the struggle as it developed till 1896 when she withdrew herself into her shell and did not join any public debate on the vital issues of the day.[5]

The article is divided into two parts. The part one deals with her confrontation with the missionaries of Athanasian Creed, who baptised and sheltered her in England till she moved to America in search of support to her scheme to establish a home for the destitute Hindu child-widows on secular lines. The second part examines her intellectual duels with the champions of Hindu orthodoxy, especially concerning the Age of Consent Bill and the Sharada Sadan, in which she thoroughly exposed the hollowness of the Shashtras, especially their bias against woman which subjected her to all kinds of humiliation and reduced her to a mere object of lust.

I

Against the background of her early trials and tribulations, as well as disgust with popular Hinduism, Ramabai joined Brahmo faith, while in Bengal. She states that both she and her husband, Bipin Behari Das Medhavi, did not believe at that point of time in Hinduism and got married under the Brahmo Civil Marriage Act. She came in contact with the Rev. Issac Allen, a Baptist missionary, at Silchar, and through him with Christianity. When she returned to Bombay in 1882, after her husband's death, she aligned herself with the Prarthana Samajist leaders and worked for arousing the consciousness of the women through her lectures and *Puranas* under the auspices of the Arya Mahila Samaj. It was at Pune she came in contact with the Wantage sisters of the Community of St.Mary the Virgin(CSMV). It was a branch of an Anglican missionary society founded at Wantage in England. Miss Hurford, who was on their staff, used to teach English to her and Ramabai Ranade, introduced her to the Wantage sisters. Ramabai's interest in Christianity gradually increased with her new found contact with the Mission of the Wantage Sisters at the St. Mary's Home and the Cowley Fathers of Panch Hauds Mission at Poona.[6] It was through these Sisters that Ramabai's visit to England was arranged with the intention of studying medicine.

Pandita Ramabai left for England in April 1883, along with her daughter and a friend, Anandibai Bhagat. There, she was put in the CSMV at Wantage, under the care of Sister Geraldine (1843-1917), whom Ramabai affectionately called *Ajeebai.*[7] In June 1883, one Mr. Coles was asked to instruct Ramabai on Christian theology. Not until 13 July, that she expressed her desire to get baptised. She was made a Cateshuman on 23 July and from then until the end of September 1883, was put under instructions preparatory to baptism. Ramabai, along with her daughter Manorama, was eventually baptised on 29 September[8], by the Rev. Canon William Butler. It was a day of rejoice for her benefactors, to have converted such a high-caste and learned woman.[9] However, their happiness at this accomplishment seems to have been short lived.

The correspondence between Ramabai and Sister Geraldine and Butler in October 1885, reveals that Ramabai had expressed, even before baptism, her difficulties in accepting Christianity without reservations, since she had doubt regarding the doctrine of Trinity, the Divinity of Jesus Christ and the Sacraments. She had also made it very clear that she did not belong 'exclusively to one Church'. However, the Wantage Sisters and the Cowley Fathers tried to dispel her doubts regarding Christian faith in their own dogmatic way, but Ramabai found it difficult to accept their argument rationally.[10] The more Ramabai was candid in addressing her difficulties, the more her Christian benefactors became suspicious of her conversion to their faith. The rift between them ever widened in the succeeding period, with both parties taking unconcilliatory positions. On the other, Ramabai's superiors among the Wantage Sisters and Cowley Fathers took upon themselves the responsibility of taking decisions regarding her future without consulting her, which she resented. This made her sullen and withdrawn, as she was unwilling to surrender her freedom to decide for herself.[11] Consequently, it was decided in early 1884, by her benefactors that she be put Ramabai in the Ladies College at Cheltenham[12], under the care of Principal Miss Dorothea Beale (1831-1906). It was here that her stay was perhaps happiest while being in England. Unlike at Wantage, she could breathe free at Cheltenham from the dogmatic clutches. Also, in Dorothea Beale, she found a very congenial and sympathetic friend, in whom she could freely confide. Beale welcomed Ramabai's long letters which addressed her questions and difficulties regarding religious issues and tried to answer them at equal length.

In one of her letters, Beale wrote, "Ramabai is very learned and thoughtful, and (Ramabai) says how powerless most missionaries are, for want of knowledge of native philosophy and religion..."[13] No wonder, she deeply mourned Beale's death in 1906 and paid her a glowing tribute.

What infuriated Ramabai in mid-1884 was the serious discussion among the members of Church hierarchy – Sister Geraldine, the Dean of Lincoln Rev. Canon Butler, the Lord Bishop Rev. Dr. Mylne, the Bishop of Bombay, Rev. Thomas V., the Bishop of Lahore, the Mother Superior of Wantage Sisters, and lastly, Dorothy Beale — without ever bothering to seek Ramabai's consent. This apparently a trivial matter, nevertheless, created distrust in Ramabai's mind and made her rebellious against the arbitrariness, racial prejudices and pontifical attitude of the Church authorities, with whom she was in association. Beale informed members that Ramabai planned to stay for a few years in England and return to India as soon as some plan is devised to establish a home for education of Indian widows. All the Sisters at the Wantage felt that it was prudent to keep Ramabai there until she was firmly established in Christian faith. Although Beale did not think the time was ripe enough for her return to India as she was not sufficiently established in the faith, nevertheless, felt that Ramabai would not accept to lead a life of dependence and inaction any longer. The fact that some ladies belonging to the Unitarians wished Ramabai to come down to London, Beale cautioned Sister Geraldine to be very discrete and that any suppression of her individuality on the part of Church authorities could be counter-productive and might make her more rebellious. She, therefore, proposed to Geraldine that Ramabai be allowed to teach Sanskrit and native languages to girls and boys at Cheltenham for two reasons — firstly, she would not get the feeling of being dependent for her daily sustenance, and secondly, she would be helping many prospective evangelist English women, who otherwise spend several years studying Indian conditions— native language, religion and philosophy— better. Beale also suggested that "boys" at the Working Men's College, who are preparing to go to India, would also be benefited by her lectures. Between May 1884 and June 1885 this question of teaching assignment was hotly discussed by the people in "authority". On this seemingly non-descript issue their opinions do reflect boorishness and also exhibit most biased attitude which did hurt Ramabai very deeply.

The Rev. Mylne, the Bishop of Bombay, wrote to Beale,

> "I most earnestly hoped that the evil would be minimised in her case...I am sure I cannot do wrong in saying that all publicity, anything which indirectly tends to make silly people treat her as a lion, is of all things most to be avoided".

In fact, he thought, not only would she be most marginalised by the fellow-countrymen if they would learn about her lectures to young men, but "may cause scandal even among the better sort of native men".[14] The Bishop of Lahore, Rev. Thomas V., felt the question was prejudged, what could be done was "to plead for modifying and limiting to the utmost possible ill-effects which could not wholly be avoided..." His complain was that young 'Christian Hindoos' should not be sent to England, "as they have almost uniformly scorned work among their own countrymen, and become wholly denationalised". Since he knew Ramabai, he did not think that she would settle down and become an English lady. However, concurring with the objections raised by the Bishop of Bombay, he felt that Ramabai's professorial assignment in the Men's College "might lead to a little undue self-exaltation" and suggested that "a less prominent position for a short time, with an humbler title such as teachership, making no demonstration in any way, would probably lessen the danger of elation of mind very considerably".[15]

Knowing Ramabai's inquisitive mind about Christian theology, Sister Geraldine, who was vexed with Pandita Ramabai's theological queries, was more anxious for her being rooted in the faith. Writing to the Lord Bishop, Canon Butler, she complained against Beale's liberal attitude towards Ramabai, expressed helplessness and asked him "whether the disputed point is to be conceded or no."[16]

Hinting a strict and watchful eye, Bishop Butler conveyed Beale the opinion of Sir George Hunter, the Director of Indian Medical Work, one who knew Ramabai that "her influence as a fellow countrywoman with the Indian natives is utterly at an end. She will have no more access than an English woman. Therefore, bring her up as much as may be, in English thought and ways and let her go out as a part of the staff of some English institution."[17] Although Butler conceded that Ramabai's knowledge of Indian ways would give her an advantage over the English counterparts, he nonetheless felt, **"All that she needs is an English development of her Indian brains."** He also told

Ramabai that she would be kept in England till she was thirty years of age; and consequently held her future in a state of abeyance.[18]

Ramabai's reaction was one of caution and disdain. When Geraldine told her that the Bishops were right in deciding against her teaching "boys", she expressed her repugnance in no uncertain terms,

> "I cannot do a single thing without knowing what I am to do. It is very difficult for an old pupil (at least for me, if not for you) to go on working, when I do not know the thing which I have to do... I am arguing with those people who give their opinion or decide anything for me without knowing my will, and above all God's will."[19]

The matter seemed to rest for a while as Ramabai was allowed to teach but the distrust of the Superiors remained deep in her. Even Beale assured Geraldine that she will be sorry "if anything is done that would be disapproved by those who have stood '*loco parentis*' to Ramabai, or be in any way disloyal to the Community..."[20]

The Wantage Sisters and Cowley Fathers threw Beale's caution to wind and continued to arbitrarily control Ramabai's day to day movements, which she felt as an infringement on her freedom. It was only after a remonstrance that Ramabai was allowed to stay with her Unitarian friend Mrs. Gilmore, for the Easter holidays in April 1885, whom Geraldine held responsible for Ramabai's "mental and spiritual disturbances".[21] When Ramabai went to see Rev. Issac Allen, a Baptist missionary and a friend of Ramabai's husband, Geraldine high-handedly reprimanded Beale for giving more freedom to her.[22] In April 1885, after completing one year at Cheltenham, the question regarding her continuance and teaching assignment came up again. Beale advised against Ramabai to be taken out of Cheltenham and put in a smaller school, as contemplated by the Church Superiors and expressed her apprehension to Geraldine that, "*If she(Ramabai) does not find someone to whom she can speak freely, she will be silent and might easily pass into Unitarianism.*"[23] (Emphasis is mine) Geraldine, in concurrence with the Mother Superior and Bishops of Lahore and Bombay, informed Ramabai that she has to learn as a Christian and is bound to accept the authority of those over her in the Church; and asked Beale "to make this an occasion to giving her a little teaching on submission to authority".

Pandita Ramabai termed Geraldine's behaviour as "unbecoming of being civilised", and in utmost contempt retorted her,

> "it does not follow that because we are friends we ought not to have our own judgment and mind...(and) advising me under the WE to accept always the will of those who have authority etc. ***This however I cannot accept. I have a conscience of my own; I must myself think and do everything which GOD has given me the power of doing. Although priests and Bishops may have certain authority over the church yet the Church has another Master who is Superior even to the Bishops.*** I am, it is true, a member of the Church of Christ, but am not bound to accept every word that falls down from the lips of priests and bishops. If it pleases you to call my word liberty as lawlessness you may do so, but as far as I know myself, I am not lawless. Obedience to law and to the Word of God is quite different from perfect obedience to priests only. ***I have just with great effort freed myself from the yoke of the Indian priestly tribe, so I am not at present willing to place myself under another similar yoke by accepting everything which comes from the priests as authorised command of the Most High.***[24] (Italics are mine)

So much hurt was she that Ramabai was not ready to take the things lying low, and further asserted, **"If you and your country people do not trust the people of India, it matters little, but for my part, I do trust and love my country with all my heart. I know very well trust brings trust and love brings love with it..."** She reminded Geraldine and her ilk that the title *Saraswati* was bestowed on her by Pandit Tara Nath in a large gathering of Pandits who examined her in Sanskrit shashtraic learning. Further she wrote,

> "It was the example set by the good Brahmos which kindled my spirit and made me able to plead the cause of women before my countrymen. It is true, it is not necessary for me to be a teacher of men, but when either in India or England I can get women as well as men for my pupils there is no reason why I should not teach both... *It surprises me very much to think that neither my father nor my husband objected to my mother's or my teaching young men while some English people are doing so...* ***I am not anxious to give lessons to young men, but I am anxious to do away all kinds of prejudices which deprive a woman in India of her proper place in society...*** *To help the women to come forward in the society I must first of all urge upon men, teach men of poorer classes. Then when men are convinced of the necessity of elevating the condition of their women, I shall have access to their Zenanas...*"[25] (Italics are mine)

However, the orthodox missionary friends were in no mood to mend their attitude. Instead, Geraldine wrote to the Mother Superior suggesting that Ramabai should her return to India, and advised Beale that it was important to keep her interested in some scheme of work in which, though she cannot be the organiser, she could carry out her ideas for the training of Indian women. It was a 'crisis', thought Beale and urged Geraldine, "I may have been wrong but it seemed that not to yield would have been to provoke and perhaps bring about a result which some yielding might avert". It seems, it was beyond Geraldine's comprehension to comprehend Ramabai in proper perspective. Instead, in a manner of complain to the Dean of Lincoln, she blamed Beale for not reporting to her for decision; for 'injudiciously' giving Ramabai freedom and making her independent of the Wantage Sisters in financial matters; and firmly held that "when Ramabai has thrown us off (as) she is certain to do if Miss Beale continues the attitude she is at present taking with her, Ramabai will at the first rub with Miss Beale throw off her authority too".[26] To Bishop Mylne, Ramabai was both "wrong and obstinate", but the question in his opinion was, "*how to minimise an evil which we cannot wholly prevent*".[27] Bishop Canon William Butler attributed the real danger to the courting she receives. But his comment, "to a neophyte in the Faith that self-reliance is intensely dangerous", was too injurious to Ramabai and showed how he was not ready to think in any sympathetic manner. Beale who sympathised Ramabai, cautioned Butler that, "her life accustomed to question and debate the deepest questions of philosophy... A little impatience on our part might throw her back into the Unitarian teaching of the Brahmo Samaj".

Ramabai was pained for being "arbitrarily" controlled and her genuine difficulties concerning faith termed as being influenced by the "Devil". She conveyed her displeasure to Bishop Butler in no uncertain terms :

> "I have not forgotten the lessons which my dear parents had taught me in my childhood, i.e. to honour and be grateful to those who led me to the life immortal. I honour and am grateful to my parents first, and next to them, I honour those who are my spiritual parents and who brought me to Christ and to God. But at the same time, I should never hesitate to ask them some questions and to tell honestly to them that I could not agree with them in every point of faith...*God has given me*

an independent conscience, not to accept everything slavishly that other people say, but "hear and see" for and by myself... This freedom of thought I honestly say I was not allowed to have by my Wantage friends. The moment I asked any questions they would either mistake me or say I was sinning against such and such commandment of God. Consequently, I dared not to ask you or Sister Geraldine any question concerning the doctrines taught by the church, and *so laboured for a time, and underwent many afflictions of my troubled conscience.* After I came here, I found a friend in Miss Beale...so I placed my difficulties before her, which I had never mentioned to Sister Geraldine or to you... These my questions reached Sister Geraldine through Miss Beale, and from her to you..."[28] (Italics are mine)

Since Ramabai felt that the misunderstanding was alarmingly aggravating, "too formidable not to be corrected", she considered it necessary to clarify her benefactors the circumstances which had led her to embrace Christianity :

"I was indeed impressed with the holy life of the Sisters, and their sublime unselfishness, but I must say for the sake of truth that their life was not the cause of my accepting the faith of Christ. It was Father Gore's letter that proved that the faith which I professed (I mean the Brahmo faith) was not taught by our Veda as I had thought, but it was the Christian faith which was brought before me by my friends disguised under the name of Brahmo religion. Well, I thought if Christ is the source of this sublime faith, why should not I confess Him openly to be my Lord and my Divine teacher ?... But this confession does not mean that I believe also all the doctrines taught by other people, unless they be proved to be true from Christ's own teachings..."[29]

In an effort to make Butler realize what kind of mental trauma one has to undergo in accepting an alien religion, Ramabai pointed out that, "You have never gone through the same experience of choosing another religion for yourself, which was totally foreign to you, as I have". She questioned Butler : "If a Hindoo theologian - however learned and holy and good he may be - comes and tells you that your religion was a false one, and that you were to accept humbly everything that he taught, could you do it?" She soon realised that even her inadvertent comments were seen in lurid light.[30] She pleaded with Butler that "if you agree not to be a lawyer but a searcher after the truth in all your arguments, I will most gladly bring my difficulties before you... The examples that you give about which the Bible has not said anything in details seem to me not to be of great consequence or essential to the faith."[31] The pain caused by the 'decision' of not allowing Ramabai to teach boys is well reflected in her letter to Beale

> "There is no doubt I am (pained). Because it is saying plainly that those people who are not of that country know India and its people far better than I do who am born and brought up in India and among its own people. And that they whoever they are do not trust me and my people and that they are the masters to decide anything for me and I ought not to have a voice of my own to speak against their decision... But to say that if I teach boys it would weaken my influence on my country people is simply absurd... And I shall not allow anyone to lay hand on my personal liberty. Although I am poor and weak in body I have a mind strong enough to resist all these meaningless social customs which deprive a woman of her proper place in society.... 'This decision', as Sister Geraldine names it, I consider as a *personal insult* and I shall not act according to it.[32]

From the beginning Ramabai had her differences with Sister Geraldine and others of the Athanasian Church, a faith into which she was baptised, on issues concerning Christian faith. She observed that Sister Geraldine was dogmatic and more worried about the rituals and sacraments, exhorting "earnestness of purpose", attributing her questioning spirit to "the influence of Devil" and insisting her to learn "Christian warfare" to combat it.[33] Butler's bigotry created a fright in her mind. He was very often not ready to listen to Ramabai's reasons for not believing in the 'Divinity of Christ', and on the contrary accused her of denying God Himself. When she asked whether she should not have a voice of her own in such matters, he emphatically said, "Decidedly not! You ought humbly to accept the Church's teaching, you are not cleverer than the Church." He paid least attention to her appeals and contemptuously told her, "Go and work or stay with the Brahmos, or do what you like." Ramabai felt pity that for a 'man of his age should have behaved so uncharitably, and her anguish is reflected in her letter to Beale :

> "I do not hate the Brahmos as he does. I shall if it be God's will and shall have to go and live and work among my people, though they be hated and called humbugs by some pious Christians because they

are either Brahmos or Hindoos, and are not willing to submit to the Church doctrine, without proving its accuracy."[34]

Ramabai's "appetite for philosophy", to quote Beale's words, her enthusiasm and unsparing devotion to the cause of her unhappy sisters in India, touched Beale's heart deeply.[35] It is with her that Ramabai bared her heart and mind regarding the vexed issues concerning Christian faith. Ramabai's concise ideas on Christian faith are found in her long letters to Beale. She explained her dilemma :

> "You can very well imagine how hard I have to struggle sometimes between the Prayer Book, the Bible and Hindoo religion and my different understandings about them, with no one but with my own limited knowledge of these books and the spiritual language of the Spirit of God which passes my understanding to help me... I have of late, as you know, after realising the sublime truths of Christ's teachings, become one of the least of his disciples, and believe in Him as the Messiah of God, and therefore, am bound to receive every word which falls from his lips as the command of God which comes to me through His meditation...I call myself a Christian, though I do not know if after hearing my creed my fellow Christians would call me so. But that does not matter. It is not for others and for other's opinions that I have accepted Christianity....[36]

The dilemma that Ramabai faced on accepting Christianity, was because of her inquisitive mind. In the manner she studied Hindu Shashtras and philosophy which revealed to her how it was unkind to womanhood, Ramabai felt that she should study Bible herself instead of being instructed by others.[37] But her reasoned beliefs differed from the Athenasian Creed of Christianity into which she was baptised, on the issues, namely, the doctrine of Trinity, or the divinity of Jesus, for she found that such a mode of prayer was not prescribed in the Bible. During Ramabai's short stay at Wantage in September 1885, when Manorama, her daughter recited her prayers in the Trinitarian way, Ramabai became furious and protested to Sister Geraldine for teaching some thing which she did not believe. She did not object to her saying the Apostle's Creed, the Lord's Prayer, and other prayer to God through Christ, but objected to praying to Christ, and to the Holy Ghost, as a person separate from Heavenly Father, for she felt it was not commanded by Christ in the *New Testament*.[38] Since her relations with the orthodox Wantage Sisters had been ruptured, she saw a sinister design in it, an attempt to alienate her daughter Manorama from her. In fact, Geraldine's refusal to bind herself not to teach the Trinitarian principle, was partly responsible for her leaving England.[39]

The reason she advanced for refusing to do sacraments and rituals such as Confession and thanks-giving was, she wrote, "From the Bible I can derive the necessity of confessing sins or faults to *one another* and to God, and not to a particular priest in India". In her opinion, India was not ripe enough to practice such things.[40]

From the beginning itself Ramabai did not believe either in Athanasian Creed of the Church of England or any other Christian denomination, for she believed in the Universal Church of Christ. The disparaging way the Wantage Sisters, the Cowley Fathers, and members of other Christian denominations such as Baptists, Congregationalists, Wesleyans, and Unitarians, spoke and wrote against each other, made her sick. She once requested Geraldine, "You profess to be a Sister of Charity. Do you have a little more charity towards your brethren of all denominations ?"[41] Sister Geraldine (*Ajeebai*) was almost mad with anger when Ramabai once told her that she had no right to call the Dissenters heretics, because she herself belonged to a Church which is but a Dissenting sect of the Roman Catholic.

Such fundamental differences as this between her and her Christian patrons soared their relations. The correspondence of Ramabai with Geraldine, Butler and others in September-October 1885, is full of accusations and counter-accusations. It reached to such a level that Geraldine accused Ramabai of caste prejudices for not having animal food. Against this background it is easy to understand what Ramabai wrote to Geraldine, "You may if you like trace my pride in pies and puddings, butter and milk, water and rice, shoes and stockings... I confess I am not free from all my caste prejudices, as you are pleased to call them. I like to be called a Hindoo, for I am one, and also keep all the customs of my forefathers as far as I can."[42] On the other hand, the Church authorities ordered her to submit for their scrutiny her correspondence with Unitarians and more importantly the 'theistic' Brahmo Indian friends. She was forbidden to read literature on Christianity which they considered detrimental to her settling into the Athanasian faith and the Lord's Divinity. Her studies at Cheltenham were discontinued and was asked to return to Wantage. Her idea of starting a school for Indian sisters was put in cold storage, and she was told that her future course of action would be communicated to her once she was soundly grounded in Christian faith. They repeatedly reminded her of their "generosity" towards her and her daughter. Ramabai realised that staying for another year in England meant more expenses, and she being penniless, has to depend more and more on others. She did not wish to live on charity. "***It is a shame***, she wrote to Dorothea Beale, ***to live as a beggar when I have sound health and strong limbs to work with***."[43] (Emphasis is mine)

By July 1885, Ramabai had realised that it was time for her to leave England. It seems, she arranged an invitation to America, under the pretext of witnessing the convocation ceremony in which her 'cousin' Anandibai Joshi was to be awarded a degree in medicine and with whom she seems to have been in correspondence for long. In her invitation letter Dr. Rachel Bodley, wrote, "**The impression I have received from your relatives concerning you is that your mission in India is that of an inspirer rather than that of a teacher.**"[44] This must have pleased Ramabai. She left for America in February 1886.

With influential and sympathetic friends like Dr. Bodley, America offered to Ramabai much freedom and latitude in her thought and mission, which was denied to her in England. Here, she read about and met a multitude of Christian denominations but with less bigotry, which made her a public figure and that widened her vision. Though her stay was initially planned for six months, she stayed for nearly three years as she found the atmosphere congenial for collecting monetary help for starting up a school for child-widows in India. No wonder, Rev. C.E. Gardiner, a Cowley Father known to her, author of *Life of Father Goreh,* wrote that Ramabai lost her spiritual footing amidst a wild sea of antagonistic opinions, which brought laxity of thought, not holding truth as a supreme Divine reality.[45] Having the same kind of belief that Ramabai was losing her faith, even Father Goreh wrote a letter which was later published in 1887, under the title- *Proofs of the Divinity of our Lord, stated in Letter to a Friend*. But she did not seem to think so.

America offered to Ramabai much freedom of thought and latitude in her mission. Here she read about and interacted with the people belonging to other Christian denominations, those having much less bigotry. Ramabai's interactions made her a public figure, widened her vision and found atmosphere congenial for collecting monetary help for her dream of starting a school for child-widows in India. She well informed the American public on this issue by writing a book – *The High-Caste Hindu Woman*[1887], to which Dr. Rachel Bodley wrote a foreward.

In America, she met illustrious persons such as Frances Willard (1839-1898)[46] and Harriet Tubman (1821-1913)[47]. Frances Willard was remarkable lady - educator, reformer and founder of the World's Woman's Christian Temperance Union. She was committed to temperance reform, women's suffrage, and improved industrial code for women. She not only helped Ramabai in organising her lectures through out America, on the condition of Indian women, but later became one of the founding members of the Ramabai Association of America which was formed in Boston on 28 May 1887. Willard's perceptible influence is reflected in Ramabai's letter to *Ajeebai* regarding temperance and Eucharistic meal.

> "I think and thousands of my countrymen think that it is good to totally abstain from intoxicating liquor. We term it sinful to use it, not because that which God made is bad, but man has turned it into an evil...I very much doubt whether it is God's work to corrupt and decay the grapes and similar other things, ferment them and turn them into a poison, namely, alcohol... I think the Mother has mistaken pure juice of grapes which the Lord used and sanctioned for use in the Eucharist, for the fermented drink is called wine now... It appears to this heathen to be the Christian's work, and it is high time the Church and Church people tried to remove this horrid enemy by setting the example and show the world that the saloon and brothel are not included in the 'Creation'.[48]

Ramabai also met many abolitionists, and in particular, Harriet Tubman, "Moses of her people", one who fought against slavery, spoke for women's rights, and founded schools for emancipated slaves after the Civil War.[49] She also met Miss Anna Hallowell, a lady connected with Sub-Primary School Society. Meetings with such persons seem to have inspired Ramabai to work for woman's proper position in India with renewed zeal.

It seems that Ramabai was well acquainted with the writings and works of Theodore Parker (1810-1860), the Unitarian clergyman, social reformer, abolitionist and freethinker, and one whose writings influenced the two principal reform movements in Western India, namely, the *Prarthana Samaj* (1867), and the *Satyashodhak Samaj* (1873) of Jyotiba Phule, the founder of the low caste protest movement.[50] Parker, who derived the special authority of the Bible and the supernatural origin of Christianity, had said in his first ordained sermon, "the God who created earth and heaven had never spoken miraculously in Hebrew words bidding Abraham kill his own son and burn him for sacrifice, and that Jesus of Nazerath was not a finality in the historic development of mankind". Further he demanded that "we worship, as Jesus did, with no mediator, with nothing between us and father of all". For saying this he was denounced as an "Infidel", a "Deist", an "Atheist", a "blasphemer". Even the Unitarians denounced him and excommunicated him by striking off his name from their Almanac.[51] In taking Christ as her "Guru" and rather as a mediator with God, her disbelief in the doctrine of Trinity and Divinity of Jesus, and her belief "in a progressive state of soul", Ramabai takes a position very similar to that of Parker's. For instance, she wrote to Ajeebai in 1896, "I believe in the Universal Church of Christ which includes all the members of His body,... The dry discussion about sects and differences has never been an attractive one to me since I was converted". Perhaps, she may have read Parker's sermons while in England, which Geraldine calls as un-Christian books given to her by the so-called Christian friends.

Despite her conversion, Ramabai remained a staunch nationalist and yearned more than ever to reach out her people. As early as in 1884, Ramabai refused to wear the cross with the Latin words inscribed "Sacrament and Priests". Her objection was that it ought to be replaced with Sanskrit words. She said, "I stick fast to Sanskrit, not because I think it to be sacred or the language of Gods, but because it is most beautiful and oldest language of my dear native land...I do not myself understand the Latin, and neither do my countrymen." When Geraldine told her that it (the Cross with Latin words) was approved by Father Nehemaih Goreh, Ramabai replied,

> "I am not going to find fault with Father Goreh about the words 'Sacrament and Priests'. I know quite well the feeling of those people, who when they make up their mind to leave some bad things of their custom, etc., are entirely blinded by the new atmosphere...Father Goreh no doubt is good, old and wise and perhaps he(Goreh) thinks is right, but I am sorry to say in some things I do not agree with him...Father Goreh who does not and will not sympathise with Indian feelings, but I am just plucked down from Hinduism and Brahmoism, so I know very well and sympathise with their feelings. So I am not

inclined to do anything, which will lead my fellow Indian Christians into wrong ideas."[52]

No wonder, Ramabai did not associate herself with Father Goreh, anytime after her return to India. Even though both were at Pune until Goreh's death in 1894, it is not strange that Ramabai never ever invited him to Sharada Sadan, nor did she keep relations with Panch Haud Mission where he lived.

Even as a Christian, whenever Ramabai learnt of any racial discrimation against the fellow-Indians, her anger came out openly. When Ramabai learnt that Dr. Anandibai Joshi was refused at London, to board the ship going to India, she expressed her displeasure to Beale, "I too cannot realise that any ship could have refused to take Dr. Joshee on board simply because she was a Hindu woman, but when I remember the daily occurrence of misbehaviour of many a short-sighted English toward my country people I do not wonder if such a thing has indeed taken place in England."[53]

Ramabai did not align herself with any other Christian missionary sects in India, but sought to develop something like a 'Church of India'. Her experience with the Wantage Sisters was so distasteful that she did not allow Manorama to visit Wantage in 1898. She also translated the *New Testament* from Hebrew into Marathi. Ramabai attempted to show to the missionaries as well as her own people, that in becoming Christian, it was not necessary to denationalise oneself.

II

Though for several reasons, Ramabai had become a Christian; her approach to social reform was essentially secular and humanitarian. On 11 March 1889, she founded with American financial help the Sharada Sadan, which was designed to be a secular and philanthropic institution for the upliftment of destitute Hindu widows. It was shifted to Poona in November 1890.

For the Hindu orthodoxy, Ramabai was a rebel and a renegade, and her teachings were considered subversive of traditional order.[54] From the very inception of Sharada Sadan in 1888, leaders like B.G.Tilak and his followers not only held her intention of working for Hindu widows in suspicion but always accused her for using the

Sadan to proselyte for Christianity. Through out, they lost no opportunity in launching virulent attack on Ramabai and her Sadan.

Mahatma Phule was one of the earliest reformers who openly admired Ramabai[55], but did not live to defend her during the turbulent days of Sadan. Since her arrival to Bombay in 1882, in general, all the reformers — M.G. Ranade, Dr. R.G. Bhandarkar and their Prarthana Samajist friends, Gopal Ganesh Agarkar, and many other— actively supported Ramabai, not only in founding *Arya Mahila Samaj* but even after her return from England as Christian. They also admired her for attending Indian National Congress held at Bombay in 1889 with a view to mobilizing public support in the cause of women's emancipation. The public debate that she entered through the columns of *Sudharak* in early 1891 for lending support to the reformist group on the issue of Age of Consent which had begun with the publication of "Notes on Infant Marriage and Enforced Widowhood" by Beheramji M. Malabari in 1884, shows how Ramabai confronted the *shashtri* class and the leaders of orthodoxy; and thereby laid the foundation of the feminist movement along with Tarabai Shinde.[56]

Ramabai's exposé against the orthodoxy and their leaders came against the background of the Age of Consent Controversy (1884-1891). In November 1890, Lionel Ashburner, who was a member of the Governor's Executive Council, wrote an article in *National Review* entitled — "Reform of the Marriage Laws in India"[57] in which he debunked the whole corpus of Hindu shashtraic injunctions on marriage etc. and wrote most condescendingly of the Hindu society in general and Hindu widows in particular by calling them "**charted libertines**". It would be worthwhile to quote him. He wrote :

"The real reason why the Indian widow declines to be reformed by philanthropic legislation is that she is a chartered libertine, she is allowed greater latitude of conduct. Society is very tolerant of her frailties; they are ignored and condoned, and she is by no means inclined to relinquish the Bohemian freedom of an amateur member of the *demi monde*.... This is of course very shocking, but it is the root of the whole matter, and we can hardly afford to stone the Indian widow, at least till we can find some immaculate person to cast the first stone. I do not assert that all widows are unchaste—many are perfect models of domestic virtues. But society does not enforce a very high standard of morality and they do not presume to dictate to society, they accept the position."

It was Agarkar who wrote two articles in *Sudharak*,[58] taking Lionel Ashburner task for writing not only indecent but positively mischievous and false accusations against hapless Hindu widows. He regretted that a person like Ashburner, who has spent three decades in civil service in this presidency and has interacted with Indian people, should dare to stigmatise orphaned Hindu widows and that the publishers of *National Review* should print such sweeping generalizations without determining the veracity of such claim. He did not think such writing was not worth responding and pointed out that the very phrase "enforced widowhood" is suggestive of the innumerable disabilities imposed on them. To accuse them of being "chartered libertines" is not only to paint them in poor taste but to castigate entire Hindu society.

Ashburner's article prompted Justice K. T. Telang to respond in a different way. In a letter to the editor of *Sudharak*, writing under the pseudonym ***Shankit***[59] (one who has doubts), Justice Telang complimented Agarkar for his fitting reply to Ashburner, and raised some fundamental issues. He pointed out that expression similar to that of Ashburner are evident in the writings of some of the ancient *shâshtrakârâs*, and that while Ashburner writes uncharitable expressions against widows, the purport of the ancient *shâshtrakârâs* as mentioned in *Manusmruti* [*Adhyâya* 2, *Shloka* 213 and *Adhyâya* 9, *Shloka* 14] and *Gobhil Gruhasutra* [*Prakaran* 2, *Ka*. 5, *Sukta* 7] is aimed at hurling invectives at even married women. He asked the editor of *Sudharak*, namely Mr. Agarkar, three fundamental "doubts"[*shankâ*] — whether such ancient *shâshtrakârâs* need to be exposed ? Is it to be supposed that the opponents of the Age of Consent accept these vulgar expressions against the married women as enjoined in *shâshtrâs* ? And if it is so, whether the high-caste women from Poona, who are thinking of sending a memorandum to the Government against the Age of Consent Bill, accept this *shâshtrâic* view ? In his view, Telang felt, a proper reply to these queries could immensely help the current movement.

The reply appeared in the next issue of *Sudharak*,[60] on 23 February 1891, not from any one belonging to orthodox section or the opponents of the Bill, but from one who championed the cause of women's emancipation, Pandita Ramabai, under the pseudonym of ***Nisshank*** [one without doubt].[61] Agarkar has identified in his letter written to his former teacher Vishnu Moreshwar Mahajani of Akola that these both letter belong to Justice Telang and Pandita Ramabai respectively. If Justice Telang was "sceptical" about their indecent references to women in the ancient *shashtras*, Ramabai was "confident' about their positive vulgarity towards womenfolk.[62]

Orthodox newspapers like *Jagadhitechhu* or conservative *Kesari* not only did not reply to the queries raised by *Shankit* but refused to publish the letter. In this regard, Ramabai realised that they were not ready for an intellectual debate. She wrote, "those who do not want to admit that there is falsehood in many an ancient and modern practices and on the contrary, they justify in the name of religion a practice which is morally, medically, economically, and practically proved very harmful. For them there is not even slightest room for doubting the expressions enjoined in the *Manusmruti* or such other texts...I doubt if one can find a single known Sanskrit text in which womenfolk are not derided or abused...." By sarcastically describing B.G. Tilak, *Mahâmahopâdhyâya* Ramshashtri Apte, and K.R. Kirtikar as "God-fearing Modern *Maharshi*", Ramabai questioned whether matters which are depicted by the ancient "*Maharshis*" are acceptable to them. She had no hesitation to believe that they would not only accept as true such things hundred times over, but would hold them in reverence. Since the passages quoted by Justice Telang in Sanskrit could be difficult for the general reader, she thought it prudent to quote from the ancient texts in support of Telang, with a view to educate the womenfolk and also for the reference of the "Modern *Rhushis*". In this regard, she copiously cited verse after verse from those ancient texts which are considered as authoritative, such as *Manusmruti, Rg Veda, Daksh-smruti, Shruti-Smruti, Mahâbhârat, Bhâgwat Purân, Renukâ Mahâtmya* from the *Sahyâdri* chapter of the *Skanda Purân, Bruhad-Parâshar Samhita*, in support of her argument. With a view that general readers and especially women should be able to follow, she also rendered its Marathi translation and showed how all those texts are unanimous in bringing women into disrepute. A few of the passages quoted are as follows: "With regard to women their companionship cannot be trusted, for they have hearts of wolves. Hence, like cruel enemies their companionships are replete with deceitfulness of wolves. How can modern *Maharshis* be at variance with the description given about cruel nature women ? [*RgVeda Samhita, M.* 10, *Adhyaya* 8, *Sukta* 95, *Rhucha* 15] Ramabai further commented, " Since, it is better to distance oneself as early as possible from the wolf-like, cunning, treacherous and impure women, the injunction pointed out by respectable Mahamahopadhyaya Zalkikar from *Dharmashashtra* that there is no harm having relation with a girl of eight years, in fact, is designed as a good ploy to put away womenfolk from this world. Such an act would serve interest — both material and spiritual." What has other *shashtras* say about women's nature ? Ramabai pointed out that in *Dakshasmruti* [*Adhyaya* 9] women are described as: "Women are by nature debaucherous and devoid of love and they possess a fickle mind. Therefore, howsoever one may protect them, they will always go against the wishes of their husband. Manu has attributed to women following characteristics *Shayyâ, âsané, bhushané, Kâm, Krodha, Kapat, Dwesh and Durâcharan*. It is a religious injunction that women be not treated by Vedic rites. Devoid of Vedic injunctions and unqualified for getting them absolved from sins by the Vedic rites, these women, therefore, are untrue and impure. In *Manusmruti*, not only the fidelity of *Guru's* wife is held in question [*Adhyaya* 2] but even character of once own mother too is suspected [*Adhyaya* 9]. In *Bruhatparâshar Samhit, Adhyaya 5* it is stated that, "In comparison with men, women have eight-fold sexual urge, six-fold industry, four-fold shame and two-fold diet." The kind of work that *Manusmruti* [*Adhyaya*] attributes to women is, "For women and *Shudras*, six types of works such as chanting of prayer, meditation, pilgrimage, renunciation of worldly life and daily *pooja* are sinful." In *Adhyaya* 5 & 9 of *Manusmruti* is stated that "whether a female is a girl, or young or an old, it is undesirable to give her independent. In every household, men-folk must strive day and night to reduce women to dependence and hence should be enslaved. Unless kept under clutches they may become libidinous. If you slightly depend on them they might go out of hand and that might bring ruin and disrepute to both the families of husband and father."

The *Mahabharat*, which is commonly believed by the Hindus as the fifth *Veda*, is held in reverence as much as the *Vedas*. In its *Anushashan Parva* [No.38.39 and 40] it is stated in a dialogue form that no matter how old they are, women have a strong urge for immorality. The conversation goes like this : Yudhishthir urges Bhishma to opine on the nature of women, as *Rg Veda* holds them as the root cause of all evil. Bhishma chooses to reply him in the form of a dialogue that took place between Nârad and the Panchachudâ, a courtesan in Heaven. Nârad asks her to comment on the disposition of women. After much denials on the ground that being herself a woman, it would be unfair to deridingly comment on members of her own sex, she gives in to cajoling and coaxing of Nârad. In this dialogue, following derogative words have been put in her mouth : "Dear Narad, it is the fault of women that they cannot control themselves despite being from high families, good-looking and married. They are the root causes of all evil things. Even though the husband is wealthy, respectable and one who listens to them, they slip into depravity at the first opportune moment. It is our wicked disposition that we carry sex with sinful men by shedding all indignity... Without caring for even a single thing such as fear, affection, selfishness or wickedness , they are not truthful to their husband... The worth of women is that which is the result of combining such things as *Yama* [wicked person], *Utpât*[calamity], *Vâyu* [wind], *Mrutyu* [death], *Pâtâl* [hell], *Vâdvâgni* [big fire] *Kundâche Mukh* [mouth of a fire altar], *Vastryâchi Dhâr* [edge of a blade], *Veesh* [poison] and snake...." After listening to Narad-Panchachuda conversation, Yudhisthir tells Bhisma that, "Similar to the way cows sprint to eat newly grown hay women catch hold of new person every-time...." Thereupon, Bhisma expresses his concurrence to this view.

In the *Sahyâdri-khanda* of *Renukâ-Mahâtmya*, the famed sage Jamadagni orders his sons to kill their mother—Renuka, for suspecting her fidelity without any substantial reason. This was not obeyed by all his elder sons. By narrating that Parshurâm, one who is considered as an incarnation of God Vishnu, murdered his defying brothers and supposedly immoral but chaste mother, Pandita Ramabai further added, "had not *Maharshis* like Jamadagni held extreme animus against womenfolk such inhuman and barbaric deeds such as the one referred above would not have committed by them."

Pandita Ramabai did not express any surprised regarding the public meeting of women in Poona to oppose the Age of Consent Bill and also about their memorial to the government to that effect. On the contrary she wrote: "When male-folks created characters like Panchachudâ in whose mouth words demeaning to womenfolk were inserted, it was neither impossible then nor is it difficult today for the males of the same ilk to get a memorial sent through their womenfolk... In such period of crisis, the leadership that is provided by the defenders of orthodox Hindu religion for protecting the 'prestige of women' would not hesitate to insert into their mouth debasing expressions of the same kind, should they get a new and modern *Apsarâ* to preside over the meeting of their womenfolk." The substance of Pandita Ramabai's other quotes was that women ought to be kept in perennial subjection and should they be let free, they would be damaging to the families of both, her parents and in-laws.

Ramabai not only demonstrated the malice against women as expressed in the writings of ancient but also the modern *Shâshtrakârâs*. Quoting passages after passages from *Vidhawâpan Anâchâr* authored by Vyankat Rango Katti and *Vedokta Streedharma Prakâr* written by Vinayakshashtri Velankar, and Ramabai explained how those texts were hurtful the fair sex. The purport of a few expressions in them was: "Woman is a special and sanctified object of pleasure... If she enters heaven, it's not for her own sake but for the pleasure of her husband...Similar to the countless shops of material enjoyment in the market, women too have shops. On the contrary, such shops of men are not traceable, and therefore, it seems to be true that man is an independent entity."

After taking stock of all ancient and modern *Shâshtrakârâs*, Pandita Ramabai launched a frontal and scathing attack on the opponents of the Age of Consent Bill. In this regard, her pen was acerbic, frank, fearless, and most logical. By openly naming B.G. Tilak, Ramshashtri Apte and their ilk as 'defenders of Hinduism', she sarcastically wrote, "Hurry for the defence of Hinduism. These *Sudhâraks* [reformers] are injuring their own cause by defending hapless women, whom God Brahma [the Creator] created for the enjoyment of man's lust! Take out your God given weapon in the form of *Shastrâs*. Oh, Tilak, Apte, Kirtikar and others, be prepared for weeding out the womenfolk while they are still tender with the help of firearms in the form of clever speech and such other things, lest if this poisonous shoot gets going it could prove dangerous! Hence, oh, the chivalrous, the defenders of faith, at least in the interest of your *Arya* ancestors and to respect sages such as Manu, Parashar, Yadnyavalka, Dakshgobhil, Bhishma, Narad and others, do something to defeat these unfortunate and innocent women...."

While taking note of all these 'authoritative' *Shâshtrâs*, Pandita Ramabai refuted their infallibility. What she showed was that in a patriarchical society these biased *Shâshtrakârâs* created a powerful ideology to legitimise their social position by debunking the entire womanhood. What reflects in the exposé of '*Nisshank*' is Pandita Ramabai's deep understanding that female sex as such was browbeaten : women had only parasitical existence and had little education. She seemed in work and in motherhood more a servant than an associate. Almost all writings were more male chauvinistic and charged them with laziness, coquetry, and lewdness. Woman was made to yield to man and to put up with his injustice. Consequently, Ramabai showed that neither persons such as Tilak, Zalkikar, Vyankat Rango Katti, Velankar nor the traditional class of womenfolk themselves, which remained mentally feeble, could challenge the anti-women ideology.

Neither *Kesari* nor any orthodox newspaper came forward in defence against such sarcastic and audacious attack of Pandita Ramabai. For it was difficult to stomach such scathing intellectual assault.

It is important to note that as one of the influential feminist theorist of twentieth century, Simone de Beauvoir (1908-1986),[63] French novelist, playwright, autobiographer, and essayist, in her book showed that since patriarchal times women have in general been forced to occupy a secondary place in the world in relation to men, and that this secondary standing is not imposed of necessity by natural feminine characteristics but rather by strong environmental forces of educational and social tradition under the purposeful control of men. This has resulted in the general failure of women to take a place of human dignity as free and independent existents.[64] What she attempted to show in her book was, how ever since the time of classical antiquity to the modern times, the arguments have been loaded in defence of male hegemony, and that attempts were made to legitimise that position by creating a mass of literature in support of that claim. To substantiate her argument, Simone de Beauvoir interspersed her exposé with examples from Western history and mythology. Such an exposition became an important tool in the feminist armoury in combating all ideological constructs in support of male supremacy. The importance of Pandita Ramabai's writing under the pseudonym of *Nisshank,* in 1891, lays in fact that she has used methodology to counter argue by challenging the very texts which sought to legitimise male dominance, a method similarly used by Simone de Beauvoir in 1949. This is a pioneering contribution of Pandita Ramabai to the feminist movement in India.

III

In conclusion, Pandita Ramabai detested any kind of infringement on her liberty, be that from the Hindu orthodoxy or her so-called Christian benefactors. Her concern for destitute child-widows was sincere and earnest and when she found that the Wantage Sisters and their male counter-parts - the Cowley Fathers were very cold to idea of founding a school for Hindu hapless widows, she did not hesitate to move to America for realising her goal. For Ramabai's Christian patrons, she was a very hot property to maintain. They were ecstatic over her conversion and attempted hard to inculcate in her the "Christian warfare" to combat "satanic influences" that tried to unsettle her into her new faith. But she was not a "lamb from the herd" who could be taken in by such talk. Although, almost all Indian converts to Christianity were marginalised in the social history of Maharashtra, perhaps with a possible exception of Pandita Ramabai, for she did not align herself with any other Christian missionary sects in India. What Ramabai attempted to show to the Christian missionaries as well as to Hindu orthodoxy was that in becoming Christian it was not necessary to denationalize oneself. During the Age of Consent controversy, she not only supported the cause of women's emancipation, but exposed the hypocrisy of the orthodoxy and also of the ancient Hindu *shashtrakaras*, and thereby questioned their cultural hegemony.

References

1. The brief life-sketch of Pandita Ramabai is as follows. Ramabai was born in Gangamul village near Mangalore on 23 April 1858. Her father, Anantshashtri Dongre was a renowned Pandit and a 'conservative' reformer who believed in the education of women. He fought against the obscurantism of his fellow Brahmins and taught Hindu scriptures to his wife and daughter, which resulted into his family's endless peregrinations. By the time Ramabai was sixteen she had lost both her parents and also elder sister, and was left only with her brother, Shrinivas, to continue wanderings. She arrived in Calcutta in 1878. The pandits of Calcutta, in appreciation of Ramabai's vast learning and scholarship in Sanskrit philosophical and religious texts, conferred on her the titles of – 'Saraswati' and 'Pandita'. After her brother's death the lonely Ramabai got married in June 1880 to Bipin Behari Das Medhavi under Brahmo Civil Marriage Act. She gave birth to a daughter, Manorama, in April

1881. She came in contact with Christianity through the Baptist missionary at Silchar, Rev. Issac Allen.

2. Pandita Ramabai(PR) to Sister Geraldine (SG), 3 July 1885, "It was Father Goreh's letter that proved that the faith which I professed (I mean the Brahmo faith) was not taught by our Veda as I had thought, but it was the Christian faith which was brought before me by my friends disguised under the name of Brahmo religion. Well, I thought if Christ is the source of this sublime faith, why should not I confess Him openly to be my Lord and my Divine teacher?" Pandita Ramabai, *The Letters and Correspondence of Pandita Ramabai* (hereinafter *LCPR*), Compiled by Sister Geraldine and Edited by A.B. Shah, Maharashtra State Board for Literature and Culture, Bombay, 1977. This is also reiterated by Ramabai in *A Testimony*, Pune, [first published in 1907] 11th edition, 1992, p.24.

3. PR to SG, Ash Wednesday, 1884, *LCPR*, pp.23-4.; PR to Dorothea Beale (DB), 22 May 1887, *LCPR*, p.178.

4. PR to SG, 12 May 1885, *LCPR*, p.60.

5. Following works have also been referred : Meera Kosambi, "Women, Emancipation and Equality – Pandita Ramabai's Contribution to Women's Cause" *Economic and Political Weekly*, Vol. XXIII, No.44, October 29, 1988, pp. 38-49, and the all the references mentioned therein; Ram Bapat, "Faith and Reason in the Shadow of the East and West", in Vasudha Dalmia and H. von Stietencrorn (ed) *Presenting Hinduism : The Construction of Religious Traditions and National Identity*, Sage Publication, New Delhi, 1995, pp.224-252.

6. The Society of St.John the Evangelist, popularly known as the Cowley Fathers, was founded by Richard Meux Benson in 1866. In 1859 Benson offered himself to Bishop Cotton for two years' missionary service in India, but the Bishop of Oxford, Samuel Wilberforce, persuaded him to be at Cowley, which was developing into a suburb of Oxford. Benson, who was the Vicar of Cowley, was joined by like-minded friends in 1866, who formed themselves into the "Society of St John the Evangelist". Father Page and Biscoe came to Bombay in 1874 and mainly worked among poor Europeans and Anglo-Indians at Mazgaon. The most notable Indian recruit to the Cowley Fathers was Nehemiah Goreh. S.S.J.E. had been called to work in Bombay by Bishop Douglas, but he died in 1876. They found a bishop still more after their own heart in his successor, Louis George Mylne, who at the time of his appointment was a senior tutor of Keble College, Oxford. In 1882, Father Goreh was at the Panch Hauds at Poona. The Cowley Fathers were devoted workers, but their churchmanship was aggressive and

extreme. For further details see Gibbs, M.E., *The Anglican Church in India 1600-1970*, ISPCK, Delhi, 1972.; Also Sengupta, Padmini., *Pandita Ramabai Saraswati - Her Life and Work*, Asia Publishing House, Bombay, 1970, Pp.116-17; 'The Community of St Mary the Virgin', a female counterpart of the Cowley Fathers, was founded by Bishop Canon William Butler. The Wantage Sisters started working at Poona since 1878.

7. Originally, it was thought the Ramabai be put under the care of Sister Elizabeth, who had been the Sister Superior at Poona, and Superior of St.James' Diocesan Home, Fulham. Since the Fulham Home was meant for fallen women it was thought by the competent judges to be unsuitable for a high-caste woman. So she was sent to Mother House of the Community at Wantage, where Sister Geraldine was the only sister available for work. Sister Geraldine (1843-1917) of the CSMV at Wantage, came to Poona in 1878, was invalidated in 1883, but before returning to England had already come to know Ramabai and her infant daughter Manorama in 1882. She had been wholly in an European and Eurasian school and had no experience of work among the native Indians;

8. Ramabai was baptised into the Athanasian Creed. This Creed was one of the three ancient Creeds of the Christian Church. Mainly a definition of Trinity and Incarnation, it was written many years after the death of Athanasius, but was attributed to him as the chief up holder of Trinitarian doctrine.

9. The letter of the Rev. Mother, CSMV, to the Exterior Sisters of the Community, 1 October 1883. The baptism of Ramabai was witnessed by Rev. Father Page, the Mother Superior of St.Mary's, Sister Elizabeth and Geraldine. The Child's sponsors were the Rev. Thomas Henry Archer-Houblon, Sister Mary, Sister Agnes and Emily. The news was immediately telegraphed to the Sisters at Poona, so that 'all could sing their *Tri Deum* on the same day'. Ramabai's confirmation took place in early December, and her first Communion was made on the Christmas Day 1883.

10. Pandita Ramabai (PR) to Sister Geraldine (SG) (Both at Wantage), 22 September 1885, Pp.89-90 and SG to PR, 5 October 1885, *LCPR*, p.98.

11. SG to Dorothy Beale (DB), 18 December 1883, *LCPR*; Originally, Ramabai had in mind to study medicine, so that she could be service able to her country women. But her impaired hearing ruled this out. Ramabai's mental state is reflected in the letter written by Sister Geraldine to Dorothea Beale : "Since her conversion she has so shrunk from being in any way considered a public character, and has evinced

such a desire to walk quietly and hiddenly, and has been pained when she has at times come to know that the eyes of many are upon her and her future work, that the less the future is alluded to, the happier she will be at Cheltenham...." , *LCPR*. Against such a background, Ramabai must have felt pained with anybody talking about her future with out even consulting her.

12. It was Prime Minister W.E. Gladstone, who sanctioned from Royal Bounty Fund, a grant for Ramabai's educational expenses at Cheltenham. DB to SG, 3rd January 1885, *LCPR*.

13. Ramabai held Beale in high esteem, which is reflected in the glowing tribute she paid while mourning Beale's death in 1906: "It is over twenty-one years since I saw Miss Beale for the last time. But her sacred memory is quite fresh and I seem to hear her pray and give Bible instruction. Her love and influence, her words of encouragement and her prayers on my behalf, have helped me much in my life and work." Raikes, Elizabeth., *Dorothea Beale of Cheltenham*, Archibald Constable and Company Ltd., London, 1908.p.301.

14. The Rt.Rev. Dr.Mylne (in England) to DB, 26 May 1884, *LCPR*. Since Beale agreed with the Bishop of Lahore, Mylne wrote to her that for his suggestion, she should not think of him as a "terrible wet blanket".

15. The Rev. Thomas V., The Bishop of Lahore to DB, 9 May and 25 May 1884, *LCPR*.

16. SG to the Lord Bishop, Canon Butler, (n.d. probably 1884, writes SG in her annotations.) She wrote : "She (Beale) could not guard her, neither could we had she been with us, from the subtle influences of those who calling themselves Christians have been at work to undermine her faith and our influence with her... I had felt that she had been getting out of hand, and so tried to make the difficulty which arose an opportunity for showing her that she could not act independently but must defer her judgment to those in authority." *LCPR*.

17. Butler to DB, 15 June 1884, *LCPR*.

18. *Ibid.*, 17 June 1884.

19. PR to SG, 9th March 1885, *LCPR*.

20. DB to SG, August 1884, *LCPR*.

21. PR to SG, 9 March 1885, *LCPR*.

22. SG to DB, 10 May 1885, *LCPR*. Rev. Issac Allen was a Baptist missionary at Silchar, and was a friend of Ramabai and Bipin Behari Das. He had come to England to recuperate from malaria. He was put up

with Mr. & Mrs. Glover, a Baptist Minister of Clifton. He had wished to call on her.

23. DB to SG, 22 April 1885, *LCPR*.

24. *Ibid.* 12 May 1885. *LCPR*.

25. *Ibid.*

26. SG to the Dean of Lincoln, 1 June 1885, *LCPR*.

27. Mylne (in Bombay) to SG, 5 June 1885, *LCPR*.

28. PR to Butler, 3 July 1885, *LCPR*.

29. *Ibid.* She also reiterated Father Goreh's influence in her getting converted to Christianity in the *Testimony* which she wrote in 1907. Since she had a purpose to write the *Testimony*, she does not make any reference to her confrontations with the Superiors in Church, and even her differences in matters of Christian faith.

30. *Ibid.*

31. PR to Butler, July 1885. (No exact date given), *LCPR*.

32. PR to DB, 8 May 1885, *LCPR*.

33. SG to PR, 21 June 1885, *LCPR*.

34. PR to DB, 15 August 1885, *LCPR*.

35. Raikes, Elizabeth., *op.cit.*, p.299.

36. PR to DB, 21 June 1885, *LCPR*.

37. "Some thoughts on Ramabai's Life and Work with extracts from her letters and writings" by Sister Geraldine, *LCPR*, p.407.; Later Ramabai also translated the *New Testament* from Hebrew into Marathi, as *Navâ Karâr*.

38. PR to SG, 20 September 1885, *LCPR*.

39. PR to DB, 21 September 1885, *LCPR*.

40. PR to SG, 25 June 1885, *Ibid.*

41. PR to SG, 7 November 1885, *LCPR*.

42. PR to SG, October 1885, *LCPR*.

43. PR to DB, 12 December 1885, *LCPR*.

44. Dr Rachel Bodley to PR, 28 December 1885, *LCPR*; Dr. Bodley was so impressed by Ramabai that she not only helped in organizing finances for her endeavour for Hindu child-widows, but also wrote a beautiful foreword to Ramabai's book — *The High- Caste Hindu Widow* [1887]

45. C.E. Gardiner, *Life of Father Goreh*, Longmans, Green & Co., London, 1900, p.276.

46. Willard, Frances Elizabeth Caroline (1839-98), American educator and reformer, born in Churchville, New York, and educated at North-western Female College. In 1874 she gave up a successful teaching career to become secretary of the National Woman's Christian Temperance Union (WCTU). An indefatigable crusader on behalf of prohibition, she was elected president of the WCTU in 1879, founded the World's Woman's Christian Temperance Union in 1883, and was elected president of the latter organization in 1891. Willard was identified also with the movement for woman suffrage and the Prohibition Party, which she helped to organize in 1882. She became president of the National Council of Women in 1890. Her writings include Woman and Temperance (1883) and Glimpses of Fifty Years (1889).

47. Tubman, Harriet Ross (1820?-1913), an African American who fled slavery and then guided runaway slaves to freedom in the North for more than a decade before the American Civil War (1861-1865). During the war she served as a scout, spy, and nurse for the United States Army. In later years she continued to work for the rights of blacks and women. Harriet Tubman, originally named Araminta Ross, was one of 11 children born to slaves Harriet Greene and Benjamin Ross on a plantation in Dorchester County, Maryland. She later adopted her mother's first name. Harriet was put to work at the age of five and served as a maid and a children's nurse before becoming a field hand when she was 12. A year later, a white man—either her overseer or her master—hit her on the head with a heavy weight. The blow left her with permanent neurological damage, and she experienced sudden blackouts throughout the rest of her life.

    In 1844 she received permission from her master to marry John Tubman, a free black man. For the next five years Harriet Tubman lived in a state of semi-slavery: she remained legally a slave, but her master allowed her to live with her husband. However, the death of her master in 1847, followed by the death of his young son and heir in 1849, made Tubman's status uncertain. Amid rumours that the family's slaves would be sold to settle the estate, Tubman fled to the North and freedom. Her husband remained in Maryland. In 1849 Harriet Tubman moved to Pennsylvania, but returned to Maryland two years later hoping to persuade her husband to come North with her. By this time John Tubman had remarried. Harriet did not marry again until after Tubman's death.

In Pennsylvania, Harriet Tubman joined the abolitionist cause, working to end slavery. She decided to become a conductor on the Underground Railroad, a network of antislavery activists who helped slaves escape from the South. On her first trip in 1850, Tubman brought her own sister and her sister's two children out of slavery in Maryland. In 1851 she rescued her brother, and in 1857 returned to Maryland to guide her aged parents to freedom. Over a period of ten years Tubman made an estimated 19 expeditions into the South and personally escorted about 300 slaves to the North. The Fugitive Slave Law of 1850 had created federal commissioners in every county to assist in the return of runaways and provided harsh punishments for those convicted of helping slaves to escape. Harriet Tubman was a likely target of the law, so in 1851 she moved to St. Catharines, a city in Ontario, Canada, that was the destination of many escaped slaves. By the late 1850s a number of Northern states passed personal liberty laws that protected the rights of fugitive slaves, so Tubman was able to purchase land and move with her parents to Auburn, New York, a center of anti-slavery sentiment.

Tubman faced great danger guiding slaves to freedom, as Southerners offered large rewards for her capture. Tubman brilliantly used disguises—sometimes posing as a deranged old man and, at other times, as an old woman—to avoid suspicion when travelling in slave states. Tubman constantly changed her route and her method of operation, though she almost always began her escapes on Saturday night for two reasons. First, many masters did not make their slaves work on Sundays and thus might not miss them until Monday, when the runaways had already travelled a full day and a half. Second, newspapers advertising the escape would not be published until the beginning of the week, so by the time copies reached readers, Tubman and the fugitive slaves were likely to be close to their destination in the North.

Tubman never lost any of her charges and seemed to have an unusual ability to find food and shelter during these hazardous missions. Among African Americans she came to be known as Moses, after the Biblical hero who led the Hebrews out of enslavement in Egypt.

Tubman also served as an inspiration to both white and black abolitionists. She worked closely with black antislavery activist William Still in Philadelphia and with Underground Railroad conductor Thomas Garrett, a Quaker who lived in Wilmington, Delaware. Abolitionist John Brown gave her the title "General Tubman." She consulted with Brown on his plan to start an armed rebellion against slavery in the South, but illness prevented her from joining him at Harpers Ferry, Virginia (now West Virginia), in his ill-fated 1859 raid.

When the Civil War began in 1861, Tubman served as a nurse, scout, and spy for the Union Army in South Carolina. She helped prepare food for the 54th Massachusetts Regiment—composed entirely of black soldiers and known as the Glory Brigade—before its heroic but futile attack on Fort Wagner in 1863. She later received an official commendation, but no pay for her efforts. In 1869 she married an African American war veteran, Nelson Davis. He died in 1890.

Tubman spent the years after the war in the North, where she continued her work to improve the lives of blacks in the United States. She raised funds to assist former slaves with food, shelter, and education. Tubman also established a care facility for the elderly at her own home in Auburn. Tubman was not able to read or write, but in 1869 her friend Sarah Bradford helped her publish her biography, *Scenes from the Life of Harriet Tubman*, so that her achievements could be an inspiration to others.

Tubman became active in promoting the rights of women, particularly of black women. In 1895 she was a delegate to the first and only meeting of the National Conference of Coloured Women in America (NCCWA), a group formed to combat attacks, made by the press and others, on the morality and civic pride of African American women. The NCCWA evolved into the National Association of Coloured Women in 1896, although Tubman had only limited involvement in this organization. She also became a strong supporter of woman suffrage. In 1974, more than 60 years after Tubman's death, the Department of the Interior designated her former home in Auburn as a national historic landmark. In 1978 the U.S. Postal Service inaugurated its Black Heritage Series with a stamp honouring Harriet Tubman.

48. Helen S. Dyer, *Pandita Ramabai : The Story of Her Life*, Morgan and Scott, London, n.d., p.23; This is a contemporary source, since Helen Dyer and her husband Alfred Dyer were close friends of Ramabai during 1890s. Alfred Dyer was the editor of the Christian weekly —*the Bombay Guardian*. Sister Geraldine write about these friends of Ramabai, in her annotations, most contemptuously.

49. PR to Manorama, 8th January 1888, *LCPR*. (Harriet Ross Tubman (1821-1913) was born a slave in Maryland. She escaped to Philadelphia in 1849, where slavery was out-lawed. She set up the Underground Railroad, a secret network of sympathizers to help slaves escape to the North and Canada. During the Civil War, she spied for the Union Army).

50. J.V. Naik, "Influence of Theodore Parkar on the Ideologues of Religious Dissent and Social Protest in 19th Century Western India", *Proceedings of the Indian History Congress*, 55th Session, Aligarh, 1994, pp.590-94.

51. *Ibid.* The quotes of Theodore Parker are taken from this article.

52. PR to SG, October 1884, *LCPR*. Father Goreh's biography is written by his fellow Cowley father C.E. Gardiner. One also finds a dilemma similar to that of Pandita Ramabai. But Father Goreh, despite his scholarship, had weak character to counter the Cowley Fathers in pressing his doubts regarding Christian religion. His letter quoted in extensor by Gardiner reflects his being unsettled in Christian doctrines and are full of self-pity as a sinner for having doubts. In the last years of his life, after 35 years in Anglican Church, he wished to convert himself to Roman Catholicism but lacked courage.

53 PR to DB, 22nd May 1887, *LCPR*. When Beale refused to believe the story, as an evidence Ramabai submitted the account of the happening stated by those who had personally witnessed it.

54. The Christian missionaries carried a venomous campaign during the second half of the 19th century against Hinduism and claimed that "Hinduism was incapable of initiating any social reforms". To such criticism, the mood generated by the revivalist Conservative leadership contributed to counter such criticism in more aggressive way. It is in these conditions, that many people became suspicious of Ramabai's intentions, for she had publicly stated that in going to Christian her purpose was not to become Christian.

55. Jyotirao Phule, *Satsar* or The Essence of Truth, Issue No.2, in *Mahatma Phule Samagra Vangmaya*, Dhananjaya Keer, S.G. Malashe (ed), Maharashtra Rajya Sahitya ani Samskriti Mandal, Mumbai, Third Revised edition, 1988, pp.310-14

56. Tarabai Shinde, *Stree-Purush Tulana* (1882), S.G. Malashe (ed), Mumbai Marathi Granth Sangrahalaya, Mumbai, 1975.

57. "Reform of the Marriage Laws in India" *National Review*, Vol. XVI, No. 93, November 1890, pp.367-81.

58 *"Mister Ashburner âni Anâth Hindu Vidhawâ" Sudharak*, 29 December 1890, Issue No. 10, Year 3; *"Ânakhi Ek Shahânyâchâ Kândâ"*, *Sudharak*, 12 January 1891, Issue No. 12, year 3. In the second article, he not only criticised Ashburner for his indecent and filthy remark but also pointed out how there are many other Europeans of the ilk to write similar things. The example he gave was of Mr. Augustus Willard, a military official during Lord Bentinck's regime, who interpreted the display of amorous sentiment in Indian music (*shrungâr*) as debasement of Hindu social system and sexual morality. Therefore, Agarkar felt that there was hardly any difference between both Ashburner and Willard.; Also, G.G. Agarkar, *Agarkar Vângmaya*, M.G.Natu & D.Y. Deshpande (ed),

Maharashtra Rajya Sahitya Samskriti Mandal, Mumbai, Vol,1, 1984, pp. 398-401 and 402-407.

59. *Sudharak*, 16th February 1891. Agarkar in a letter to Vishnu Moreshwar Mahajani, dated 3 March 1891, identified that the letter of ***Shankit*** as belonging to Justice K.T. Telang. *Agarkar Papers.*

60. "*Shankitâs Nisshankâche Uttar*", *Sudharak*, 23rd February 1891. This public debate between Telang and Pandita Ramabai was first time brought to the notice of scholars in 1995. Aravind Ganachari, "*Shankit âni Nisshank*" *Loksatta*, Chaturang, 7th January 1995, Translated into Marathi by Prof. Surekha Sabnis.

61. *Ibid.* Agarkar wrote : "I may tell you that this letter of *Nisshank* [this word is written in Marathi] is from the pen of Pandita Ramabai, the one appearing over the signature of *Shankit* [this word is written in Marathi] in the previous issue being from the pen of the Hon'ble Mr. Justice Telang"., *Agarkar Papers*. At the beginning of her article, Pandita Ramabai deplored that Telang's letter was not accepted for publishing by *Kesari, Jagathitechhu* and similar other papers, for his letter pointed out the mischievousness of the religious texts which have been held in reverence by them.

62. The issue of *Sudharak*, dated 23 February 1891, which carried Pandita Ramabai's exposé, also carried a letter from Dr. R.G. Bhandarkar entitled – "The Age of Consent". In support of his argument when Dr. Bhandarkar quoted from certain *shastras*, Tilak in reply called them "expressed texts" and hence spurious and unacceptable. He commented thus in utter exasperation : "I have been carrying on literary controversies since 1864; but never did I hitherto meet with an opponent who treated me with such studied discourtesy as Mr. Tilak has been doing."

63. Beauvoir, Simone de (1908-1986), French novelist, playwright, autobiographer, and essayist. One of the most important writers of her generation, she became known as an influential feminist theorist and a key exponent of existentialism, a movement in philosophy that emphasizes individual freedom and choice. Her autobiographical works are essential for an understanding of her era because they illustrate, with actual circumstances and events, the fundamental tenets of existential philosophy.

    Beauvoir was born in Paris and spent her life there. She studied at the *École Normale Supérieure* and the Sorbonne, graduating in 1929 with a degree in philosophy. While at the Sorbonne she met French philosopher and writer Jean-Paul Sartre, with whom she shared intellectual interests. The two became lifelong companions. Beauvoir taught high school until 1943, when she published her first novel, *L'invitée* (translated as She Came to Stay, 1949).

Beauvoir and Sartre remained in Paris during World War II (1939-1945), writing about and discussing philosophy with friends. They also were active in the Resistance movement against the German occupation of France. During these years they refined the principles of existentialism: one exists first, and through one's acts, one becomes something. They reasoned that in a godless world, one has absolute freedom and must exercise that freedom in order to live authentically.

After 1947 Beauvoir became a committed writer and devoted herself to analyzing the philosophical, social, cultural, and political problems of her era. She collaborated with Sartre on the political and literary journal *Les temps modernes* (*Modern Times*) and travelled with him throughout Europe and to the United States.

Le deuxième sexe (1949; translated as *The Second Sex*, 1953), Beauvoir's existential analysis of the situation of women in the world, drew significantly from personal experience and was extremely influential in the formation of feminist theory. Her novel Les Mandarins (1954; The Mandarins, 1956) received the prestigious Prix Goncourt, a French literary award. In her later years, she also wrote essays on aging, including *Une mort très douce* (1964; *A Very Easy Death*, 1966), which recounts her mother's death, and *La vieillesse* (1970; *Old Age*, 1972), which railed against Western society's poor treatment of older people.

64. Simon de Beauvoir, *The Second Sex*, translated and edited by H. M. Parshley, Alfred A. Knopf, New York, 1957, [first written in 1949].

11

The Panch Haud Tea Episode : An Index of Social Tension

This article deals with the Panch Haud Tea Episode, a sequel to the Age of Consent Controversy (1884-1891), which caused a storm in the upper-caste society in Maharashtra. The paper attempts to highlight the consequent social tension arising out of caste prejudices as well as the dichotomy that existed between thought and practice of the Nineteenth century social reformers. More importantly, the episode provides an idea of the methods of social reform advocated by different schools of thought.

The facts of the episode may firstly be briefly discussed. On October 14, 1890, Gopalrao Joshi, a post-master by profession, well known for his eccentricities and quaint sense of humour, organized a lecture programme at the Panch Haud Mission School at Pune, an Anglican missionary centre headed by the Rev. Revington. Almost all the worthies of Poona, including Prarthana Samajists like M.G. Ranade, G.V. Kanitkar, and C.N.Bhat. The leaders of orthodoxy like B.G.Tilak, and others like G.K. Gokhale, V.K. Rajwade, totaling 52 attended the function. The sisters of the Mission served them with tea and biscuits on the occasion. Because of the caste prejudices, many felt embarrassed but they did not want to show themselves as conservatives by refusing it. So, while a few drank tea, others merely accepted but refused to drink. The event went unnoticed for six months.

A few days after the passing of the Age of Consent Bill (March 19, 1891), Gopalrao Joshi published the report of the Panch Haud Mission gathering in *Pune Vaibhav*,[1] an organ of the orthodoxy, giving the names of those who drank tea. He charged the reformers with deliberate intention of going there to break caste distinctions and to trample upon Hindu religion by making common cause with Christian Missionaries. Joshi had double intention of ridicule in making public exposure of this event: if the orthodoxy would not take objection, it would expose their hollow threat of ex-communication; and secondly, to expose the hypocrisy of the reformers in the event of their apology.

The opponents of social reform seized this opportunity to settle scores with the reformers and blew the event out of proportion. The hard-liners among the orthodoxy clamoured for deterrent punishment with the sole intention to humiliate the reformers and to ridicule their cause. Public meetings of the orthodoxy declared the participants of the tea party as out-castes. The reformers resented this. They addressed a remonstrance to the orthodox people and sought to remove the dispute from the 'lynch-law tribunals' of the self-constituted leaders of the orthodoxy to the regularly constituted quasi-judicial court of ecclesiastical authority. Eventually, Balasaheb Natu, the leader of the orthodoxy, and ten others referred this matter to the *Shankaracharya* for arbitration, who in turn appointed a Commission of enquiry consisting of two noted *shashtris*. The proceedings of the Commission prolonged for more than six months. The final number of whose drinking of tea was called in question was forty-two.

Those who disputed the right of *Shankaracharya* to sit in judgment over them and did not bother the Commission, proved to be most happy. Among the sixteen of them was Gopal Krishna Gokhale. A few wished to defy but could not do so due to social pressures. The episode evoked much interest in Maharashtra as it brought both Tilak and Ranade together before the religious authorities.

B.G. Tilak, a social conservative, belonged to the Mandlik School of social reform: "Reform from within".[2] During the Age of Consent debate, he had countered social legislation and had opposed the social reformers for seeking to force "reform from without" on an unwilling community. His attitude in this episode was quiet expected. At the outset, he welcomed the reference to the *Shankaracharya*, but felt outrage of the die-hard orthodoxy as more borne out of malice than religious sanctions permitted. Since the Commission gave individual decisions, Tilak deposed that he had obeyed the dictates of the *shashtras* on his own, accordingly had performed *prâyaschitt* (expiation) while being at Benares, and had performed certain rites in Pune. The Commission accepted his claim and gave him no further punishment. His differences with them mainly concerned with the nature of evidence tendered.[3] Tilak unexpectedly embarrassed himself by being in the company of reformers, whom he had so far ridiculed. But he enjoyed the mockery of the reform party. Hence his *Kesari* maintained a low profile. Perhaps, one would have seen him in different light had he not been involved.[4]

M.G. Ranade, who was earlier ex-communicated for his role in the widow marriage of 1870, refused to take *prâyaschitt* for nearly a year. However, in May 1892, he decided to join a group of seven others[5], who wanted to submit to the authority of the *Shankaracharya*, regardless of the impending criticism. The *prâyaschitt* taken by them evoked sharp criticism from other reformers, and was viewed to be a big jolt to the reformist cause. The sharpest criticism came from *Subodh Patrika*, an official organ of the Prarthana Samaj. It termed their act as betrayal. Angry letters of criticism also appeared in *Sudharak*, which termed the action as "constipation to the reform movement".[6] The orthodox paper like *Pune Vaibhav*, *Jagadiddhichhu* and others, pounced upon the reformers and exposed the dichotomy in their conduct.

In reply to the editorial written by the *Bombay Gazette*, Ranade wrote a letter to that paper on May 26, 1892, explaining his position on this issue.[7] While citing his role in the 1870 widow marriage, he wrote, "it was not the fear of offending the caste which influenced my friends and myself in accepting the award of the *shashtrees*..." He felt that the other social issues were far more important than the *prâyaschitt*; that "we have always been in bad odour with the orthodox majority..." and hinted that there were other matters of more or less confidential character which he was not at liberty to disclose. On this issue, he also spoke at the Hirabaug meeting, suggesting that his own turmoil reflected that of the Indian society at large... the difficulties of acting under the conflict of -

> "two ideals of life, of two civilizations, of two modes of thought, acting upon us forcibly and calling on all to make the choice of alternative courses... We cling to the past, we are drawn to the present. Both have their claims on us and we seek to reconcile these claims as best we can by not breaking abruptly and finally with either".[8]

However, the other reformers found it hard to accept his argument.

Ranade was ever ready to follow all possible method of social reform. If the case demanded, he would support social legislation, or would support those who believed in self-help. He would not forsake an opportunity if any help could be sought from the caste leaders.[9] His positive view of the *Shashtri* class could be understood from his letter written to K.T. Telang :

> "The position that reformers ought to regard all ecclesiastical authorities as their open enemies, is one which nobody in active life will venture on urging for one moment. These authorities have their uses and no great or good purpose is served by ignoring them or treating them with contempt. There are some matters in which we must stand out, but there is no reason why we should stand out on all matters simply for the fun of the thing. It is these public interests which move me... Even if the Swami was not prepared to help me on all lines, I should prefer to see him in a mind to realise that we had a side to be considered and to be agreeable to fair compromise."[10]

Ranade's action was motivated by two reasons - 1. he was interested in getting as much as possible the support of the religious leaders to the cause of reform by submitting to their demands. He also wanted to make use of Tilak's position in this regard; and 2. he believed in showing futility of 'ex-communication' by accepting the *prâyaschitt* without changing one's normal behaviour, and thereby making a dent in the orthodox camp.[11]

A different strand in thought on this issue was presented by G.G. Agarkar.[12] His approach was rational, balanced and moderate in tone. While expecting the discussion on this episode on the lines of the Age of Consent debate, he called the commissioning of enquiry by Shankaracharya as retrogative step; the entire episode and behaviour of orthodoxy as 'concealed oppression'.[13] He felt that the attitude of the orthodoxy as the outcome of ignorance of social reality, mendacity and blind faith; and hence 'self-destructive'. In the course of evolution, he wrote, not only the ideas and institutions - social and religious, ought to change but even the social restrictions should change to meet the demands of time. The transition is smooth if there is no head-on collusion. to understand such a change needs minds enlightened by Western liberal education rather than disputing the lines of antiquated *shashtras*.[14] By citing the example of the whole-sale oppression by the French social aristocracy in the pre-1789 period, Agarkar reminded the dictum that "too much oppression breeds revolution" and urged the orthodoxy to forestall revolutionary change.[15] He pointed out that they must learn lesson from the ex-communication of Vishnu Parshuram Pandit in 1870; and that the punishment should be aimed at reforming the offender, a principle most absent in their out-look.[16] Agarkar ridiculed the whole issue : the arguments for and against before the Commission, as the question of deciding the "cost of breaking the religious injunctions by way of *prâyaschitt.*"[17]

Though Agarkar considered the ideas of the Christian missionaries no less fatuous than the ignorant orthodox Brahmins, he warned that the hard-line attitude of the orthodoxy would not only alienate the liberal brahmins but also the ignorant ati-shudras, and would consequently drive the latter closer to Christianity.[18] While expressing this opinion Agarkar was most forthright yet without Jyotiba Phule's vituperation. For Agarkar, the days of ostracism and *prâyaschitt* were over, and hence the perpetrators themselves were in the fear of being ostracized by the masses. Equally, he urged the angry reformers not to expel from their camp those who had taken *prâyaschitt*, instead asked them to understand their situation.[19]

Agarkar felt that the people can hardly be faulted for criticising Ranade, for he belied their hopes. He did not think that Ranade had taken the decision in haste or without reason. If Ranade had decided to take *prâyaschitt* to save other members from ex-communicated, he gave undue importance to the whole question. Neither his acceptance would retard the progress of reform nor would it exert positive influence on the orthodoxy. If non-acceptance were to result in the formation of a different sect, the acceptance of *prâyaschitt* would have been the ideal method of reform. But Agarkar did not think even for a moment, as past experience showed him, that Ranade's refusal would have ever produced such a result.

Although Agarkar expected the leaders to lead behaviour of conformity, he thought it unwise to blame Ranade, for he was no Buddha or Luther since he lacked their courage of conviction. When Ranade finally accepted the *prâyaschitt*, Agarkar called his action as a "puzzling mystery"[20] While citing the example of the Irish leader, Charles Stewar Parnell, whose affair with Miss O'Shea got him into trouble; and of Sir Charles Dilke, who faced a similar situation, Agarkar pointed out that the leaders have to be careful or else their faults get over-projected under public scrutiny. His final perceptions are very important : "If progress could be possible by this 'compromise' (of which Agarkar was most sceptical), Ranade would be eternally remembered for the action for which he is blamed today. Or else, unquestionably his biographer would have to make reference to this episode with great difficulty and anguish". In Agarkar's view, Ranade had missed his date with history. Nevertheless, he accepted Ranade's action as a step ahead in the progress of reform movement, but 'a secondary (*gaun*) method of reform'. He seemed to believe in what J.S. Mill wrote, "the mere example of non-conformity, the mere refusal to bend the knees to custom is itself a service".[21] The ideal method, according to Agarkar, should have been to bear the inconveniences caused by ex-communication and to prove its futility. "Let masses be educated on the idea of reform based on reason. Clarify their doubts and bring new customs in vogue depending upon their social utility. If the situation demands, interpret the reasonableness of the *shashtras* through newspapers, lectures or books, but do not indulge in settling the finality of their meaning by appointing a 'Commission", he wrote.[22]

In the final analysis, the whole furor was an after-effect of the Age of Consent Controversy. It was important from the point of view of the method of reform. Like the earlier controversies, this episode exposed the adamant and hostile attitude of the orthodoxy to social reality; the claims of the conservatives to have social change from within, or on the lines of least resistance; the futility of the method of reform by interpreting the *shashtras*; and the inability of the society to progress on its own volition.

The orthodoxy took vicarious pleasure in causing ripples in the reformist camp, discredited the reformers, mainly the Prarthana Samajists. Despite all efforts, Ranade failed in his desired aim. "But if he erred," as N.G. Chandavarkar put it, "he erred because his soul was gentle, his heart charitable"[23] However, the social tension this seemingly minor episode created had almost educative effect on the masses. It was a conflict among the products of two different system of education - Western liberal and Shashtraic, most incompatible to each other.

If the passage of the Age of Consent Bill is to be considered as the high-point of Ranade's career, the Panch Haud episode was the first sign of his loosening grip over the social and intellectual movement in Maharashtra. The void created by Ranade's increasing loss hereafter, had to be filled in. His loss was Tilak's gain.

The episode only vindicated Agarkar's rational and secular stand : "the reformer, instead of trying to mend the ways of incorrigible leaders of orthodoxy should try to by-pass them by showing total indifference to the likes."[24]

References

1. Gopal Vinayak Joshi, husband of the first Maharashtrian lady doctor Anandibai Joshi, was well known for his capricious and vituperative attacks on public figures - both orthodox and reformers. His inventive brain included in the list the names of those who were absent. This brought *Pune Vaibhav* into a libel case in which the editor was fined Rs.200.

2. To V.N.Mandlik, the proper method of reform was, "to approach the *Swamis* and *Gurus*, the spiritual heads and the *Shashtris* of the castes, to win them over by gentle persuasion, not to irritate them or set them at naught, but to take them into confidence and proceed with the work of reform with their sympathy, support and co-operation". Chandavarkar,V.N., *The Speeches and Writings of Sir Narayen G.Chandavarkar*, L.V. Kaikini (ed.), Manoranjak Granth Prasarak Mandali, Bombay, 1911, p. 34.

3. Tilak, B.G. *Lokmanya Tilakanche Kesaritil Lekh*, Part IV, Kesari-Mahratta Sanstha, Pune,1930, Pp.127-131.

4. Kelkar, N.C., *Lokmanya Tilak Yanche Charitra*, Part I, Pune,1923, pp.288-89.

5. Deodhar, S.G., *Maza Jeevanvruttant*, Satara, 1927, p.136. The eight who applied to the Shankaracharya in May 1892, to determine a proper penance for them were - M.G. Ranade, V.M. Bhide, C.N. Bhat, G.V. Kanitkar, S.G. Deodhar, Vamanarao Ranade, Vamanrao Paranjape, and Raghopant Nagarkar.

6. A letter written by D.G.P., perhaps by Damodhar Ganesh Padhey, *Sudharak*, May 18, 1892. Many letters blamed the editor of *Sudharak* for not attacking Ranade's conduct.

7. *Bombay Gazette*, May 25, 1892.

8. Tucker, Richard P., *Ranade and the Roots of Indian Nationalism*, Popular Prakashan, Bombay,1977, p. 249; A similar thought Ranade later

expressed while commenting on K.T. Telang, "The moral interest of the checkered career of Mr. Telang lay "in the divided and conflicting life that we have to live in the midst of two civilizations". Chandavarkar, N.G., *op.cit.*, p.29.

9. Deodhar, S.G., *op.cit.*, p.136.

10. Phatak, Narahar Raghunath., *Nyayamurthi Mahadev Govind Ranade Yanche Charitra*, Nilkanth Prakashan, Pune, 2nd ed., p.317.

11. Deodhar, S.G., *op.cit.*, p.136.

12. His interest did lay in the fact that M.G. Ranade, ex-colleague B.G. Tilak and P.N. Patankar, colleagues from Fergusson College G.K.Gokhale, V.B.Kelkar and V.K.Rajwade, and friends like S.G.Deodhar and Hari Narayan Apte were involved in the episode. Gokhale was also his co-editor of *Sudharak.*

13. Agarkar, G.G., *Agarkar-Vangmaya (AV)*, Vol.2, M.G.Natu & D.Y. Deshpande (ed.), Maharashtra Rajya Sahitya Ani Sanskriti Mandal, Bombay,p.55.

14. *Sudharak*, August 3, 1891, "*Bandhane Kon Tharawinar va Tyancha Ammal Kon Karana*".

15. *Sudharak*, August 24, 1891, "*Apalya Hatane Apalya Payavar Dagad*".

16. *AV*, Vol.2, *op.cit.*, Pp.59-60.

17. *Ibid.*, p.53.

18. *Sudharak*, May 16, 1892.

19. *AV*, Vol.2, pp. 87-89.

20. *Sudharak*, June 13, 1892, "*He Gudh Kode Ahe*".

21. Mill, John Stuart., *On Liberty*, Currin V.Shields (ed.), The Liberal Arts Press, New York, 1956, p.81.

22. *Sudharak*, November 21, 1892, "*Hi Sudharanechi Disha Navh*".

23. Chandavarkar, N.G., *op.cit.*, p.350.

24. *Sudharak*, November 21, 1892.

12

Dispensing "Abstract Justice" : Erloo Bin Narayan - A Mahar's Quest for Liberal Education, Circa 1856

When Sir Erskine Perry, then President of the Board of Education proposed, that the European boys —"being fully alive to the advantages of education"— must pay an increased fee as against the Natives, and that "We are desirous of filling natives of good caste and superior classes for higher situation in life...", Edward I. Howard, the Director of Public Instruction, Bombay, in his *Report of the Director of Public Instruction-Bombay, for the year 1855*-1856 commented,

> "Such maxims may be conscientiously adopted by a private person. I do not say they are in themselves illiberal or unwise, but administrator of State Education cannot properly be guided by them. The fee of state school once fixed must remain the same for all. Poverty and talent may perhaps plead a special exemption, and public and private liberality may institute benefactions for the maintenance of "poor scholars" but Government will draw no distinction between its subjects founded on caste or religion or social rank; least of all will it tolerate the establishment of a rule whose irregular partiality shuts the School door to one because he is "fully alive to the advantages of education", and opens it to another because he is of "good caste" or belongs to the "superior class".

He, however, qualified his statement by writing in the footnote regarding "caste" : "I regret to say that, in the present state of Native feeling, it has not been found possible to adhere rigidly to this principle, but I hope that exceptional cases will shortly disappear."[1] Against the background of such high sounding assumptions and candid admission of helplessness in providing social equality by the British administrators in Western India, this article seeks to analyze the case of Eroo bin Narayan, a "Mahar"[2], stigmatized as untouchable, from Dharwad District of the then Bombay Presidency, who in 1856, through the agency of the 1st Assistant Collector and Magistrate Mr. Stuart M.I. Gordon, sent a petition to the Governor Lord Elphinstone (1853-1860) complaining that he was being denied and discriminated for being a "Mahar" in seeking admission to the Marathi school run by the Government.

On the basis of the correspondence that followed this petition, this article seeks to argue that the British administration in the pre-1857 Revolt period, though prided for upholding 'rule of law' and dissemination of 'liberal education', pandered the susceptibilities of upper castes in perpetuating caste distinction in the field of education. While the administration admitted the injustice done to him and that he had "**Abstract Justice**", the officials deliberated in detail and finally decided that justice cannot be granted to Narayan in 'reality'. The article also attempts to establish that such official attitude was not a fallout of the Revolt of 1857-58 that made the British rulers indifferent to the needs of providing social justice to the weaker sections of the Indian society, as that approach existed from the beginning of their rule in Western India.

The Case of Eroo bin Narayan, though solitary, is elucidative of the official bias—not just the Bombay Government but also the Supreme Government at Calcutta, the Board of Control and the Court of Directors in London—against the lower castes and their hollow claims of "equality before law", not just in this case but ever since the beginning of the British rule. This article is based entirely on the records available in the *Maharashtra State Archives.*

Such high sounding claims were periodically made, both in the period preceding this case and after. Even later the Indian Education Commission of 1882 was ambivalent in stating the official educational policy, while declaring that all government aided schools should be open to all castes and communities,[3] it qualified by exhorting caution that it is not desirable to force a social change on an unwilling society. How this discrimination was maintained is shown by Philip Constable in his well-researched paper which deals with a period—the late nineteenth century Western India(1881-1902)— which falls after the case study taken for discussion in this paper.[4]

The facts of the case are like this : On 18th June 1856, Erloo bin Narayan, a resident of Dharwar, which formed a part of the Bombay Presidency and presently is a district of Karnataka State, submitted a petition to Lord Elphinstone, the Governor of Bombay, through the instrumentality of Mr. Stuart M.I. Gordon, the 1st Assistant Collector and Magistrate at Dharwar, complaining of his having been refused admittance into the Government Marathi School on account of being by birth a Mahar, a social outcaste or untouchable.[5] He also appended the copies of the correspondence carried with the officials of the Education Department, who had not paid serious attention to his request earlier.

The 'Minute' of C.J. Erskine, the then Director of Public Instruction, on this petition is quite illuminating in showing ambivalent attitude of the officials. Erskine first attempted to find fault in the arguments made by the petitioner. Fully aware that the Education Department's policy was quite contrary, Narayan wishfully had stated that "there would be no objection on the part of the parents to send their children to schools along with him". Erskine questioned the basis of such a statement. Without denying the justness of Narayan's request Erskine's dilemma was, "what present measures will most good and least harm be done to the cause of Education". He states in the 'Minute' that Mr. Gordon, the 1st Assistant Collector of Dharwar was conveyed with his sympathies and predicament :

> I am as anxious as any man can be to contribute to the removal of prejudice which he (Narayan) denounces. But a less propitious moment for attempting to force on the people an agreement which is distasteful to them could hardly be chosen than the present, when we are solicitous to conciliate the wealthier members of all communities and induce them to contribute toward the education of their poorer neighbors, and we have intimated that no new school will be established except with the cooperation of local residents.

The administrative policy Erskine alluded to was that of grant-in-aid under Wood's Despatch of 1854, which announced that to educate the natives would not be the responsibility of the government but that of the people themselves. The Government would only give the native endeavor a partial grant as aid. Hence, Erskine felt that the problem of such an admission would hold back the 'wealthier' upper classes. Shifting the onus of proving the soundness of such a request, Erskine wrote with helplessness and resignation,

> "If the writer of this petition be seriously persuaded that the Government system can from this day be worked on the terms which

> he (Narayan) contemplates, **he would perform a real service if he would attempt to give practical proof of the soundness of his views in the establishment of a partly self-supporting School into which all castes shall be equally admissible.** I do not say that a zealous man might not succeed in effecting this in a particular locality. But I am sure of two things that it would not be expected to succeed generally at once ; and that would be a great step towards the annihilation of caste prejudices throughout the Presidency… It will not be supposed that I contemplate the toleration for a long period of the exclusive prejudices referred to. I believe to cease without very great delay. But it seems to me that decisive measure on this subject can best be adopted after the new system has been allowed to spread in some degree, and not in the very act of appealing for support to the classes whose prejudices it is proposed to disregard in the outset. I should accordingly prefer that **the question were not pushed to a decision immediately.**"[6] (Emphasis is mine)

The solution he suggested was to establish a school exclusively for the low-caste boys. Obviously, Erskine's remarks were guided by the official unwillingness to disregard the caste prejudices of the upper classes and also by abdicating state responsibility to educate the lower classes in favour of the utilitarian concern—the financial support of upper classes for indigenous educational institutions.

Equally ambivalent was the resolution adopted by the Bombay Government. At the outset, the resolution acknowledged that, "There can be no doubt that the Mahar petitioner has '**abstract justice**' on his side" and sympathetically hoped for an early removal of prejudices which prevented him from availing the existing means of education. This confession, without spelling-out the nature of that "abstract justice"—something that can only be notional, theoretical and conceptual, and cannot be translated into reality—reflects how the British administrators were trapped in their high sounding ideals they boasted to uphold and their unwillingness to put into practice those very principles for fear of reaction which could create problems for the continuance of their rule. While repeating the same argument that "to interfere with the prejudices of ages in a summary manner for the sake of one or a few individuals would probably do great damage to the cause of education", they tried to extricate themselves from the blame of relinquishing moral responsibility by saying that "the advantages under which the petitioner labours is not one which has originated with this Government…" and hence refused to act in favour of Narayan. It endorsed the arguments expressed in Erskine's report and purport of the resolution was conveyed to Mr. Gordon, who had taken much initiative on behalf of Erloo bin Narayan.[7]

The matters did not rest here. The correspondence was forwarded for guidance both to the Government of India (GOI) and Home authorities, namely, the Court of Directors.[8] Mr. Cecil Beadon, Secretary, Home Dept., GOI, conveyed Governor General's opinion that 'probably' the BG acted wisely in the matter but stated that "the boy would not have been refused admission to any Government School in the Presidency of Bengal". He expressed satisfaction that BG had not opened schools exclusively for the low-castes, as suggested by Erskine, for "to adopt it would be to encourage and perpetuate the prejudices which the Government is every where seeking to overcome".[9] The second part of Governor General's observation put the BG in a quandary. It felt offended that the GOI should put them in an odious light—illiberal and exclusivist.

It was immediately resolved that the GOI should be informed that the BG is "most unwilling to neglect any means of rendering the ordinary village schools less exclusive than they practically are in the case of caste, provided this can be reflected without bringing the Government Schools into general disrepute and thus destroying their efficiency." By this time, Erskine was replaced by E.I. Howard as the Director of Public Instruction. Gleaning over the entire correspondence, he concurred with Erskine's report and felt that the GOI had made light of his observations regarding practical difficulties. The 'harm' apprehended, he thought, was "nothing less than the estrangement of wealthier and more influential classes" from the schemes in grant-in-aid introduced and that the declared policy was not to start any new government school or college unless the native community was willing to liberally subscribe half the funds. Further, he remarked acerbically

> Even if the influence of education does not itself soften the prejudices of Caste, the influence of Railway much destroy them. In the 3rd Class carriages of every train Brahmins are to be seen in the close contact with Mahars and the other *outcastes* (underlining his). The effect of this must be to eradicate those ideas of uncleanness and pollution with which the very sight much less the actual touch of the despised Pariah have hitherto been associated with. The present generation will surely not scruple to send their children to school with the sons of those with whom they are brought daily in close and immediate bodily contact in the Railway carriage.[10]

The Governor of Bombay expressed his agreement with Howard's views. The GOI was further approached with the purpose of soliciting an opinion on a host of questions : "Whether the admission of such pupil in the Bengal Presidency has met with opposition from natives of caste & if so, whether or no this has been found to affect the usefulness of Government Schools generally, and in what proportion boys of the lower castes are in general or in particular places found to take advantage of the means of education afforded by Government Schools." It was also asked what kind of response in terms of financial contributions it elicited from the upper and wealthier classes to the schools of mixed castes.[11]

Interestingly, the draft shows that one more point was added and later deleted : "With this letter I am directed to submit copies of a Minute by the Right Hon'ble the Governor (Sir Robert Grant) dated 17 September 1837[12] and of one by the Hon. Mr. (J.G.) Lumsden concurred in by the Hon. Mr. (Arther) Malet, under date the 19th Idem." This was dropped as it was not felt worth sending. Unfortunately, the Minutes of Governor Robert Grant (1835-38), of J.G. Lumsden and Arther Malet, Members of Lord Elphinstone's Executive Council, are not traceable.

On receipt of this letter, the GOI made express inquiries and forwarded a 'Minute' scripted by the Lt. Governor of Bengal, Mr. Fred Jas Halliday.[13] The GOI was quick to realize the trap and not only was there complete volte-face from the stand taken in Cecil Beadon's letter, but there was a total surrender to the continuance of a predominantly caste Hindu construction of education and society. Mr. Halliday confessed that there was no rule of the government, or the DPI, prohibiting the admission of boys of low-castes into any of the Government schools, except as regards certain special institutions in Calcutta, reserved for particular classes. He reiterated that "the avowed ultimate policy of the Government was that its schools and colleges should be open to every caste, class and creed." But what he stated further in the Minute amounted to not just a virtual surrender but in actuality a justification of the prejudices of the upper castes :

> Practically, however, this has never yet been carried into full effect. It has been left to the several local Administrative Authorities to regulate the admission to our schools according to rules which contain no allusion to any question of caste or creed. And these Local Authorities being in one way or another, largely open to the appreciation of native feelings and influences, have in the matter of Hindu caste, undoubtedly so managed the admission of Hindu boys into the schools, as to prevent any offences to Hindu prejudices, not by the

adoption of any declared and unvarying system, but by a tacit accommodation of local practices to local opinion. Thus it has come to pass, without any irritation or doubtful disputations, that while those castes which the Hindus consider vile, are no where presented for admittance into our Schools, *the line of tacitly understood exclusion is differently drawn at different times and places, according to the varying tenor of social feelings*; certain castes being admitted in some places, without any offence to Hindu local prejudices, while some castes are excluded, or more properly not encouraged to apply for admission in other places... In this wholesome and natural process much aid is afforded by the Natives attached to the Department, whose leanings are certainly in favour of catholicity, and who are often able to influence the general feeling and incline it more and more liberally towards the lower castes and classes.

This quite and unobtrusive, but in the end, inevitably successful method, applicable indeed to other branches of Administration in India besides that now in question, is, I apprehend, in accordance with the general policy of the GOI, and is, I firmly believe, the best and wisest way of ensuring a safe and steady progress towards civilization and social improvement. A rigid and violent enforcement of philosophical liberality in the management of our Schools, would, I fear, like any over-logical and aggressive reform attempted in other matters, social, political or religious, produce reactions and revulsion, and would thus delay, if not imperil, the ultimate attainment of the great object in view. (Emphasis is mine)

Mr. E.I. Howard, DPI, BG, felt Mr. Erskine justified. He suggested to the Secretary Mr. Hart that the printed copy of the above Minute be placed in Editor's room as "the local press misled by the first statement (Beadon's letter) of the Supreme Government, severely and as it now appears, unjustly censured the late Board of Education as inferior in liberality to the educational authorities in Bengal. Mr. Halliday's Minute commented by the Bombay Government shows clearly that there was no foundation whatsoever for that charge.."[14] Over-ruling Mr. Howard's suggestion and outraged at the last paragraph of Halliday's Minute, Mr. Hart wrote, "I very strongly dissent from the *'modus operandi'* advocated by Hon. Halliday. I consider it a virtually amounting to an <u>exclusion</u> (underlining his) of boys of the so-called low caste classes. I trust it should not be acted on in this Presidency." In a manner of admonishing Mr. E. I. Howard, "*the publication of Mr. Halliday's minute with the approval of this Government will completely prevent justice being obtained by the low caste children.*" (Emphasis is mine)[15] In the final analysis the British administrative hierarchy refused to act on the plea for liberal education by Erloo bin Narayan.

When referred, the East India Company's authorities did not specifically commit on this case.[16] But later, they proved no less explicit in defining the stand than Mr. Halliday. In a letter by Lord Ellenborough, President of the Board of Control addressed to the Chairman, Court of Directors, stated :

> Education and civilization may descend from the higher to the lower classes, and so communicated may impart new vigour to the community, but they will never ascend from the lower classes to those above them; they can only, if imparted solely to the lower classes, lead to general convulsion, of which foreigners would be the first victim. If we desire to diffuse education, let us endeavour to give it to the higher classes first. There are two ways of doing this;—by founding Colleges to which the higher classes alone should be admitted, and by giving, in the reorganization of the Army, commissions at once to such sons of native gentlemen as may be competent to receive them. I am not apprehensive of adopting both these plans; on the contrary, I think that both judiciously carried out, might greatly tend to give a natural character to our Government, and to unite the higher classes in its support."[17]

Perhaps, expressions such as these could be attributed to John Stuart Mill, an intellectual giant of the time, famed author of *On Liberty* and apostle of individualism, one who drafted many of the despatches on education while working as a Senior Examiner in East India Company's office in London. By 1850s J.S. Mill was convinced that, "Indian beliefs, fears, and ideas were not be ignored or discarded. The British had to recognize that Indian desires, founded on customary beliefs and traditional knowledge, were as important for the improvement of India as the creation of new social order."[18] Hence the official support to the prejudices of upper classes.

Obviously this kind of reaction was not just due the on-going Revolt of 1857 but one which has been consistently maintained by the British rulers—both in London and India—and which has been described by Nurulla and Naik as the *"downward filtration theory"*[19] dating it to the debate between Mountstuart Elphinstone and his Council Member, Francis Warden in Bombay.[20] The conflict was between medium of instruction in vernacular and English. Around the period when Elphinstone left India in

1827, it was decided in favour of Warden who wanted it to be given exclusively in English.[21] Elphinstone saw education as a good opportunity to draw the traditional elites into the British system, for he was deeply worried about the problem of disaffection of the Brahmin class. Although he gave considerable place to English education, he always thought that the vernaculars were of more far-reaching importance as means of instructions for 'the lower orders'.[22] During his period, although education was mostly opened to all, partial financial support to Brahmin orthodoxy continued in the form of Daxina fellowship as it was done during the Peshwa period. It is interesting to recall what Dadoba Pandurang Tarkhadkar,[23] noted social thinker, founder of *Paramhansa Sabha* and Panini of Marathi Grammar, recorded in his autobiography about his recollections on school life which coincides with the post-Elphinstone times. While he was a student in the Native Education Society's Marathi School, an order was issued by the Bombay officials that children belonging to S*hudra* class—Marathas, Kolis, Kulambis, Bhandaris— should be removed from School and nor are they to be admitted in future.[24] Children belonging to these castes, who fared well in the studies, had to forgo education. Reverend John Wilson confirms what Dadoba Pandurang has described.[25] The reason for this action, writes Dadoba Pandurang, was the caste considerations of Dadaji Dhakjee, a well-known businessman, a senior leader of the Prabhoo caste, and one who was also the member of the Committee for Native Education Society. He threatened that should the lower caste children be admitted to the School, he would ask all children of his caste to withdraw, to which the Parsee, European and other Native members acceded. His obvious consideration was that the education of the low castes would leave few employment opportunities to the upper castes. Dadoba bemoans that though this rule did not last long, the caste prejudices discernibly increased in the later period among the educated classes.[26]

A realization of this concern is reflected in a letter that appeared in the *Bombay Gazette* on 23 March 1857 under the title – *Is Caste to be recognized in the University?*[27] The question it raised was most poignant :

> As I always look with satisfaction upon measures conducive to general welfare of the educated masses of my countrymen and as the rules and regulations for the government of that excellent institution (University of Bombay) are probably yet to be framed, may I start a question which is in my opinion, deserving of the most serious

attention of the authorities and of the public at large—viz, "whether young men belonging to the lower caste, such as Pariahs Mahars, Mangs, Mochees, Sweepers, etc. etc. and converts to Christianity from these castes, shall if qualified, be deemed eligible to admission in the said University ?"

Although Madras young men belonging to some of these castes have actually been admitted both into the institutions at Presidency and these in the Mofussil, still here in Bombay the Government pays so much respect to the caste prejudices of the Brahmins, Prabhoos, and others, that the lowest classes are altogether shut out from the Zillah schools as well as from the Colleges. I admit that, for he present, boys of the aforesaid classes may not be admitted to the vernacular and the Zillah English schools, the main object of which is to create a taste for education among the great majority of population and that an admission of this kind into these school would perhaps, excite the antipathy of the people against the Government system of education. But I can see no reason why the doors of the University, the main object of which is not the same with that of the minor institutions, should be closed against this long neglected portion of the subjects of enlightened Government of Great Britain.

The above discussion shows that the British administrators in India sacrificed their noble ideals of "reason and social justice" even before the Revolt of 1857-58. The unwillingness of the British government to do "natural justice" to Erloo bin Narayan and the concerns expressed in the letter in *Bombay Gazette* were, in deed, a continuance of an educational policy which was based on promoting caste distinction. There are instances on record of low-caste children being admitted, but that was dependent on local reactions similar to those mentioned by the Lt. Governor of Bengal.[28] The statement of Nurulla and Naik that Wood's Despatch of 1854 'regretted the adoption of *downward filtration theory*', and that the "Government did not accept, until 1854, any *direct* responsibility for the education of the masses; on the contrary, it decided to *educate a class as a means of ultimately educating the masses*", is replete with contradictions.[29] True, neither did they take responsibility of educating masses before the Wood's Despatch nor did they do so even after, for the important excuse given in refusing admission in 1856-8 to Erloo bin Narayan was that the upper and wealthier class would not be forthcoming in supporting educational institutions if he were to be admitted. Also that Wood's Despatch did not put an end to the policy of *downward filtration theory* is evident from Erloo bin Narayan's case as well as the assertions of Lord Ellenborough in 1858. The fact that such discriminatory policy continued even after the Crown took over the administration is evident from the discerning and scathing criticism of the British Government's educational policy in Bombay which comes from the pen of Mahatma Jyotirao Phule.

In 1857, however, the Court of Directors paid lip sympathy by allocating Phule a plot of ground at Poona for erecting a school for the children of Mahars and Mangs in appreciation of his work and that of his colleagues. Phule had urged the government to grant a sanction of Rs. 5000/- to cover the cost of the building and maintenance but the 'appreciation' was not unqualified : "It seems to us undesirable that the sum contributed towards the School building should be kept on the Government books as an advance for twenty-five years, and as there is no doubt that there will be full and legitimate demands for the appropriation of any surplus of the Duxina Prize funds, we authorize you to adjust the amount as a donation by Government to the purpose of the School."[30]

In his celebrated work *Gulâmgiri*, Phule accused that "the higher European officers generally view men and things through Brahmin spectacles, and hence the deplorable ignorance they often exhibit in forming a correct estimate of them" and that not a single official of the Education Department, due to caste considerations, even dared to buy a single copy for fear of upper-caste reaction.[31]

The Memorial addressed to the Indian Education Commission under W.W. Hunter, dated 19 October 1882 articulates not only the deplorable state of affair caused by the official educational policies but reminds them of the hollowness of their "philosophy more benevolent and utopian" in assertion and "unjust and inequitable" in reality. He stated

> I wrote some years ago a Marathi pamphlet exposing the religious practices of the Brahmins, and, incidentally among other matters, adverted therein to the present system of education, which by providing ampler funds for higher education, tended to educate Brahmins and the higher classes only, and to leave the masses wallowing in ignorance and poverty...It is admitted fact that the greater portion of the revenues of the Indian Empire are derived from the ryot's labours—from the sweat of his brow. **The higher and richer classes contribute little or nothing to the state exchequer**...It is proposed by men who witness the wondrous changes brought about in the Western world, purely by the agency of popular knowledge, to

redress the defect of two hundred millions of India, by giving superior education to the superior classes and to them only... **By what contribution have these made of regenerating their fellowmen ? How have they begun to act upon the masses ? How many any of them formed classes at their own homes or elsewhere, for the instruction of their less fortunate or less wise countrymen ? Or have they kept to themselves, as a personal gift, not to be soiled by contact with the ignorant vulgar? ...My object in writing the present volume is not only to tell my Shudra brethren how they have been duped by the Brahmins, but also to open the eyes of Government to that pernicious system of high class education, which has hitherto been so persistently followed, and with broad universal sympathies, are finding to be highly mischievous and pernicious to the interest of the Government.**"[32] [Emphasis is mine]

Notwithstanding Phule's effort to awaken the Government to their lawful responsibilities, the British officials at all levels abdicated their responsibility towards the defenseless weaker sections of the society — the lower-castes and the women.

In conclusion, it must be stated that the Case of Erloo bin Narayan, one which was dealt by entire hierarchy of the British rule, showed that the colonial rulers boasted of principles of 'justice and equity' but their recipe was not for India, and that their "utilitarian and political interests" over-ruled all humanitarian considerations. It is important to note that the Revolt of 1857 was not a defining moment for British administrative policy as such discriminatory policies existed even before assurance of non-interference in social matters was given by the Queen's Proclamation [1858]. The correspondence that followed the case of Erloo bin Narayan also exhibits the daunting task Phule seemed have faced with an indifferent British Government on the one side and a hostile Hindu orthodoxy on the other. Despite repeated appeals, things did not change through out the nineteenth century, and one could state even in the twentieth century until Dr. Babasaheb Ambedkar galvanized the 'untouchables' into a political force to reckon with.

References

1. *Maharashtra State Archives* (hereinafter *MSA*), *Report of the Director of Public Instruction, Bombay for the year 1855-56*, pp. 71-72. Though the assertion of E.I. Howard was for doing away discrimination between European

children and Natives, he did include a possible similar discrimination between various castes.

2. A Mahar or Mang and such other castes were stigmatized due to their lowly occupation and with birth becoming a basis of one's social position in post-Rg Vedic period, came to be denoted as an "untouchable". Their lowly social status was accorded legitimization by much shashtraic justification in the succeeding centuries. Ever since these castes—the untouchables—have been treated with despise by the upper castes, and even their shadow or touch was considered contaminating and polluting.

3. "The educational institutional institutions of government are intended by us to be open to all classes and we cannot depart from a principle which is essentially sound and the maintenance of which is of first importance. It is not impossible that in some cases, the enforcement of the principle may be followed by a withdrawal of a portion of the scholars, but it is sufficient to remark that those persons who object to its practical enforcement will be at liberty to withhold their contributions and apply their funds to the formation of schools on different basis." MSA/ *Report of the Indian Education Commission*, 1882, pp.515-6.

4. Philip Constable, "Sitting on the School verandah : The Ideology and practice of 'untouchable' educational protest in late nineteenth-century western India", *The Economic and Social History Review*, Oct-Dec. 2000, Vol. 37, No.4, 383-422. The emphasis of his paper is on the decades following *the Indian Education Commission* of 1882 and deals with three case studies - 1. A dispute between Bombay Church Missionary Society in Manmad and the Manmad local Board school in Nasik (1884-5); 2. the violent attempts of the caste Hindu Patel of Ranjangaon village in Sirur Taluka of Pune district (1880-87); and 3. the untouchable protest to gain access to a government primary school in Dapoli village in Ratnagiri district (1892-1901).; Ellen McDonald's article similarly deals with the period after the establishment of the University of Bombay and analyzes mainly the curriculum. But she does not make any mention about the socially deprived class— the untouchables. "English Education and Social Reform in Late Nineteenth Century Bombay : A Case Study in the Transmission of a Cultural Ideal", in *The Journal of Asian Studies*, Vol. 25, No.3, May 1966, pp. 453-70.

5. *MSA/ General Department (GD)/* 1856/ Vol.28/ Compilation No. 637. The actual condition of this petition is very bad as the paper used is very thin and the ink has made impressions on both sides, and that makes it very difficult to read. Philip Constable makes an oblique remark about this case in his article : "In June 1856 another petition was made to the Bombay government by a Christian Mahar convert who had been refused entry to the government school at Dharwar. Missionaries were again seen to be behind the petition. This exclusion occurred in direct contradiction of the Wood Despatch of

1854 which, as a result of increasing missionary pressure over low-caste and untouchable education..." *op.cit.*, p.399. The author does not cite any documentary evidence and wrongly ascribes to the Missionaries the effort to write this petition. In fact, the official records in the Maharashtra State Archives do not make any mention of the Missionaries, not even vaguely, in this entire correspondence.

6. C.J. Erskine's Minute, No. 1652 of 1856, Director of Public Instruction *(DPI)*, Poona (now Pune); *MSA/ GD/*1856/ Vol. 28/ 637.

7. Resolution of the DPI, *BG*, dated 10 July 1856. The Governor in Council endorsed the view expressed in the Resolution, vide No.2439, *Ibid.*

8. It was informed to the GOI vide, No. 3292, dated 13 November 1856; The dispatch to Court of Directors in London, vide No. 101, dated 2 December 1856; *Ibid.*

9. Cecil Beadon, Secretary, Home Department(Ed.), GOI, to W. Hart, Secretary, GD, BG, dated 23 January 1857. *MSA/ GD/* Vol. 28/ 283.

10. Minute by E.I. Howard, DPI, 17 February 1857, *Ibid.*

11. W. Hart to Cecil Beadon, No. 599, 12 March 1857. Page is partially torn here, *Ibid.*

12. The Minute referred to, by Robert Grant, the then Governor of Bombay, is not traceable. *Selection From Educational Records (1815-1840)* edited by R.V. Parulekar and C.L.Bakshi, Asia Publishing House, Bombay, 1953-55, do not make reference to the education of the low-castes. And J.G. Lumsden and Arther Malet were Members of the Governor Lord Elphinstone's Executive Council. Even their Minutes on Erloo bin Narayan's petition are not traceable.

13. J.W. Dalrymple, Under Secretary to GOI to W. Hart, Secretary, GD, BG, dated 5 February 1858. The appended Minute of Mr. Halliday dated 20 May 1857. *MSA/GD/* 1858/ Vol.24 / 287.

14. *Ibid.*

15. *Ibid.*

16. In the Despatch from the Court of Director, Public Department No. 36 of 1857, in the reference made by the Bombay Government vide letter No. 101 of 1856, paragraph No. 6 which referred to Erloo bin Narayan's petition, nothing was mentioned. *MSA/GD/ Letters from the Court of Directors/* 1857/ Vol. 74.

17. In a Memorandum dated 28 March 1858, Sir G.R. Clerk, Secretary of the Indian Board stated similar views. Both these are reproduced in the *Report of the Director of Public Instructions, Bombay for the year 1857-58*. pp. 10-11.

18. Lynn Zastopil, *John Stuart Mill and India*, Stanford University Press, 1994, pp.48-49.

19. According to this theory, culture was supposed to spread naturally from the upper classes of society to the lower ones and the government need only educate a few persons in the upper strata in order to educate the people as a whole. Curiously, it needs to pointed out that the exact phrase *'Downward filtration theory'* does not figure in the records of Mountstuart Elphinstone, Francis Warden, James Adams who was appointed by William Bentinck to investigate into the affairs of indigenous education, Lord Macaulay, Lord Auckland the Governor General, or the Charles Wood's Despatch of 1854, though most of them shared the view which believed in giving education to the upper classes. The origin of this phrase is either shrouded in mystery or must have been coined by Nurulla & Naik to denote this view.

20. S. Nurulla and J.P. Naik, *A History of Education in India*, Bombay, 1951, pp. 82-83.

21. According to Mountstuart Elphinstone, was to be confined to the Brahmins, banias and agricultural classes. He was not against any free education to all classes but he feared it might create a suspicion among the orthodoxy of some concealed design on the part of the Government. R.D. Choksey, *Mountstuart Elphinstone – The Indian Years [1796-1827]*, Popular Prakashan, Bombay, 1971, pp. 374-5. Either in the schools run by the Bombay School Book and School Society with the assistance of the Government or the Engineer Institute which Elphinstone started it had students from the lower classes.

22. Further details regarding Elphinstone—Warden controversy Kenneth Ballhatchet, *Social Policy and Social Change in Western India 1817-1830*, OUP, 1957, pp. 248-275.

23. Dadoba Pandurang Tarkhadkar (1814-1882), was one of the illustrious Tarkhadkar brothers, the others being Bhaskar and Dr. Atmaram. Dadoba was one of the earliest products of English education in Western India. Along with Durgaram Mancharam and Dinmani Shankar, he started Manavdharma Sabha in 1844. He was also the founder of *Paramhansa Sabha(1848)*, the first anti-caste movement and main creed was to denounce caste distinction. He advocated "universal humanism".

24. Anant Kakba Priolkar (Editor and Biographer), *Raobahaddur Dadoba Pandurang – Purvardh : Autobiography; Uttarardh : Charitra*, Mumbai, 1947, pp. 45-47.

25. Cited by A.K. Priyolkar in the footnote, *Ibid.*, Wilson wrote in *Evangelization of India*, 1849, p. 338, "The youth of certain castes, however well washed and clothed, dare not enter the Elphinstone Institution. The Vernacular Pantojis drive the children of certain tribes altogether from their schools. None but the Brahmins, 'the Gods upon earth', are admissible to the Sanskrit College of Poona."

26. *Ibid.*

27. *Bombay Gazette*, 23 March 1857. The letter is sent from Ahmednagar and perhaps could be by somebody who is close to the Missionary of the American Mission.

28. *Report of the Government Marathi Schools in the Deccan and Konkan* signed by Capt. Joseph Candy, Supdt. Of Government Marathi Schools, Poona, 27 May 1840, gives caste-wise break-up of students – Brahmins-1848, Shenvi-21, Prabhoo-131, Sonar-132, Wanee/Vaishya-194, Gujar-42, Kunbee-335, Koshti-17, Kasar-56, Shimpi-87, Sutar-9, Salee-9, Teli-25, Tamboli-19, Tambat-7, Lohar-11, Dhangar-3, Koli-9, Pardhee-1, Jangam9, Bhandari-77, Nhavi-7, Marwadi-31, Khatri-2, Mali-2, Kamatee-12, Telangi-2, Parsee-2, Mussalman-80, Isrealite-3, Native Christians-4. Although the number of the lower-classes is fairly small, this list gives no mention of the Mahars, Mangs and other untouchables. *MSA/GD/* Vol. 13/ 530. The Missionaries admitted these lower caste including the untouchables—Mahars and Dhers— along with that of higher castes in their educational institutions.

29. Nurulla and Naik, *op.cit.*, pp. 164-5 and 182-83. This work has been held as most authentic by most of the historians.

30. From Court of Directors to Governor in Council, Bombay, No. 7 of 1857, Public Department, in reply to BG letter to the C of D, No. 141, GD[Public], 15 November 1855. *MSA/ GD/ Letters from Court of Directors/* 1857/ Vol. 74.

31. Dhananjaya Keer, S.G. Malshe (Ed.), *Mahatma Phule Samagra Vangmaya*, Maharashtra Rajya Sahitya ani Samskriti Mandal, Mumbai, Third revised edition, 1988, p. 83 & 144.

32 *Ibid.*, pp.182-195.

Index